The Abusing Family

Revised Edition

Blair Justice, Ph.D.
and
Rita Justice, Ph.D.

With a Foreword by
John Bradshaw

 **INSIGHT BOOKS**

Plenum Press • New York and London

Library of Congress Cataloging-in-Publication Data

Justice, Blair.
    The abusing family / Blair Justice and Rita Justice ; with a
  foreword by John Bradshaw. -- Rev. ed.
      p.   cm.
    Includes bibliographical references.
    ISBN 0-306-43441-5
    1. Child abuse. 2. Family psychotherapy.   I. Justice, Rita.
  II. Title.
  HV6626.5.J87 1990
  362.7'63--dc20   89-26659
                                                            CIP

10 9 8 7 6 5 4 3

© 1990 Blair Justice and Rita Justice
Plenum Press is a Division of
Plenum Publishing Corporation
233 Spring Street, New York, N.Y. 10013

An Insight Book

Published in cooperation with Peak Press
Houston, Texas

Printed in the United States of America

We are grateful for permission to reprint brief passages from the following:

Cicchetti, D. (1987). A chart from: The sequelae of child maltreatment. In R. J. Gelles and J. B. Lancaster (Eds.), *Child Abuse and Neglect: Biosocial Dimensions*. New York: Aldine de Gruyter. (© 1987 Social Science Research Council)

Daro, D. A. (1988). A chart from: *Confronting Child Abuse.* New York: The Free Press. (© 1988 Deborah Ann Daro)

Mrazek, P. and Mrazek, D. (1987). Excerpts from: Resilience in child maltreatment victims: a conceptual exploration. In *Child Abuse & Neglect*, Volume 11. New York: Pergamon Press plc. (© 1987 Pergamon Press plc)

Helfer, R. E. (1987). A diagram from: A developmental basis of child abuse and neglect: an epidemiological approach. In R. E. Helfer and C. H. Kemp (Eds.), *The Battered Child*. Chicago: University of Chicago Press. (© 1987 Social Science Research Council)

Foreword

I welcome the opportunity to write a foreword for the revised edition of *The Abusing Family* by Blair and Rita Justice. In my opinion, there is no area of human concern which demands greater explication than the trauma of physical violence. Blair and Rita are perhaps the most knowledgeable people in the country on the nature, extent, and consequences of physical abuse. Their partnership itself is a model of how we should proceed, for the Justices combine expertise in the fields of public health, sociology, psychological theory, and psychotherapy. For two decades they have painstakingly been involved in the research and treatment of the abusing family. Working with such families is often a brutal task. I'm thankful that Blair and Rita have chosen to continue their work.

This book complements their pioneering volume *The Abusing Family*, first published in 1976. That book opened our eyes to the extent and sociological implications of the problem. This new edition offers us the most current knowledge available in treating and preventing child abuse.

The discussion in Chapter 7 of children who have escaped the devastating consequences of early child abuse is a major contribution. It has always been believed that the "power of love" could go a long way toward mediating violence. Now the Justices offer us empirical data which prove that "a loving and supporting adult" can be the crucial factor in preventing the reenactment of a child's abuse on society or on the child's own children. This is the kind of data we need to have if we are to mount an effective campaign to stop the abusive depletion of our greatest natural resource—the mental health of our children.

I recently heard someone say that the most dangerous place for any child in the United States is the American Family. The Justices help us to take that statement seriously. More importantly they offer us hope for the future. I predict that this book will be the reference point for treating physical abuse for many years to come.

John Bradshaw

Preface

In the nearly two decades we have been working with families who abuse their children, we have seen a new "can do" attitude emerge toward the problems of child abuse. It has been most noticeable in community organizations and programs formed to prevent abuse. When we started the first group therapy for abusing parents in 1973 in Houston, no one even thought that prevention was possible. As for treating parents to control recurrence of abuse, the prevailing attitude was "Why bother? These people are incorrigible."

Both treatment and prevention are far from being effective in many cases, but we are convinced that the "can do" attitude is justified. The combination of clinical skills, scientific rigor, and community effort is making a difference—both among the families where abuse has occurred but can be stopped and among those at high risk where abuse can be prevented.

To "heal" a family is a tall order, and we do not pretend we succeed in doing so. Our experience has been that abusive families can change and be repaired, and the foundation for healing can be laid. Making progress with such families requires not only identification of the problems underlying the abusive behavior but establishment of a therapeutic relationship that permits positive change to take place.

The rewards we have enjoyed in this work come from watching such change start, grow, and then endure. We still hear from some of those we treated when we first began this work. They say their lives are different as a result of therapy. We know ours are too from having the opportunity to treat and, we hope, to heal.

We owe much to many who helped make our work possible and who encouraged the publication of *The Abusing Family* in 1976 and, now, this thoroughly revised edition. We wish to acknowledge our families, friends, and colleagues who gave their support over the years. We thank all the dedicated CPS (children's protective services) workers and administrators who referred clients to us and shared in our efforts, particularly Judy Hay, director of community relations at Harris County Children's Protective Services, and Gene Daniels, regional director of the CPS of the Texas Department of Human Relations.

John Bradshaw has done much to help people across the country understand how abuse in their childhoods impairs them later as adults and parents. We applaud his efforts and are pleased that his voice has reached so many.

Without the diligent efforts of Rice University librarian Rita Marsales, the referencing and bibliography in this book would have been impossible. We also would like to thank our secretaries, Barbara Fredieu and Barbara Taylor, and Diana Tuchman for their steady support in handling the many mundane tasks that go into making any book a reality.

Blair and Rita Justice

Houston, Texas

Contents

Introduction

In 1980 a national objective was set to reduce child abuse injuries and deaths at least 25% by 1990.[1] Several years later, a midcourse analysis indicated that this objective would not be met.[2] Now, under the leadership of the U.S. Department of Health and Human Services, national health objectives for the year 2000 are the focus. The question is: Will we do any better in the next decade than we did in the last on the reduction of child abuse?

Mounting evidence suggests we will, although serious problems hampering progress remain. On the positive side, a number of advances can be listed, and these will likely continue if public concern with the problem does not diminish and available funds for research, prevention, and other programs grow. At the top of the list of advances is increased knowledge, based on empirical research, of how some kinds of child abuse can be prevented.[3] This revised edition of *The Abusing Family* focuses on what is known about prevention as well as treatment and

what we are learning from children and adults who have survived abusive environments with the least damage.

What we know about prevention is being enhanced by findings on both "resilient" children and adults who grew up in
violent homes but are not abusive in their own families. Among
children who were abused but do not suffer many of the consequences common to maltreatment, several factors have been
found to offer protection. As we discuss in Chapter 7, the effects of abuse seem to be buffered by a child's finding some
adult who is loving or supportive.[4] The child is able to
develop and hold on to a conviction that he or she is loved
and worthwhile.

The resilient children also learn to "reframe," to look at their
painful experience in such a way that they do not blame themselves—for example, they may come to realize that their beatings
were not for their "own good" but due to their parents' being
alcoholic. Another buffer seems to be the ability to break the
isolation that characterizes the abusing family and to form relationships that help in crises.[5]

Similar protective factors are being found among adults who
were severely abused as children but do not maltreat their own
children.[6] They also managed to bring some loving adult into
their lives when they were children. They were able to find a
supportive spouse, and they "own" or reclaim the trauma of
their past and are willing to work on getting it out and letting
it go. Programs that show promise of preventing abuse have incorporated some of these basic protective elements. Support
programs for new parents, for instance, offer to the family the
services of a nurturing adult who can model competence and
care.[7]

The growth of child abuse research itself, with better-con-
trolled studies and more generalizable findings, is an encouraging development in meeting a new national objective on violence
toward children. No less important are community organizations

and the development of coalitions to mount programs that work and to increase public awareness.[8] What may prove to be most valuable for assuring increased financial support for such projects is the ability to demonstrate the tremendous savings a community realizes from effective prevention and treatment programs in child abuse (see Chapter 9).[9] Also on our progress list must be the recognition by the surgeon general of the magnitude of child injuries and deaths inflicted by abusing parents and of the pressing need for action. It was under the leadership of U.S. surgeon generals, past and present, that the first step of setting national health objectives, including those for reducing abuse, was taken.[10]

WHAT IS HAMPERING PROGRESS?

Although national attention and resources are now being focused on child abuse, there is still the question of how long it will last. The public is fickle in terms of its interest in unpleasant problems, regardless of the fact that the welfare of so many children is at stake. Newspaper and magazine headlines are still reserved for extreme cases of abuse, leading many people to assume that "typical" cases involve bizarre treatment or torture of a child, with death as the outcome. "The Horrifying Steinberg Trial," which *Newsweek* featured in a cover story of the abuse and death of a couple's 6-year-old adopted daughter in New York, is an example of the widespread publicity that extreme cases receive.[11]

Many parents distance themselves from the problem by believing that only people who are sick, psychopathic, or drug-crazed can commit abuse. The public still does not see abuse as a problem that occurs in many "average" homes where a child is not bizarrely treated but is subject to frequent episodes of anger or physical punishment that leaves lasting emotional damage, if not physical scars.

A number of people would prefer to pretend that child abuse does not exist or that it is none of their business. Why this attitude prevails is related to the negative feelings that most humans have about their own children and how they may treat them.

> Is there any mother or father who has not been "provoked" almost to the breaking point by the crying, wheedling, whining child? How many parents have not had moments of concern and self-recrimination after having, in anger, hit their own child much harder than they had expected they would? How many such incidents makes a "child abuser" out of a normal parent? There may be a tacit agreement among us not to meddle in each other's private matters unless it is simply impossible to ignore the behavior involved.[12]

Despite the inclination to ignore the problem, public attention has been galvanized during at least two previous periods of recent history. One period lasted for several years after radiologists began reporting in 1946 that subdural hematoma (brain hemorrhage) and abnormal X-ray findings in the long bones were commonly associated with trauma in early childhood. A second period of greater concern and attention occurred after the American Academy of Pediatrics conducted a symposium on child abuse in 1961 and C. H. Kempe coined the headline-making term the battered child to describe the kind of damage being done in American homes.[13]

In the wake of the second wave, the Children's Bureau of the U.S. Department of Health, Education and Welfare drafted a model law on child abuse for states to consider. Between 1963 and 1968 all the states enacted legislation that required the reporting and investigation of cases of abuse and the provision of protective services for children.[14] But both periods of attention, after reaching a high pitch, subsided again to levels of public and professional apathy.

KEEPING ABUSE A PUBLIC ISSUE

With the passage of the Child Abuse Prevention and Treatment Act in 1974, and its reauthorization in 1984, we are once again trying to keep the problem of abuse on the national agenda. The national health objectives, which include those for abuse, are part of this effort. But drawing public and legislative attention to child abuse continues to raise thorny issues that many people would prefer to ignore. For example, spanking and discipline are inextricably involved in the problem. One point of view is that the line between a spanking and beating is a thin one indeed, that abuse is often a spanking that simply went too far.[15] Thus, corporal punishment and how parents are to discipline their children are matters for national debate if the problem of abuse is to become a truly public issue.

How discipline may be related to abuse easily stirs up intense public feeling. Historically, children have been viewed as the property of their parents, and parents have the right to rear their child as they see fit.[16] As for discipline, "parents have the right to punish their child however they like."[17] In Texas, for instance, there has been a law on the books since 1974 that says "the use of force but not deadly force against a child" by a parent or stepparent is justified "when and to the degree the actor reasonably believes the force is necessary to discipline the child."[18] By custom, as well as by law, parents' rights are well established. Only recently have the rights of children received equal attention.

National surveys have shown that a majority of people believe almost anyone could deliberately injure a child in his care.[19] If discipline or punishment is so severe that it amounts to abuse, do parents forfeit the right to raise their children as they see fit? The easy answer is yes, but a sampling of national opinion has shown that most people believe abused children should be removed from the home only as a last resort, not after having been abused only once.[20]

Alongside the view that children are the property of their parents and that removal from the home should be a last resort is the sense of outrage the public reserves for anyone who abuses a child. If these two phenomena appear to be contradictory, they simply reflect society's ambivalence toward the question of whether parents have the right to treat children as they see fit and are entitled to use whatever physical discipline they believe is necessary.

WHAT CONSTITUTES ABUSE?

Confusion as to "caseness" still exists—questions of what constitutes a case of physical abuse, sexual abuse, neglect, or emotional maltreatment.[21] In this book, we focus only on physical abuse, which we regard as any nonaccidental injury to a child by a caretaker.[22]

What constitutes an "injury" is often a matter of judgment—the judgment of children's protective services, the police or, finally, a judge. The ability to predict abuse and to develop instruments for accurately assessing which families are at high risk continues to be impaired by the absence of a reliable, operational definition of abuse.[23] Public attitudes toward physical discipline and disagreement over whether spanking and corporal punishment qualify as abuse continue to make the problem difficult to define.

And the lack of uniform and objective criteria for defining abuse feeds into the question of whether anyone really knows how much there is. That there is too much is indisputable, but estimates of incidence vary ten- to twentyfold.[24] National representative surveys, based on household interviews, report many more times the amount of abuse than do official registries.[25] Unreported cases of abuse thus remain a serious problem. Some findings suggest that for every reported case, there are 30 unreported incidents of child abuse.[26]

Despite the steps taken by the surgeon general's office, which heads the U.S. Public Health Service, local and state public health departments have done little on the problem of child abuse at the grass roots level. In 1976, when *The Abusing Family* was first published, next to nothing was being done by public health professionals.[27] Today, with a few exceptions, the record is hardly better.[28]

Another problem remaining is the continued use of children's protective services staff with limited training to work with abusive families.[29] Children's protective services (CPS) across the country have also been charged with being either too intrusive or too lax in dealing with parents. CPS workers in many states are being accused of invading the rights of parents and picking up children without adequate cause. In some cases, custody court battles between estranged parents are behind charges of abuse, with the child and CPS caught in the middle. National organizations, such as Victims of Child Abuse Legislation, have been formed to restrict CPS activities.[30] Meanwhile, attacks on CPS also are coming from the opposite direction, from groups— such as Justice for Children—arguing that the agencies are not diligent enough in removing children from the homes where abuse is suspected.

WHAT IS WORKING?

Although many problems remain, progress is being made on several fronts. One of the most positive steps in reducing the incidence of child abuse is the development of support programs for new parents. New parents deserve special focus for several reasons: Many first-time parents lack information on the needs and development of infants and children and have no background in parenting skills, many are young and isolated, there is greater willingness to accept guidance from outside the family around the birth of the first child, and the consequences of abuse are greater for younger children and have a longer-lasting influence on development.[31] Evaluation of support programs for new parents indicate that they can constitute an effective means to prevent abuse on the primary level.[32]

The support offered takes the form of "parenting enhancement services."[33] A health visitor or parent aide is assigned to a couple and, if possible, becomes acquainted with them in the hospital before birth of the child. After birth, the health visitor acts as a role model for good parenting, provides them with relevant information on child care, and serves as a resource for getting them help on a wide range of problems that new parents can have. Chapter 9 gives details on some of the best of these support programs and evaluations that demonstrate their effectiveness in primary prevention. In the same chapter, we also discuss the kind of savings that a community realizes from offering programs for parents.

With the growth of parenting services and evidence of their effectiveness in primary prevention, there is increasing awareness that prevention deserves major attention if child abuse is to be reduced. Treating the problem after abuse has already occurred will never make the impact that prevention will. The National Child Abuse Prevention Committee now has chapters in a number of cities and all states. In Houston, for instance, primary prevention programs have been instituted through efforts of the Child Abuse Prevention Council, a chapter of the NCAPC. The council gives an annual national award for a prevention program in the United States that has demonstrated outstanding effectiveness. The director is invited to Houston to speak and to encourage similar programs in that city.

PHYSICAL EFFECTS OF SUPPORT

On the research level, mounting evidence is confirming the importance of support for families and confirming the role of social isolation as a factor in child abuse.[34] Social isolation plays a part in both child neglect and child abuse, and interventions by lay health visitors show some effectiveness in cases of nonorganic failure to thrive.[35] Both abuse and lack of nurturing of a child can produce serious consequences in growth. Evidence shows that improper mothering and touching can result in abnormal endocrine function and growth hormone release, contributing to psychosocial dwarfism.[36]

The effect of tactile stimulation and wholesome touching on growth and development has been demonstrated in recent years. In psychosocial dwarfism, which signals the absence of adequate nurturing and touching, excessive hydrocortisone is released under stress from the adrenal cortex, and growth hormone diminishes.[37] When the child is moved to a more favorable emotional climate and receives positive touching, the anterior hypothalamus is activated, leading to normal release of growth hormone from the anterior pituitary gland.

When a child lives in an unsupportive, abusive environment, the stress is likely to keep catecholamine levels high and increase the risk of illness. On the other hand, a supportive home, with wholesome touching, dampens the posterior hypothalamus and release of stress chemicals. The anterior hypothalamus is engaged, and the parasympathetic nervous system, which is associated with relaxation, turns on.[38] Research on the biological mechanisms of support and good touching, as mediated by the brain, is making clearer what happens in the body of a child subjected to abuse and neglect.

PURPOSES AND APPROACH

One limited but important purpose of this book is to distinguish the factors that help explain how some people have survived abusive environments without the disabling consequences that are common to such experiences. Both resilient children and adults who come from abusive backgrounds but are functioning well can help teach us what they brought into their lives to protect them against those consequences. *The Abusing Family* also presents what has to be done in therapy to help heal the children who did not get buffered from the effects of abuse. Only recently have findings emerged on what issues must be focused on in treating the abused child.

A broader purpose of the book is to emphasize the systems nature of child abuse so that causes and "cures" can be understood and interventions designed for both primary and secondary prevention. The family and its social and physical environment are a system in the sense that what affects one part of it has an influence on all parts.

Child abuse requires a systems or ecological approach for several reasons: (1) The entire family is involved, not just a mother, a father, or some other caretaker who deliberately injures a child. The mother, the father, the child—and the environment—all play a part. The interlocking symbiosis that develops between spouses and between spouses and child can be understood and broken up only through working with all parts of the system. (2) On the community level, any effort at primary prevention will succeed only if the different parts that make up the system of host, agent, environment and vector are properly identified. No family exists in a vacuum. Environmental stresses as well as community resources and support must be considered. (3) On the societal level, the cultural "scripts" that are given parents and children must be identified—the messages that largely determine what parents expect of children and themselves. The messages about use of violence are also part of scripting—the idea that family members can be hit if they persist in doing wrong, the notion that if all else fails, violence will solve the problem.

Violence throughout the world is influencing the lives of individual families as never before. Instant communication not only has made people inhabitants of a global village, it also has spotlighted the way individuals are bound into a single network system, with one part affecting all others. But instant communication is just one reality in the sweeping technological changes that have overtaken all of us. A kind of "future shock" continues, and child abuse is one of its manifestations.

Another purpose of *The Abusing Family* is to demonstrate how too much change coming too fast plagues the lives of families in which child abuse occurs. That families are under high stress is evident from the rise in divorce rates, the level of unemployment, the number of school dropouts and the epidemic of alcohol and substance abuse. The high mobility of American families continues, and a sense of impermanence contributes to isolation and a lack of social support—both of which, as we have noted, are risk factors for abuse. Stress is not the cause of abuse, but in families where coping skills are deficient, it can play an important role.[39] Helping parents cope with the stress is part of the group therapy we have done with parents.

Describing what we do in therapy—both with children and with parents—and discussing what techniques work is another aim of this book. We also provide a conceptual framework for therapy that is derived from our model on the causes of abuse. How Goal Attainment Scaling is used therapeutically and as an evaluation tool is presented. We will show how GAS provides an objective assessment for determining when a home is safe for a child after abuse has occurred and the parents have been treated in therapy.

In this book we attempt to present important advances from child abuse research and clinical practice that have had an impact on treatment and prevention approaches. After Chapter 1 discusses the role of stress in child abuse, we present in Chapter 2 current ideas on causation. Chapter 3 describes the theoretical model we have followed in explaining and treating abuse. In Chapter 4 we review epidemiological features of the problem. Our group therapy interventions and techniques, as well as goal-setting and evaluation measures, are discussed in Chapters 5 and 6. Chapter 7 focuses on characteristics of children and adults who have survived abuse with the fewest scars. In Chapter 8 we describe therapy with abused children and the issues that must be addressed. Chapter 9 presents advances in primary prevention, and in Chapter 10 we discuss the important contributions of nonprofessional caregivers and children's protective services.

1

Child Abuse as a Response to Stress

What distinguishes the abusing family from the nonabusing one? Parents who abuse their children are not cruel maniacs, nor do they lack love for their child. Furthermore, the vast majority of them are not what most people would call crazy. "It is striking how few relationships discriminate between abusing and nonabusing families.... This implies that in many ways abusing families are 'just like everyone else.'"[1] So how are abusing parents different from parents who do not physically abuse their children?

One of the main differentiating factors is that abusing families not only are under high stress but also are more likely to respond to pressure with violence.[2] In virtually every theoretical approach to child abuse today, stress is seen as playing a role, but how a family deals with it is more important than the stress itself.

Stress alone is not a necessary or sufficient cause for abuse.[3] Murray Straus,[4] one of the foremost researchers on violence in the American family, argues that stress does not directly cause child abuse. "Violence is only one of many possible responses to stress. Among the alternatives are passivity, resignation, or just leaving."[5] Many families experience high levels of stress and do not abuse their children. In a study of 1146 parents, Straus found that for stress to result in violence, these factors were present:

1. The parents had fathers who used physical punishment and who observed their fathers hitting their mothers, thus training parents to respond to stress with violence.
2. The parents believe that physical punishment of children and slapping a spouse are appropriate behavior.
3. The marriage is not an important and rewarding part of the parents' lives.
4. The parents engage in physical fights with one another.
5. The parents have a combination of low income, education, and occupation.
6. The parents believe that husbands should be the dominant person in the marriage, and, to a lesser extent, when husbands actually are in such a position of power.
7. The parents are socially isolated.

To test for the influence that attitudes toward the use of violence have in child abuse, we compared 23 abusive couples with a matched control group of 23 who had not abused their children. The two groups were given these instruments:

1. Social Information Form
2. Recent Life Changes Questionnaire
3. Clarke Parent/Child Relations Questionnaire
4. Family Environment Scale
5. Social Support System Inventory
6. Self-Description and Mate Description

The Recent Life Changes Questionnaire was used as the measure of stress. Questions on the use of physical force in child rearing were taken from the Clarke Questionnaire. Questions on the use of violence as a socially acceptable response to stress or to solve problems were taken from the Family Environment Scale and the Clarke Parent/Child Relations Questionnaire.

There was a statistically significant difference between abusers and nonabusers on the level of stress, as measured by the Recent Life Changes Questionnaire. There was also a statistically significant difference between the two groups on violence as a socially acceptable or programmed response to stress or as a means to solve a problem (Table 1).

The results of the study supported Straus's contention that violence occurs under stress because parents see it as a legitimate way to solve a problem or have been socialized to use it. While life crises and the stress of excessive change may be predisposing factors, abuse occurs among parents who have been socially scripted to respond to stress with violence or who see violence as a legitimate means for solving a problem. The abusive parents in this study who had high levels of stress were more likely to answer "yes" to such items as "Family members sometimes hit each other" and "Did you ever see your father strike your mother?" (in their family of origin).

The kind of stress that abusing parents seem to have the most difficulty dealing with is change. In an earlier study, we compared a group of 35 abusing parents and an equal number of nonabusers who were similar in age, education, and income.[6] Although the nonabusive parents also had problems with their children, none had ever been physically abusive. We asked the parents in each group to fill out a questionnaire containing 39 questions and the Social Readjustment Rating Scale developed by Holmes and Rahe.[7] The most striking differences between the groups centered on their responses on the rating scale, which represents 43 different changes that could occur in a year's time in the lives of the parents—chan-

Table 1. Factors Analyzed for Their Value in Predicting Child Abuse
(N = 46)[a]

Variable	Group	Mean score	Standard deviation	t value	Two-tailed prob-ability
Stress					
Normative	Abusers	562.89	172.00	2.924	.0045
weighting	Nonabusers	438.80	231.00		
Self-weighting	Abusers	115.87	42.40	2.662	.0093
	Nonabusers	89.85	51.00		
N of changes	Abusers	15.33	4.72	2.987	.0037
	Nonabusers	11.96	6.02		
Dependency	Abusers	14.46	27.07	−0.230	.8160
	Nonabusers	16.21	23.65		
Physical force	Abusers	3.63	7.23	0.010	
	Nonabusers	3.61	9.55		
Maladaptive	Abusers	43.61	33.70	−0.790	.4310
coping	Nonabusers	49.87	17.16		
Violence as a	Abusers	.70	3.15	−2.190	.0340
social script	Nonabusers	3.13	4.30		
Symbiosis	Abusers	4.74	5.04	−2.200	.05
	Nonabusers	7.78	4.69		

[a] From Note 22.

ges that require readjustment as a means of coping (see Tables 2 and 3).

It was evident that the abusing parents had undergone too much change too fast. They had either experienced many more changes or had undergone more serious changes than the nonabusers. The number and magnitude of the changes they had to adjust to constituted a "life crisis," which preceded the onset of abuse. The nonabusing parents had not experienced a life crisis and had not been exposed to an excessive number of changes.

As we shall see in Chapter 2, one theory about the cause of child abuse is that parents are under too much economic

Table 2. Distribution of Life-Change Scores for Abusing and Nonabusing Parents[a]

| Parent group | Life-change scores | | | |
	No crisis 0–149	Mild crisis 150–199	Moderate crisis 200–299	Major crisis 300+
Abusers (N = 35) $\overline{X}$ = 233.63	4	9	14	8
Nonabusers (N = 35) $\overline{X}$ = 123.62	25	5	3	2

[a] χ^2 = 25.69, $p < .001$; t_{ind} = 4.28, $p < .001$.

stress. Those who take this position argue that a disproportionate amount of abuse occurs in poor families. A review of the literature by Straus[8] concludes that not all research supports this view.

While it may be true that there is a higher incidence of abuse reported among lower socioeconomic families, if economic stress were the overriding factor, little abuse would occur among the middle- and upper-income families, and most, if not all, poor people would abuse their children. This is clearly not the case.

When the abusing and nonabusing parents (the poor and the affluent were equally represented in the two groups) in our earlier study were compared, we found that change, not economic or environmental stress, was the distinguishing factor.[9] Change requires constant readjustment. Although it is possible to adapt to chronic stress, excessive change constantly throws people off balance. It is as though they never have time to catch their breath or mobilize their resources before they are confronted with a new change. Because change requires decision making and problem solving, people must be constantly on the alert, waiting for the new and unexpected to happen. The result is what Toffler described as a kind of numbness caused by sensory overload.[10]

Table 3. Social Readjustment Rating Scale

Rank	Life event	Mean value
1	Death of spouse	100
2	Divorce	73
3	Marital separation	65
4	Jail terms	63
5	Death of close family member	63
6	Personal injury or illness	53
7	Marriage	50
8	Fired at work	47
9	Marital reconciliation	45
10	Retirement	45
11	Change in health of family member	44
12	Pregnancy	40
13	Sex difficulties	39
14	Gain of new family member	39
15	Business readjustment	39
16	Change in financial state	38
17	Death of close friend	37
18	Change to different line of work	36
19	Change in number of arguments with spouse	35
20	Mortgage over $10,000	31
21	Foreclosure of mortgage or loan	30
22	Change in responsibilities at work	29
23	Son or daughter leaving home	29
24	Trouble with in-laws	29
25	Outstanding personal achievement	28
26	Wife begin or stop work	26
27	Begin or end school	26
28	Change in living conditions	25
29	Revision of personal habits	24
30	Trouble with boss	23
31	Change in work hours or conditions	20
32	Change in residence	20
33	Change in schools	20
34	Change in recreation	19
35	Change in church activities	19
36	Change in social activities	18
37	Mortgage or loan less than $10,000	17
38	Change in sleeping habits	16

Table 3. Continued

Rank	Life event	Mean value
39	Change in number of family get-togethers	15
40	Change in eating habits	15
41	Vacation	13
42	Christmas	12
43	Minor violations of the law	11

[a] *Source:* T. H. Holmes & R. H. Rahe. The social readjustment rating scale. *Journal of Psychosomatic Research, 11,* 213–218 (1967).

At the time we did this earlier study, the Social Readjustment Rating Scale was one of the most widely used instruments for measuring the role of life stress in psychosomatic illness, injury, and accidents. It has since been used extensively as an instrument for assessing the role of stress in child abuse.[11] Our study suggested that a large number of life change units in a year is also associated with the onset of abusive behavior.

We do not mean that excessive change—constituting a prolonged life crisis—is the cause of child abuse (see Chapters 2 and 3). However, change is a predisposing factor. A rapid series of changes is more difficult for a person to deal with than a situational crisis. In a situational crisis, which may involve divorce, loss of job, or sickness, a person's defenses are weak when the stress is most severe, but the individual has time to mobilize new resources to deal with the problem. In dealing with it successfully, that person achieves a higher level of functioning, with greater emotional equilibrium, than before.[12] A life crisis, however, consists of a series of situational events that are compressed together and sometimes accompanied by maturational crises, such as marriage, pregnancy, a child leaving home, or retirement. Table 3 presents the Social Readjustment Scale given to the abusing and nonabusing groups of parents. The abusing parents we studied scored high on the Social Readjustment Rating Scale in that they experienced excessive change during the 12 months prior to the onset of their abusive behavior.[13] As Table 2 shows, the life-change scores of the abusing parents constituted a series of situational and maturational crises that exceeded the parents' ability to adapt. In fact, we postulate that, unlike persons who undergo a single situational or maturational crisis, these parents had not had time to regroup before they were hit by a new crisis. In terms of Selye's three stages of response to stress (shock and countershock, resistance, and exhaustion), they no sooner passed through the first phase of shock and countershock and entered the resistance stage than they were confronted with a new crisis, which plunged them into the third stage, exhaustion.[14] It is in this third stage that their defenses were lowest and their inner controls against acting out were weakest.

The differences in change scores between the two groups in the earlier study was supported by the results of the study comparing the two groups of 23 couples. There was a statistically significant difference between abusers and nonabusers on the level of stress as measured by the Recent Life Changes Questionnaire, using normative weighting for change events. When self-weighting and number of life changes were used instead of normative weights, there were still statistical differences between the two groups. In other words, the abusive parents both experienced more changes and saw the events as more stressful than did the nonabusing couples.

Another statistically significant difference between the abusers and nonabusers in both this study and our earlier one was in answers related to the issue of symbiosis. Symbiosis, which we will discuss in detail in Chapter 3, is a relationship in which one partner tries to force the other into taking care of him or her emotionally. The partners function as if they cannot survive without the other and they establish a relationship in order to be the one receiving the caretaking. A symbiotic relationship between a mother and a baby is essential for survival of the child and can be mutually satisfying to both. But a symbiosis between the marriage partners, in which each is vying for the dependent role, or a role-reversal between the parent and child, in which the child becomes the caretaker of the parent, is socially destructive and psychologically crippling.

In the earlier study, the answers of the abusing and non-abusing parents to three questions on symbiosis differed sharply. Abusive parents were more likely to believe that their spouses had a closer relationship with the child than they had,[15] and they were more inclined to say that it was difficult to get the spouse to discipline the child.[16] In addition, the abusive parent was five times more likely to have difficulty getting the spouse to make decisions or accept responsibility. These answers are typical of persons who are involved in symbiotic relationships.[17]

In our second study, questions on symbiosis were taken from the Family Environment Scale, and from descriptions of self and mate. The difference between the abusive and non-abusive couples was significant, reflecting a struggle by one spouse to be the one receiving the nurturing. In abusing families, there is constant competition over who will be the receiver of nurturing.[18] Initially, the spouses compete with each other for the dependent role. The loser in the struggle turns to the child for nurturance. When the child fails to meet these unrealistic demands, a lifetime of frustration from unmet dependency needs may be unleashed on the child, particularly if violence is seen as a legitimate means of problem solving.

Because abusing parents chronically feel they are the losers in the struggle to be cared for, it is not surprising that they believe the spouse to be closer to the child and to be avoiding the responsibility of disciplining the child and making decisions. Those beliefs may be based on fact. Whether fact or feeling, such parents are reinforced in a lifelong feeling that they are carrying the greater burden in the family and shouldering responsibilities that belong rightfully to others. They view themselves as they always have—as losers in the competition for love and comfort.

In our work with abusing families, we have found that discipline and decision making are frequent sources of strife between the spouses. Much anger is generated in the struggle to get the other to do the parenting, to make decisions, and to take more responsibility.

The symbiotic struggle was also reflected in the way the abusive parents responded to items on the Social Readjustment Rating Scale in the first study. The most highly significant differences between the two groups of parents showed up in "sex difficulties," "change in financial state," "trouble with in-laws," and "change in living conditions."[19] The abusing group experienced many more problems in these four areas than did the nonabusing parents.

Sexual difficulties are often present because the spouses are engaged in internecine warfare to make one take care of the other. In sex, neither partner is willing to try to satisfy the other. Instead, each demands to be satisfied. The sexual difficulties between spouses also reflect unresolved problems in other areas of daily life. Because of being abused as children, many abusing parents are distrustful and have never learned to get close to anyone. Instead of talking about problems with their mates, they pout or stew in silence. The resulting emotional estrangement, not surprisingly, is reflected in sexual difficulties.

The stress from "change in financial state" reflects the tendency in many abusive families we have worked with to go through frequent financial ups and downs. Often, the fluctuations are in part a result of the problems one or both of the parents have in making decisions and assuming responsibility. One partner often tends to put things off, even critical responsibilities such as paying bills. The procrastination seems at times to be a response to an almost magical belief that someone else is going to come along and pay the bills for him. He may skip work to the point where he is fired or may change jobs often. He has trouble accepting responsibility for making ends meet and bringing in a steady income. Poor problem-solving skills and a low self-image contribute to the avoidance behavior. The result is having to face one financial crisis after another. The same dynamics result in frequent changes in living conditions.

The symbiotic struggle is expressed in problems with in-laws when the parent views the spouse's parents as competitors for attention. Abusing parents are easily threatened by others who may interfere with their quest to be nurtured. In-laws may divert the attention of the spouse or child, refuse to give the abuser any positive recognition, and indeed interfere in the lives of the couple.

As noted, sexual difficulties, change in financial status, change in living conditions, and trouble with in-laws represent the four most highly significant areas of differences between abusing and nonabusing parents in terms of life-change events. When all 43 items are taken as a whole, the abusers still differ markedly from the nonabusers. Does this mean that abusing parents are simply unfortunate victims of changes over which they have no control? No. While they may not control changes such as death of a spouse or close friend, many of the changes that characterize their lives are self-induced. An analysis of the 43 items shown in Table 3 indicates that the changes that plague them fall into several categories related to family, marriage, health, occupation, economics, residence, group and peer relationships, education, religion, and recreation. A majority of the changes represented by these categories are the product of a particular kind of personality interacting with others and with the environment.

It has been our experience that the abusive parent's view of the world and patterns of coping invite one crisis after another, all of them demanding adjustment and change. As we will discuss later, many child-abusing parents were themselves abused as children, and, therefore, they experienced others as a source of pain, not comfort and sustenance. Isolation from people became a survival adaptation, one not easily relinquished. They have not learned how to call on other people to assist them through crises or even how to plan ahead to avoid crises. They usually grew up with chaos and violence, and for them, those are the norm. The parents may not define their lives as in crisis, but being subjected to many changes exhausts them to the point where they are at the risk of chronically "going over the edge" and losing control with their children.

Any experienced stress or crisis is a result of interaction between the person and the environment, including such persons' expectations of their ability to control the situation, basic attitudes, and the context that shapes these beliefs.[20] Success in dealing with the current crises depends in part on how the current and past crises are handled.[21] Since abusive parents have had remarkably little success in handling their children or their lives satisfactorily, change for these families means acquiring a repertoire of concrete coping skills for familial and interpersonal interactions. Central to their employing these skills is breaking up the symbiotic pattern. For this to happen, however, the following considerations must be kept in mind: (1) The two spouses in the abusing family are essentially alike, regardless of which one actually strikes out at the child, (2) the family functions as a system and the child plays a role as central as that of the parents, and (3) the causes of child abuse are multidetermined and require an evaluation of social and cultural as well as psychological forces.

2

Why Child Abuse Occurs
Theories and Models

The genesis of violence against children is a complex issue, as reflected in the number of models that have been proposed to explain abuse. Theories on the causes of child abuse fall into essentially three categories.[1] One group consists of the psychodynamic theories, which attribute the source of the problem to the parents' inadequate psychological functioning and understanding of their parental role. Learning theories constitute the second group. The premise underlying learning theories is that parents abuse their children because of having had abusive role models in their own childhoods or because they have inadequate skills for appropriate parenting. The third category is composed of the environmental theories. This approach suggests that a lack of material resources or social support is the main contributor to child abuse. More recently, a biosocial theory has emerged that considers abuse from the standpoint of factors that influence the amount of investment a parent is willing to make in a child. These include the "benefits" as well as the "costs" that a child is seen as presenting to the parent.

Each of these theoretical approaches has validity, but none is complete in itself. To take into consideration the many contributing and interacting causal factors, we propose a more comprehensive causal explanation, which we call the Psychosocial System Model. Our experience has been that neither the psychodynamic, learning, environmental nor biosocial theory is complete in itself. Each of these contains a central core of determinants that is basic to causation, but they are not sufficient to explain why child abuse occurs.

One basic question involved in causation is whether people abuse children because they are driven by environmental pressures and the provocation of a child or because they are predisposed to abusive behavior by psychological forces at work from within. In the last analysis, dividing the issue of causation in this way is misleading. Both external pressures and internal dynamics play a part and interact in such a way that one cannot be considered without the other. In fact, the question involves more than the environment and the personality. It also extends to structure—that is, how a family arranges itself in terms of who is allied with whom, what coalitions exist, and who is distant and disengaged.

To complicate the picture even further, the kind of cultural cues that continuously bombard parents must also be considered. These cultural messages conjure up images of what parents should be like and how children should behave. When their own and their children's real-life behavior differs from the message parents have absorbed, all kinds of conflict can result and feed into the process of abuse. Therefore, a public health model that approaches the problem from a systems point of view, incorporating host, agent, environment, and vector, can more properly represent the interplay of multiple forces that can result in child abuse. This is not to say, however, that simpler models lack explanatory power. Each one has merit.

PSYCHODYNAMIC THEORIES

The model that developed out of the work of the earliest pioneers in identifying and describing the battered child relies on psychodynamic determinants to explain the problem. Kempe *et al.* saw the lack of a "mothering imprint" as the basic dynamic of the potential to abuse.[2] In other words, a person has been reared in a way that precluded the experience of being mothered and nurtured. Thus, as adults, such persons cannot mother and nurture their own children.

Combined with this inability to nurture is an interplay of other dynamics: a lack of trust in others, a tendency toward isolation, a nonsupportive marital relationship, and excessive expectations toward the child. According to Kempe, two other factors must be present before the potential to abuse is activated: a "special" child (the abusing parents view the child as retarded, hyperactive, or in some other way different) and a crisis (a major stress or something as minor as a broken washing machine).[3]

Thus, Kempe and his colleagues did not ignore environmental stress in formulations of what causes child abuse. However, one distinguishing feature of the psychodynamic model is that it assigns a secondary role to everything except the individual internal psychology. Those who subscribe to this model note that child abuse occurs in all socioeconomic classes. Poor people live under more stress than persons with greater income, but if stress alone explained child abuse, then what explains the fact that the vast majority of lower-income individuals do not harm their children?

An important implication of the psychodynamic model is that no matter how much environmental stress there is, the act of abuse will not occur unless the psychological potential is present. As we pointed out, the majority of people believe that almost anyone can injure a child, given enough stress and frustration. Kempe, in effect, said no, that if persons do not have the psychological potential, nothing will make them abuse. And, as we have seen, that potential rests largely on whether a person was sufficiently nurtured as a child and thus acquired the ability to nurture. One problem with this notion is that there are varying degrees of nurturing, and whether a person acquires an early "mothering imprint" is not likely to be an all-or-none matter. Persons with a less delible imprint may have some potential to abuse, and if the stress becomes severe enough, abuse may occur.

Another feature of the psychodynamic model is the recognition it gives to "role reversal," the parental expectations that the child will act like an adult and give the parent love and care rather than vice versa.[4] The reason for this behavior can be traced to the parents' own childhood, when their parents did not provide them with sufficient mothering and care and their needs for dependency were therefore unfulfilled. Helfer depicts the role of this early psychological deprivation in the causation and perpetuation of the cycle of child abuse in his World of Abnormal Rearing model[5] (see Figure 1).

The cycle begins with a child being born to parents who, for a variety of reasons, do not meet its needs but hold unrealistic expectations that the baby is there to meet the needs of the parent. The child grows up being ineffective in getting its own needs met, distrusting people, and feeling that "I'm no damn good." Obviously, those experiences affect the choice of a mate and the consequent relationship. When a child is born of the union, the parent thinks, "At last! Here is someone who will love and take care of me." And the cycle of abuse repeats itself.

Role expectations of the child, alliances, coalitions, enmeshments, and disengagements among family members are part of a family systems view of child abuse. The repeated finding that illegitimate and unwanted children are at high risk in terms of being abused[6] is related to the concept of coalitions. For example,

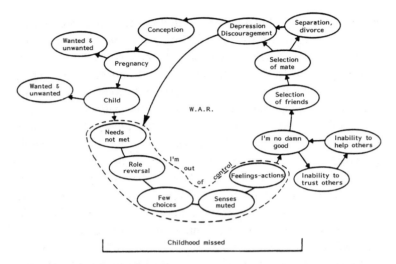

Figure 1. World of abnormal rearing, depicting cyclical nature of abuse and neglect. (From R. E. Helfer (1974). Developmental deficits which limit interpersonal skills. In R. E. Helfer & C. H. Kempe (Eds.), *The battered child* (p. 40). Chicago: University of Chicago Press. Copyright 1987 by the Social Science Research Council.)

a coalition may involve a parent who sides with one child against the abused child or both spouses who side against the abused child. Other arrangements in family structure may also result in abuse. One mother we worked with was so invested in her child that her husband literally tore the child from her arms on several occasions. The child was injured when her head slammed against a door facing.

Scapegoating is another behavior often cited as resulting in abuse.[7] Although the term may apply when a parent takes out his frustration on a child, it can also be used to describe the power struggles a child gets caught up in or an alliance that one spouse resents and makes the child pay for through physical injury. Disengagement on the part of a mother or father who declines to play a significant role in the family can also be central to child abuse. We have worked with more than one father who was on the periphery of the family and assumed little responsibility for managing his child. The wife in these cases often boils with resentment toward both her husband and her child. Since it is the child who demands her time and attention and is an easy target for her resentment, the child is the one who gets hurt.

Another psychodynamic theory is the personality or character trait model of child abuse. This model pays less attention to the factors that underlie the traits of the person who abuses than do those described above. The reason that parents abuse their children, according to the character trait model, is due to their psychological makeup, i.e., this is just the way they are. So parents are described as "immature," "self-centered," "impulse-ridden,"[8] as "chronically aggressive" and "highly frustrated," or "immature, lonely, impulsive, suspicious and untrusting people...."[9]

Merrill divided abusive mothers and fathers into three groups according to their psychological characteristics.[10] Parents in the first group were described as chronically hostile and aggressive, traits that often result in conflict with the world in general. His second group was made up of parents who were rigid and compulsive, and lacked warmth and a reasonable approach to things. The parents in the third group demonstrated a high degree of passivity and dependence, and many were depressed and unresponsive as well as immature. Merrill also had a fourth group, marked by extreme frustration. It consisted of young fathers who were unemployed and stayed at home to take care of the children. Their frustration often vented itself in child abuse.

Identifying the personality or character traits that are typical of an abusing person could end up as a form of branding or labeling unless they are associated with the context in which abuse occurs and the reasons the traits are present. Merrill's association of abuse with different personality traits describes the personality of an abusive parent but is not a causal explanation.

Many people are immature, impulsive, or self-centered, but they do not act violently toward their children. In this regard, the personality or character trait model is less helpful than other psychodynamic theories in that it does not offer an explanation of how these parents acquired these traits.

The mental illness model is similar to the character trait model in its implication that people who abuse their children are sick or mentally ill. In reality, the mental illness model applies only to a fraction of abusive parents. The overwhelming majority of them do not suffer from hallucinations or delusional systems, which characterize psychosis or being "crazy." Kempe stated that in his experience no more than 5% of abusive parents were psychotic.[11] A study in England concluded that "the attacking adult can rarely be fitted into a psychotic or parapsychotic grouping...."[12] Lascari holds that approximately 2% of abusing parents are psychotic, and Blumberg states that psychosis is rarely a factor in child abuse.[13]

The literature on child abuse does not reflect wide use of the term *mentally ill* when applied to persons who abuse children. However, there are fairly frequent references to emotional disturbances, psychopathology, character defects, personality disorders, and neuroses. Before Kempe identified child abuse for what it is in 1961, Woolley and Evans studied 12 infants with multiple fractures and discovered that they came from households with what was considered a high incidence of neurotic and psychotic behavior.[14] The suggestion was that only a mentally ill parent willfully inflicts physical abuse on a child.

Since then, mental retardation and organic brain disturbances have also been suggested as the cause of some cases of abuse.[15] Brain research indicates that the limbic system may be disturbed in some people who are excessively aggressive and show tendencies toward violence. Whether this disturbance accounts for some child abuse is still an open question. But the fact remains that everything from neurosis to organic brain dysfunction is included in the psychiatric profession's definition of mental illness. Thus, if the American Psychiatric Association's *Diagnostic and Statistical Manual of Mental Disorders* (3rd edition) is used, affective, psychotic, and personality disorders, mental retardation, and organic brain problems are all mental disorders. In this sense, some psychiatrists and other physicians argue rightly that abusive parents are mentally ill. The important point, however, is that while abusive parents are certainly not healthy emotionally, they do not fit easily into any single psychiatric classification.[16]

Many people get an odd sort of comfort in defining child-abusing parents as "sick" or "crazy." The unconscious logic seems to be that if "they" are crazy and "we" are not, then we are freed from the risk of abusing our children. Kempe once observed that "the concept stressed by us that young parents who physically abuse or neglect their small child without being necessarily 'bad' or 'mentally ill' causes a great deal of consternation."[17]

If people who commit child abuse are not "bad" or mentally ill, what are they? We believe strongly that the use of a medical model or psychiatric diagnosis to understand abusing parents and design effective intervention strategies is unnecessary. Branding these parents as sick or mentally ill may offer non-abusers a false sense of protection against their own angry or rageful feelings toward children, but the labeling also militates against the abusing parents' getting help, causing them to hide or flee out of fear that no one understands them.

There are instances in which a diagnosis of psychosis is appropriate. When a parent is cruelly sadistic to a child, tortures it with cigarette burns, bites the child, or administers bizarre punishment, that parent may well be responding to hallucinations or crazy delusional thoughts or may be on drugs. As Laury notes, "Some battering parents are mentally sick, and the child may become part of their distorted reality and delusional system. A paranoid parent may thus view his child as part of his persecuting environment and then feel justified in retaliating against him."[18] These are the kinds of stories that make the front pages of the newpapers and the headlines of the nightly news, but these are not typical behaviors of most parents who abuse their children.

In summary, the psychodynamic theory that has been adopted by a number of investigators[19] is that the root of problems within persons who abuse is the trauma that they themselves suffered as children, either physically or emotionally. More than just being rejected, adults who abuse demonstrate the kind of behavior they received as children. But it does not explain why persons who abuse express their problems in the form of violence rather than, or in addition to, other kinds of disturbed behavior, or why some abused children do not become child abusers. Being rejected as a child, developing no trust or close relationships, learning no love, having little tolerance for stress—all these factors produce problems that can and do find a wide range of expression. Some people withdraw from life, become alcoholic or paranoid, or act out in ways other than attacking their own children. Why then does a disturbed background or, in Helfer's words, "the world of abnormal parenting" express itself specifically in child abuse?[20] Other variables have to be taken into consideration.

LEARNING THEORIES

Learning theories of child abuse emphasize, rather than poor psychological functioning, the failure of abusive persons to acquire the skills and knowledge to adequately parent their children. These individuals are seen as so lacking the social skills as to "gain little satisfaction from their role as parents ... [and] are frequently ignorant of child development. They expect behavior too advanced for young children."[21] They also are inclined to use the only kind of discipline they know—physical discipline, which they received as children.

The social learning theories have considerable power in the formulation of intervention and treatment strategies. The models

based on these theories require the monitoring of specific behavior, on the part of both parents and child, that ends in abuse.
The idea is that if the immediate antecedents of abuse are properly identified, steps can be taken to modify the behavior they
represent and perhaps prevent abuse. More important to these
models, though, is the need to teach parents about childrearing
and how to modify their expectations concerning what the behavior of children and parents should be.

Nearly all couples we have worked with since 1973 have a
lack of knowledge about the stages of child development, what
children need at different ages, and how healthy parents respond, as well as many misconceptions about children and their
management. Learning theory lends itself to a behavior modification approach in working with parents and teaching them about
child management. There has been some success in both primary
and secondary prevention of child abuse by teaching parents effective childrearing practices through programmed learning and
courses in parenting.[22] (See Chapters 9 and 10.) The learning
model holds promise for treatment and prevention, and as an
explanation of why abuse occurs it has some usefulness but fails
to account for several relevant influences. Assuming that education will transform abusive parents into nurturers and good caretakers is woefully optimistic and unrealistic. People who
maltreat their children are missing much more than good information on childrearing.

ENVIRONMENTAL THEORIES

The leading exponents of the environmental stress theories
of child abuse see it as a multidimensional problem and place
heavy emphasis on stress as the cause.[23] The implication of their
models is that if it were not for adverse environmental factors,
such as poverty, poor education, and occupational stress, there

would be no child abuse. Economic stresses on poor people are seen as weakening their self-control and leading to violence against their children. The solution to child abuse, then, is sweeping programs to cure poverty, educate people, upgrade their skills, and change their style of discipline. According to Gil, focusing on the family as the only arena in which abuse occurs creates a "convenient smoke screen" that disguises the nature, scope, and dynamics of child abuse.[24]

Research in past years has suggested a causal relationship between poverty and child maltreatment.[25] Among poor families reported for abuse or neglect, the confirmed incidence rate is highest among the very poor. Also, the vast majority of fatalities occur among the very poor. Pelton argues, along with others, that the myth that child abuse is "classless" "supports the prestigious and fascinating psychodynamic medical model approach and by disassociating the problem from poverty, accords distinct and separate status to child abuse and neglect specialists."[26]

Those who subscribe to the environmental and economic stress theory note that as stress increases, so does child abuse. As economic pressures from the deep recession in 1975 mounted, an increase in child abuse cases was reported in a number of areas of the nation.[27] Fontana attributed the increase to "the stresses and strains that our society is suffering today—the frustrations, the poor quality of life, the increase in drug addiction and alcoholism."[28]

Bennie and Sclare also view child abuse as a lower-class phenomenon.[29] Blumberg and Steinmetz and Straus argue that intrafamilial violence is more common among the working class and that child abuse is part of the style of physical discipline that poor people use.[30]

While there is no doubt that environmental stresses do play a role in many instances of child abuse, the theories leave unexplained the thousands of cases of child abuse occurring in homes with no economic or environmental stress. Also, as Spinetta and Rigler point out:

> Eliminating environmental stress factors and bettering the level of society at all stages may reduce a myriad of social ills and may even prove effective, indirectly, in reducing the amount of child abuse. But there still remains the problem, insoluble at the demographic level, of why some parents abuse their children while others under the same stress factors do not.[31]

Obviously, environmental and economic stress alone is not enough to explain child abuse. Even Gil pointed out, "It should be emphasized ... that poverty, per se, is not a direct cause of child abuse in the home, but operates through an intervening variable, namely, concrete and psychological stress and frustration."[32]

BIOSOCIAL THEORY

An innovative approach to understanding the relationship among external social stressors, internal psychological stress, and child abuse is the parental investment theory. Parental investment is defined as "any investment by a parent in an offspring that increases the recipient's fitness at the cost of parental capacity to invest elsewhere."[33] The theory emphasizes the limited amount of parental resources (time, energy, attention) that can be apportioned to offspring over the course of the life spans of both parent and offspring. Earlier studies[34] supported the idea that mothers would appropriately protect and parent their children if bonding took place during a critical early period in the infant's life. Sociobiological research now indicates that there is no special period for mother-infant attachment in humans. "Bonding is not the issue but rather maternal assessment of environmental support.... Such work raised the question that it may not be unnatural for ... parents to neglect their children or even target a special child for abuse under particular sets of unfavorable contexts for parental behavior."[35] It appears that at each step of parenthood, parents are reassessing the current and future prospects of each child, and that faced with limited resources and unfavorable circumstances, they may decide to limit or cut off their investment.

Cross-cultural research suggests that certain groups of children are more likely to be undervalued and consequently seen as a poorer investment of parental resources.[35] The broad groups are as follows:

Health Status. Children whose health is inferior are more likely to receive poorer care. In societies with high infant and child mortality, the stronger child is more likely to receive preferential treatment. This observation is in part supported by the data, which show premature infants or babies and children that are difficult to care for being at higher risk for maltreatment. Malnourished children have also been found to be vulnerable. It is theorized that apathetic, anorexic, and unresponsive behaviors of malnourished children may fail to evoke a nurturing response that would improve their health as well as their behavior. This would certainly be true with abusive parents who are looking to be nurtured and affirmed by their offspring. To nurture a nonresponsive, ill child would probably demand of these parents more altruistic giving than most could put forth.

Deformed and Handicapped Children. Whether or not a deformed or handicapped child is targeted for maltreatment seems to depend on the cultural appraisal of the child. In some societies, deformities and handicaps are seen as indicating supernatural gifts, and the child is accorded special status and care. More often, unfortunately, the child is seen as a burden, an ill omen, or nonhuman. Understandably, with this sort of low value placed on the child, he or she is not likely to be cared for adequately.

Sex. The value placed on a male or female child in a particular culture influences the treatment of the child. Female children are at greater risk of maltreatment in societies with strong son preference, such as India or China. Women's economic participation and rights of land inheritance have been linked to regional differences in female infanticide and to differential access to food and medical resources. However, even though the girls are less likely to be fed as well as their brothers or to receive the same standard of medical care, those who survive are more likely to be treated warmly by their mothers in later childhood than are the sons. It is possible to assume that these mothers are more willing to invest in their daughters when they can see a greater potential return for the investment, such as helping the mothers do housework or finding sons-in-law to help care for the family.

Developmental Stage. A child in the throes of the "terrible twos" is a strain on any parent, and indeed children appear to be at greater risk of being abused as toddlers and adolescents. Toilet-training accidents, broken curfews, and oppositional behaviors of both those stages lead all parents to question—if only momentarily—whether or not the parenting struggle is worth the effort. But for parents who have unrealistic expectations and diminished emotional or social support, the answer may be a violent "no!"

Unusual, Excessive, or Difficult Births. Some children are assessed to be a poor investment from the moment of their births or even before birth. Among the Machiguenga, a difficult birth indicates an excessively angry child, which is then more likely to be killed, abandoned, or given to another family. If an infant is born face down or with a smile or teeth into the Bariba tribe of West Africa, it is labeled "witch baby" and killed or sold off. In some societies, multiple births are considered a good omen, and in others the offspring may be regarded as animal litters rather than human beings. If they are not killed at birth, they may be maltreated later. Too many children can push a parent to withhold limited resources from one or more of the offspring. Scrimshaw found that later-born children, second children of the same sex, particularly females, and children too closely spaced may be less likely to survive.[37]

Behavioral and Personality Characteristics. Parental assessment of the behavior of the child is influenced not only by the parents' own experience of having been parented but also by cultural appraisal of different behavioral or personality traits. For example, the Machiguenga of the Peruvian Amazon, who we mentioned above, devalue and disapprove of anger, and toddlers who have frequent tantrums are subjected to scalding baths. However, the Yanomamo of Venezuela highly value aggressiveness and encourage it in young male children.

While none of these observations mean that child abuse is caused solely as a result of the parent's biopsychosocial assessment of the appropriate investment in the child, they do make it clear that it is useful to look at the broad context of available investment resources. In order to understand all the factors that play a role in limiting those resources, a more comprehensive model is needed. We believe the Psychosocial System Model does that.

PSYCHOSOCIAL SYSTEM MODEL

Although there is empirical evidence that abusive families experience high levels of external stress, stress alone, as we have noted, cannot explain why violence occurs.[38] Straus presents data that refect a socialization for violence that cuts across all socioeconomic levels. He found that parents whose own fathers hit them as teenagers have a child abuse rate that is one-third higher than that of parents who were under equally high stress

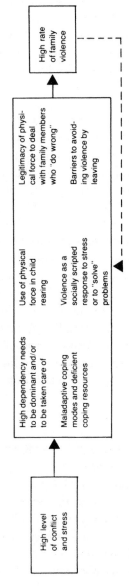

Figure 2. Adapted from M. A. Straus (1980). Stress and child abuse. In C. H. Kempe & R. E. Helfer (Eds.), The battered child (3rd ed., pp. 86–103). Chicago: University of Chicago Press. Copyright 1987 by the Social Science Research Council.

but had not experienced such treatment as adolescents. Also, the child abuse rate by parents whose own fathers hit their mothers was 44% higher than the rate of parents whose fathers never hit their mothers.

There is a legitimization of violence in abusive families. Straus found that the rate of child abuse was found to be 72% higher in families in which parents approved of slapping the spouse. The national survey he conducted determined that there was a 30% higher rate of child abuse in families in which there was an actual incidence of physical violence between parents during the year. In these families, violence is a socially scripted or accepted response to stress and a legitimate way to "solve" problems (see Chapter 1).

Certainly the role of learned behavior and the emotional consequences of living in a violent family are part of the socialization process. The relevance of each of these factors and their interaction has to be considered in order to explain what causes child abuse. The model in Figure 2, adapted from Straus's findings, shows how some of these determinants work together.

As mentioned above, the comprehensive model we propose that incorporates the factors proposed by each of the types of theories—psychodynamic, learning, environmental, biosocial—and the interaction of all of them is the Psychosocial System Model of child abuse, which we will present in detail in the next chapter. It is based on a public health model, with host, agent, environment, and the vector interacting among themselves. The host in our model is the parents and their psychological background and functioning. The agent is the child and the child's potential for contributing to the stress in the system. The environment includes the socioeconomic factors and life stresses. The vector that operates on the whole system represents cultural scripts that reinforce unrealistic expectations and legitimacy of violence. Our experience is that such a comprehensive model is necessary to understand, treat, and prevent the abuse of children.

3

A Psychosocial System and Shifting Symbiosis

As we have seen, the question of child abuse cannot be adequately examined by subscribing singularly to the idea that the abusing parent is mentally ill or by focusing only on the socioeconomic or situational stresses the parent is under, or by just looking at a set of personality character traits. Child abuse is the product of all these factors and still more. The "still more" is included in a psychosocial system model, which takes into account the shifting dynamic forces at work in the abusive family, in the environment, and in the culture in which the family lives. Abuse of a child is the end result of a system of interaction between the spouses, the parent and the child, the child and the environment, the parent and the environment, and the parent and society. What affects one affects another.

Since the family is the main system in which all the interaction takes place, it is impossible to speak of child abuse without mentioning the abusing family, the forces that operate in that total unit, and the influences that impinge on it. As Helfer points out, "The family must be considered as a total unit. Child abuse is a family affair."[1]

The precursors of abuse will be found not only in the individual parents and child and the crises they face but also in the systems and subsystems of which they are a part. As we just noted, the main system to which they belong is the family. Hence, to understand child abuse we must understand the abusing family system.

The notion of the family as a system is not new. Bowen noted that "the relationships between family members constitute a system in the sense that a reaction in one family member is followed by a predictable reaction in another, and that reaction is followed by a predictable chain reaction pattern."[2] Thus, when a parent competes with a small son or daughter for nurturance, all the other family members become part of the competition.

Our psychosocial system model is primarily concerned with two systems: the family system and the larger system of family, environment, and culture. The larger system is depicted in terms familiar to public health: host, environment, agent, and vector. Figure 3 represents this triad of interaction.

In public health, the question of whether a host suffers from a physical, mental, emotional, or social problem is the function of several considerations: the host's own resistance or vulnerability, the nature of stressful influences in the environment, the presence and potency of a precipitating agent, and a vector that transmits a stimulus to the responding host. When the model is adapted to the problem of child abuse, the host represents the parents, the environment represents physical and social influences and stresses, the agent is the child and its behavior/temperament, and the vector is the stimulus imparted from agent to host that carries the cultural "scripting" that governs interaction between the two.

Because there is continuing interaction and feedback between any two points on the triangle, as well as among all the

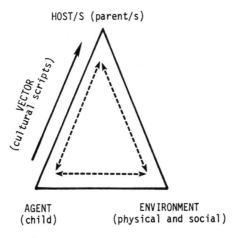

Figure 3. A psychosocial system model of child abuse.

points taken as a whole, there are subsystems within the larger system. Again, any change in one affects the other. Although the system is primarily psychosocial, it also includes a biological element. For example, as Bishop suggests, the host's childrearing abilities "are determined by her own genetic endowment modified positively or negatively by her own parenting experience; her adaptation to it; her present emotional and physical health; as well as current socio-economic and interpersonal stress."[3] Thus, the variables at any point in the host/environment/agent triad are themselves multiple. Although we do not suggest that they involve only psychological and social variables, it is in those arenas that the action takes place. But the individual's biological makeup and the physical attributes of the environment also play a part. Examples of characteristics of the environment, host, agent, and vector will be more fully developed in Chapter 4. At this point, we will present a few elements of each to illustrate the psychosocial system and how the triadal model lends itself to intervention.

Our model identifies the parents as the host in the problem of child abuse. It does not focus on the parent who actually beats or injures the child to the exclusion of the one who does not act out. As Isaacs has pointed out: "Both parents are the same.... It doesn't matter which one did the actual battering."[4] Other investigators, including Kempe, have reached the same conclusion.[5]

SCARCE EMOTIONAL GOODS

Abusing parents, as we indicated earlier, seek from their children and mates the satisfaction of their own needs for comfort, nurturing, and control. They expect them to meet their needs and to make up for the emotional deprivations and sense of helplessness they suffered in their own childhoods. The family is seen not as a place for mutual support and sustenance but rather as a competition for scarce emotional goods. The competition between the parents for nurturance may be masked by culturally accepted roles.

In public, for example, the husband may make the decisions and appear to be the caretaker of the family. At home, however, he may abdicate any responsibility for parenting and adopt a passive stance that forces his wife to become the emotional caretaker of him as well as of the children. This "Ask your mother" syndrome leaves the woman feeling helpless and unsupported emotionally. Being the "loser" in the struggle for caretaking, she directs her attention to forcing her child to meet those needs.[6] While it is the mother in this example who turns to the child, the roles are often reversed, with the father being the one turning to the child for nurturance and decision making.

The parents are locked into a shifting symbiotic relationship in which each seeks emotional satisfaction from the other and from the children. The result is that neither the parents' nor the children's needs are met.

In the environment in which child abuse occurs, the most marked feature is change. A constant need to readjust is imposed on parent and child. Defenses drop and controls weaken. Support systems are lacking. Isolation is common. The physical environment may add more stress if the home is overcrowded because of too many children, too little space, or both.

In our model, the child and his behavior or temperament are considered the agent that may trigger abuse. As we emphasized earlier, abuse results from a system of multiple interactions, but the child, and the parent's perception of the child, is the most immediate source of external stress for the abusing parent. The child's very proximity makes him an easy target for the parents whose frustrations spill over into physical aggression.

Some babies and children are of a temperament that makes them particularly difficult, aggravating, and hard to handle (see Chapter 9). They may also be more demanding because of physical problems, such as being colicky or premature. According to Flynn, the "obnoxious child" is a natural stimulus for abuse.[7] Parents who are seeking nurturing and closeness from a child may be provoked to rage and violence when the child responds with unremitting crying, sleeplessness, and agitation. A difficult baby is hard on any parent, but that same baby becomes at risk for abuse when its behavior symbolizes thwarted love and failure as a parent to the mother or the father. When the child makes unusually great demands on the potentially abusive parent, the child is in danger. Chapter 9 describes some of the high-risk children, a group that includes premature or illegitimate babies and children who are congenitally malformed or mentally retarded.[8]

The vector in our psychosocial system model represents the "cultural scripting" of the parents and carries the stimulus from the agent to the host. By cultural scripts we mean the accepted and expected patterns of interaction between individuals in a society. Cultural scripts are spoken and unspoken assumptions about human behavior that result from culturally endorsed messages, injunctions, and myths about how people should act, feel, and think.[9]

As we will explain more in Chapter 4, cultural scripts have a significant influence on the expectations of parents and their responses to their children. The myth of the Madonna Mother leaves many young mothers expecting themselves to be unfailingly loving. The Gerber Baby myth presents an image of all babies as cute, cuddly, and clean, exactly like the precious toddlers pictured on the diaper boxes and baby food jars. Parents who believe these myths may blame both themselves and their babies when their lives are vastly different from the mythical images. Another cultural script in American society is that violence is both an acceptable and a necessary method of child management, as Straus and his colleagues so clearly demonstrated.

One advantage of this triadal system model is that it offers an opportunity for preventive interventions at various levels, which occurs in public health practice. Intervention may occur at the level of host (parents), agent (child), environment, or vector (cultural scripts). We will devote more attention to this topic in our discussion of primary prevention in Chapter 9.

THE ABUSING FAMILY SYSTEM

Now that we have highlighted the features of the larger system bearing on child abuse, we can address the family system—the area of action. Jenkins and Lystad have pointed out that child abuse often occurs generation after generation in the same family, as if a cycle of violence is inherited.[10] As Helfer's World of Abnormal Parenting cycle explains, what is inherited is not a genetic propensity for abuse but a particular kind of emotional and relationship system that requires the family to absorb large amounts of tension. One expression of this tension is violence, and one target of the violence is a child. The term *emotional and relationship system* is derived from Bowen, a pioneer family therapist, who noted that "the term emotional refers to the force that motivates the system, and the relationship to the ways it is expressed."[11]

The kind of emotional and relationship system that characterizes the abusing family is one of great intensity, force, and fusion (the "stuck-togetherness" that has been found in many kinds of dysfunctional families). Either the spouses are tightly bound to one another, one parent is fused with the child, or the husband or wife is still intensely tied to his or her family of origin. This kind of fusion is healthy and necessary only when it exists between a mother and her baby. It is imperative that an infant fuse with its mother or some mother surrogate to survive. But in some families, the emotional and even physical stuck-togetherness continues far beyond infancy and sometimes throughout life. These people grow up looking for others with whom they can fuse or form a symbiotic relationship. They try to form a common self. Both are "feeling" people—that is, orienting themselves to the world and others strictly on the basis of what feels right. They are not "thinking" people in the sense of rationally planning goals and ways to meet them. Since they are not "whole" people, they do not have a defined self. They exist as part of others and are so busy "seeking love and approval, or attacking the other for not providing it, that there is little energy left for self-determined, goal-directed activity."[12]

Bowen calls these people "undifferentiated." They are undifferentiated in the sense of being fused into others who make up the nuclear or extended family. They do not have a separate self. The more undifferentiation there is, the more likely that problems will occur during stress. These problems can be expressed in three areas: marital conflict, dysfunction in a spouse, and transmission of the problem to one or more children.[13] The marital conflict takes the form of fights between the spouses as if to see which one will obtain more of the common self. Dysfunction in one of the spouses usually means that one has given in to the other. The dysfunction may be physical, emotional, or social. Social dysfunction includes acting-out behavior such as violence. When the problem is transmitted to the child, the same kinds of dysfunction may occur.

In child abuse, the dysfunction in a spouse spills over into violent behavior that is directed at the child. The family system must absorb so much undifferentiation that there may not only be violence by father or mother but a problem in all three areas: conflict between spouses, the dysfunction of one, and something wrong with the child. The root of the problem is competition within the family system over which one will be taken care of by the other. The spouses fight over who will give in to whom, who will wait on whom, who will do more for whom. The winner is taken care of, and the loser turns to more extreme behavior to obtain care. The acting-out is directed at a "special" child—the one the parent perceives as being most in need of attention or care and is therefore the most threatening competitor to the parent seeking the same thing. The parent's violent behavior toward the child represents an extreme effort to get somebody to step in and give the parent the attention and care that he or she seeks.

When there is only one parent in the nuclear family, there is nearly always some fusion between that parent and a relative in the family of origin. If that relative does not provide the parent with the desired attention and care, the parent turns to the child, who cannot possibly meet those demands. The attention and care come only after there has been abuse, and the authorities have stepped in. Even then, the care is often not the kind that is likely to promote the parent's rehabilitation and growth.

Undifferentiation, and the immaturity that results, is a multigenerational process in that the stuck-togetherness or fusion of family members that characterizes a family in one generation is passed on to the next.[14] Members in each generation fail to learn how to individuate, become whole people, meet their own needs, and overcome the need to fuse with others. Thus, the cycle of dysfunction perpetuates itself.

IMBALANCE BETWEEN TWO BASIC NEEDS

The family system is the arena in which two fundamental issues must constantly be addressed: how to meet one's need to belong and simultaneously individuate or become one's own person with a distinct self. Whitaker identified these two issues as basic to all problems of human existence.[15] It is in the family system where these issues are struggled with most intensely. This struggle goes on in all families and in all emotional systems, whether a work, social, or cultural system. Dysfunction sets in only when fusion occurs to such a degree that belongingness becomes stuck-togetherness and individuation is obliterated.

Undifferentiation generates tension and latent anger. The tension results from the constant struggle to merge oneself with another, to incorporate the other, to become part of someone else as though in a desperate effort to meet primitive unmet needs to belong and be nurtured. The latent anger results from suppressing the opposing drive to be an individual, have a separate self or identity, and be one's own person. Because the process of individuation or separation is painful and frightening, undifferentiated people tend to view the process as impossible for them. So they try desperately to fuse with others. It is almost as if they are saying, "I can't survive without being a part of you." But simultaneously they desire a sense of self apart. The more they merge themselves (or are merged) into the undifferentiated mass of the other family members, the more their latent anger mounts. Thus, they are caught in the middle of a psychic tug-of-war. They "long for closeness but are allergic to it."[16]

The "allergy," the tension, the anger—all must be absorbed by the family system. Fights between husband and wife can absorb a certain amount. Sickness on the part of one spouse can absorb some. And physical, emotional, or behavioral problems of a child can absorb a certain quantity. But if the undifferentiation and the accompanying tension and anger are too great, the entire system becomes dysfunctional. This is what occurs in the abusing family. So much tension and anger from unmet needs must be absorbed that verbal conflict and sickness are not enough. Violence too is necessary. Yet violence occurs in some instances in families where there is no evidence of overt conflict or sickness. In these cases, the spouses express pride about how few arguments they have. Thus, the tension between them, blocked from being partially expressed through verbal conflict, must find other avenues for release. When the tension mounts to the boiling point, it is released through violent channels, sending the family system into dysfunction and partial collapse.

How does this process get started in the first place? It begins with an impaired symbiosis between mother and infant. As we stated previously, an intense emotional and physical bonding between them is necessary for the newborn's survival. The relationship becomes destructive only when the mother fails to meet the baby's needs or when the symbiotic attachment lasts beyond the time when the child should begin to establish a separate sense of self and to individuate. Mothers are not the only ones who can establish a symbiotic attachment with the infant, but someone must assume the role of a compassionate, caring nurturer if the symbiosis is to be successful in meeting the baby's early developmental needs.

As Helfer described in the W.A.R. cycle, in abusive families the parents' unrealistic expectations of the child and their own neediness result in the infant's needs not being met. The symbiosis is impaired. Where the symbiosis is insufficient or inconsistent, the baby receives little nurturing and care and is left with a hunger for dependency. As these children grow up, they keep seeking the nurturing they lacked in infancy or childhood and keep looking for someone to fill that emotional hunger. Much of their feeling and fantasy life revolves around finding and fusing with that someone. In fact, they devote so much energy to their need to fuse and attach to someone else that they remain undifferentiated and lack a defined self of their own. When they marry, they usually pick spouses who understand that neediness because of their own childhood deprivation, and the struggle for who will care for whom begins. The loser in the struggle is likely to resort to physical illness or emotional disturbance to obtain attention and care. Just as fighting is one expression of fusion between two people, sickness is another. As noted, when the tension is so great it cannot be absorbed by verbal conflict or illness, it may be expressed in violence. In the abusing family, the child who is in need of attention becomes the target of the violent tension that the system is unable to absorb. The spouse who does the actual physical abusing is losing the battle to be cared for and feels he or she must therefore eliminate competition that the child represents. Only when the entire system becomes so dysfunctional that outside intervention occurs is the tension dispersed. At that point, everyone gets attention, if only temporarily or partially.

The same outcome results when the original symbiosis is intense and prolonged rather than insufficient. In such cases, the children grow up knowing no other way to function or live than to attach themselves to someone else. Although they are dependent on the attachment, their suppressed anger over being "smothered" by the mother or some other caretaker increases. They have little differentiation as persons, little sense of self or individuation. When they marry, they choose spouses they can shift their attachment to—persons who also seek fusion and wholeness through being a part of somebody else. The same tension described above develops from the undifferentiation—from the struggle over a common self, over who is to care for whom. Mixed with the tension is the anger over being dependent and not being a separate, autonomous individual. The tension and anger are too much for the system to absorb through verbal conflict and sickness, and, again, violence is the outcome. The violence may be expressed toward the spouse or toward the child to whom the parent has turned for a continuation of the original symbiotic attachment.

At the root of the multigenerational transmission process is the merger of two persons of insufficient differentiation. In child abuse, as we have seen, the level of differentiation is so low that marital conflict and sickness—sickness of a parent, a child, or both—are not enough to absorb the tension, anger, and immaturity. This does not mean that both spouses will necessarily appear to function at an extremely low level of differentiation— that is, seem extremely dependent, irresponsible, immature, impulsive, and narcissistic. Either one or both may be poorly differentiated but may shift to a higher level of functioning in some areas.[17]

We have worked with families in which the father functionally appears to be self-sufficient, competent, and "whole." One father, a computer analyst, worked hard, showed few emotional upsets, and seemed to be quite autonomous. His symbiotic struggle with his wife took a physical form. He arranged to be cared for by having chronic back pain. He would literally be "flat on his back" for days at a time. Although he avoided emotional closeness, he was emotionally fused with his mother, calling her almost daily and never making a major decision without first consulting her. This father also had a heavy emotional fusion with his work. His work became another "competitor" in the eyes of his already emotionally deprived wife. While some of his undifferentiation was absorbed by his work, the effect at home was that the wife felt increasingly needy and desperate the more he worked. They struggled fiercely but never overtly for nurturance. When his physical illness and work were not sufficient to absorb all of the family's tension and anger, and when the wife decided she had lost the struggle to be cared for, in her frustrated rage, she jerked her infant son in his bed, breaking his arm in the process.

SOME INTERVENTIONS

Intervention in this kind of system must focus on helping the spouses gain a sense of differentiation and separateness. This is essential for the child not only to escape abuse but to gain a sense of self. As long as the same degree of fusion exists in the family, the emotional stuck-togetherness keeps all members from defining their own boundaries and becoming responsible in getting their needs met. There is much narcissism in the abusive family system in terms of "Give me" or "I want." There is little expression of individuality, as evidenced in statements such as "I am," "I believe," "I will do," "I will not do."[18] We encourage spouses to start taking "I positions" and to make statements that clearly mark where they stand and who they are.

One way to accomplish this is to use the kind of "I messages" taught in Parent Effectiveness Training.[19] We teach parents to use these "I messages" in interactions with their spouses and children. When one family member does something that is a problem for another, the "I message" is a less threatening form of confrontation and invites communication to continue. The method involves the person with the problem stating how he feels, describing the behavior that bothers him, and explaining why it bothers him. This form of direct communication about a problem is alien to highly fused and undifferentiated families because it results in clear statements of individual feelings, beliefs, wants, and needs. To make these kinds of statements requires a sense of self.

The self-definition process is enhanced further by having the parents examine their relationships with their families of origin. Although the immediate problem in abusing families is the tension, anger, or dysfunction that exists between the two spouses, the roots of the problem, as we have seen in looking at impaired symbiotic relationships, lie in the unresolved emotional bonds of childhood. Although a young family may be geographically separated from the family of origin, they still have much "unfinished emotional business" with them, in the sense of having to work through emotional bonds and unresolved feelings of deprivation and anger.

Sometimes the ties are obvious. One very young couple in our group used all their savings to buy expensive Christmas presents for their parents. It was as if they wanted to atone for being "bad children" in having abused their son. The irony is that both of these parents had been abused as children, and the maternal grandmother was given temporary custody of the child. This practice, as Martin observed, is "a dubious if not patently ridiculous therapeutic regime" since, as Helfer adds, the "relatives are rarely helpful because they created the problem in the first place."[20] The custodial arrangement, while probably unavoidable at times, only adds to the lethal family fusion.

While the couples we treat may be defensive about discussing their families of origin and their upbringing, facing the reality of their childhood experiences and their current emotional conflict with their parents is essential for differentiation to take place and the self to emerge.

Once we have explored the nature of their emotionally fused relationships with their parents, the next step is gently urging them to practice using "I messages" with their mothers and fathers. They can take tentative steps toward autonomy while being supported emotionally by the group. As they learn some facility in doing so, the parents gain a greater sense of separateness, and the tension and anger diminish.

We will discuss our other approaches to breaking up the fusion or symbiosis in Chapter 5. First, however, we will examine the process of shifting symbiosis and how this relates causally to a child's being abused.

SHIFTING SYMBIOSIS

> Basic in the abuser's attitude toward infants is the convic-
> tion, largely unconscious, that children exist in order to
> satisfy parental needs. Infants who do not satisfy these
> needs should be punished ... to make them behave proper-
> ly.... It is as though the infant were looked to as a need-
> satisfying parental object to fill the residual, unsatisfied,
> infantile needs of the parent.[21]

When children are born, their survival depends on the willingness of a parent or caretaker to meet their needs. In addition
to having a willingness to meet the child's needs, the parent must
be able to assess what those needs are without a specific request
from the infant. The infant's survival demands a symbiotic
relationship.

Symbiosis, as we discussed previously, begins as a life-sus-
taining relationship between mother and child in the earliest
stage of development.[22] An example of normal symbiosis is
when a mother awakens at her infant's first whimper and gets
up to feed, change, or in some other way attend to its needs.
Symbiosis can be experienced as meeting mutually shared needs,
the infant's to be nurtured and the mother's to nurture.

When the symbiosis is impaired through premature separation, a lack of parental responsiveness, neglect, or overprotection,
the child is unprepared "to function as an independent person
who can solve problems in the world."[23] With no individuation,
there is no sense of autonomy. The difference between meeting
one's needs through symbiosis and through autonomy is that
autonomous persons are aware of their needs and consciously
take steps to meet those needs. This requires an awareness of
an ability to meet one's needs. In a symbiotic relationship, these
persons manipulate others into meeting their needs without considering whether the other person is willing or able to do so.
Relationships recreate the dynamics of infancy—a demand that
another respond to one's needs.

The demand takes the form of passivity. Passivity, in the context of symbiosis, means devoting one's energies to reestablishing a symbiotic relationship—as opposed to taking direct action to meet one's own needs.[24] There are four significant categories of passive behavior. They are (1) doing nothing, (2) overadaptation, (3) agitation, and (4) incapacitation or violence. Persons who "do nothing" mobilize all their energy to avoid responding when confronted with a problem. Doing nothing is usually accompanied by not thinking. Persons who "overadapt" try to solve a problem according to someone else's expectations rather than deciding on their own solution and carrying it out. Again, these persons are not thinking about their ability to come up with a solution. "Agitation" is non-goal-directed activity, such as wiggling one's foot or chain-smoking. Both behaviors may relieve tension but do nothing to solve the problem that is the source of the tension. Although "violence" and "incapacitation" seem to be opposites, they both serve to discharge the pent-up tension and anger that Bowen describes as resulting from fusion, helplessness, and an inability to think of any other effective way to get one's needs met.

Since "not thinking" about a solution underlies each of the passive behaviors described here, the result is that someone else is left with the task of solving these persons' problems for them. Extreme forms of passivity—insanity, violence, physical incapacitation—demand that society do something to stop or contain the problem. Mental institutions, prisons, and hospitals exist to ensure that people who are unable to come up with acceptable solutions to their problems are cared for appropriately. The man who batters his child forces the community to come up with a solution. The response may be either punitive or therapeutic, but either way, his behavior demands what is, in essence, a symbiotic response.

When infants or children repeatedly experience ineffectiveness in their efforts at getting needs met, the logical result is a belief that they are incompetent in taking care of themselves.

They discount their ability to come up with competent solutions to their problems. In symbiotic passivity, there are four ways in which people discount.[25] They discount the problem, the significance of the problem, the solvability of the problem, or the person. Discounting the existence of the problem is involved when parents insist that they are adequate parents, although authorities have removed their infant after it was hospitalized for multiple fractures, lacerations, bruises, or failing to thrive. "She bruises easily" is discounting the significance of the problem. Insisting that children will not learn respect unless they are spanked discounts the solvability of the problem. Protesting, "That kid's impossible! I couldn't help it!" discounts both the child and the parent.

SYMBIOSIS IN TRANSACTIONAL ANALYSIS TERMS

Transactional analysis is one approach we have found very effective in enabling abusive parents to think more clearly about their emotions and the life problems they are facing. Its concepts of ego states, transactions, and games are readily grasped by most people and help them make sense out of the emotional struggles they experience in trying to resolve their conflicting needs for closeness and autonomy.

Berne, the originator of the theory of transactional analysis, saw people having distinct and differing aspects of their personalities. He called these aspects ego states and labeled them Parent, Adult, and Child, after the kind of "personality" each ego state appeared to represent. Berne noted, "Parent-Adult-Child are all ego states which are observable realities that can be consciously experienced...."[26] The three ego states are distinguishable by "skeletal-muscular variables and the content of verbal utterances. Certain gestures, postures, mannerisms, facial expressions and intonations, as well as certain words, are typically associated with one of the three ego-states."[27]

The Parent ego state is the judgmental, opinionated, rule-making part of the personality. It is essentially a videotaped recording of the parenting—words, feelings, and mannerisms—received by the child. When people are in the Parent ego state, they use words like *should, ought, right,* and *wrong, everybody, nobody, always,* and *never.* The Parent performs both caretaking/nurturing and critical/disciplinary functions. Mannerisms accompanying the Parent ego state are a wagging forefinger, a stern, critical, or nurturing facial expression, and an attitude of bossing, telling what to do, or taking over. When a person has a history of physical or emotional abuse, the Parent is often very shaming, as in "I knew you couldn't do that, you little wimp!" The Parent is also woefully lacking in nurturing messages.

The Adult ego state is basically an emotion-free, value-free computer. It is the part of the personality that asks questions about how, when, where, and why and seeks to find the answers. The Adult represents the objective ego state. It obtains information necessary to achieve a goal. When there has been the kind of impaired symbiosis discussed earlier, the Adult ego state is underdeveloped. By learning to think about their feelings and problems, abusive parents lessen their discounting and strengthen the Adult ego state.

The Child ego state expresses feelings, both spontaneous and learned. Anger, sadness, fear, rage, love, joy, and all other human emotions are experienced in the Child. Abused children have had to modify many of their feelings and the expression of those feelings in order to survive in the family environment. The feelings and behaviors they do express are more often "adapted" than natural. The Child part is the seat of the emotional struggle for nurturing and individuation.

When persons have matured and differentiated successfully, they use all three ego states appropriately. They can parent with both nurturance and limit-setting, can ask appropriate questions and get information for problem solving, and can express and experience a wide range of feelings. They function and experience themselves as "whole" persons. Clearly, the ability to use all three ego states freely is severely limited when a person has not successfully grown beyond a symbiotic relationship.

WIN/LOSE STRUGGLE

Symbiosis as understood in transactional analysis terms is when two people "share" one complete set of ego states. One person uses two of the ego states and the other uses the remaining one.[28] Figure 4 represents this symbiotic arrangement. Typically, one person or spouse functions as the Parent and Adult and the other assumes the Child role. The former assumes the responsibility for solving and handling problems in the family, ignoring or discounting his feelings of neediness. The latter discounts her own ability to think and to be responsible.

An example would be the husband who repeatedly gets injured on the job and cannot work, while his wife works steadily in a responsible management position, putting in overtime whenever possible to help meet financial obligations. When the husband becomes depressed and abusive to the children, the wife becomes "Mom" to him by trying to appease him and control the children so that their behavior does not set him off emotionally. She stays stuck in the Parent and Adult roles, discounting her feelings of anger and neediness and suppressing them with food by overeating. The husband, in the Child role, is discounting his ability to figure out why he keeps getting injured and to be a responsible provider for his wife and children.

The symbiotic relationship may develop around one or many issues, but in abusive families it is pervasive. There is often a shifting from "top dog" (Parent and Adult) to "underdog" (Child) in different areas in the life of the family,[29] but one

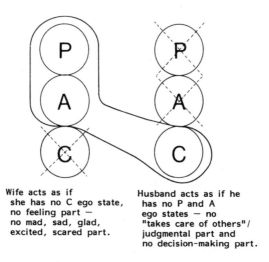

Wife acts as if
she has no C ego state,
no feeling part —
no mad, sad, glad,
excited, scared part.

Husband acts as if he
has no P and A
ego states — no
"takes care of others"/
judgmental part and
no decision-making part.

Figure 4. A symbiotic relationship at one point in time.

partner usually wins out in the struggle to be cared for by being more passive than the other. The loser in the struggle shifts the symbiotic attachment to the child in hopes of getting the nurturance so desperately sought.

A win/lose belief underlies the symbiotic struggle: "Either I get what I want or you do. We can't both be satisfied." This belief is founded on the abusive parents' early life experience. Getting their needs met became a struggle over which they often had no control. In order to receive caretaking, mother's needs had to be met. One tragic example of how the symbiosis shifts is seen in the case of a 3-month-old baby who died of malnutrition and dehydration because his mother fed him only when she and her husband got along well together.[30] She would assume the role of Parent to her infant only when her husband sufficiently nurtured her Child. Youngsters learn that they can receive or be in their Child ego state only after they have been Parent to their parents.

SCRIPTS AND INJUNCTIONS

These early life experiences of role reversal are accompanied by implicit or explicit messages of how life is to be lived. These messages, called life-script injunctions in transactional analysis, are parent-conveyed dictums about how to survive. Since these dictums or injunctions are basically unconscious, they motivate people's actions and thoughts outside their awareness.[31]

Because abusive parents have similar parenting, they receive similar or interlocking life-script injunctions. They see their survival as dependent upon fusing with another. Their lives are therein interlocked. One cannot act independently of the other, just as one Siamese twin cannot move without affecting the other and may risk death if separated.[32] The partners must tacitly agree on what each will do when, behaviorally and emotionally. The agreement is made even if only one takes action and the other implicitly agrees on the course by doing nothing to stop the first one. The couple described above illustrates this type of Siamese-twinning arrangement. She, by her acceptance of his behavior, agreed that she would carry the responsibilities in the family and he would express the anger and neediness in the family. His rageful feelings and abusive behavior are as much hers as they are his. It is typical of abusing families that one person does the acting-out of the negative feelings, but both parents are responsible for the abuse.

Figures 5 and 6, based on one of the couples we treated, demonstrate how injunctions that reinforce symbiotic patterns are conveyed from the biological parents or parent-surrogates to the child.[33] The messages conveyed from the parent's Parent to the child's Parent are usually verbal. Those from the parent's Child to the offspring's Child are most often nonverbal and are the major determinants of how life goes for the person. The injunction from the Adult to the Adult is given in the form of

Mother or surrogate   Father or surrogate

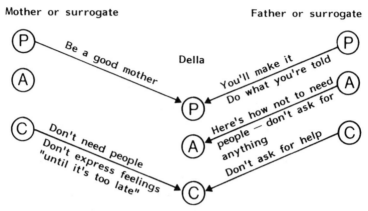

Figure 5. "Siamese twinning" script matrix of a child abuser.

behavior that demonstrates how the script messages are to be carried out.

These two script matrices illustrate the similarity and interlocking pattern of the injunctions of the spouses in an abusing family. Della is the young woman we described earlier who

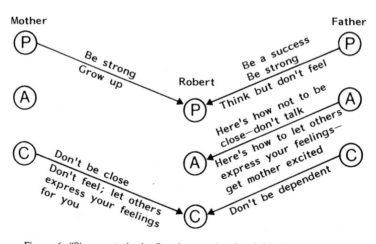

Figure 6. "Siamese twinning" script matrix of a child abuser's partner.

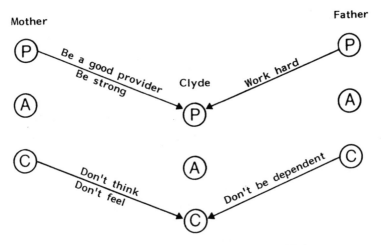

Figure 7. "Siamese twinning" script matrix of a child abuser.

broke her baby's arm when she jerked him in his crib. Robert is the "everything's under control" computer analyst. In this family, Della expressed the emotional, out-of-control, rageful Child feelings when she could no longer bear the strain of caring for

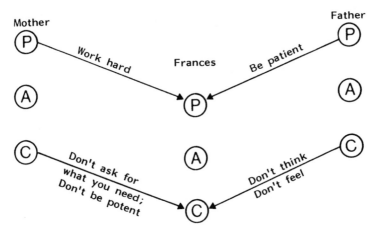

Figure 8. "Siamese twinning" script matrix of a child abuser's partner.

a constantly crying, colicky baby. Robert, functioning as the Parent and Adult, coolly took care of the problem after the child's arm was broken but did nothing ahead of time to alleviate Della's mounting tension. Both parents were programmed by their own insufficient nurturing not to ask others for help or to show feelings. Della "broke" first primarily because she had no outlet to absorb the tension, whereas Robert had his work.

An illustration of Siamese-twinning scripts and shifting symbiosis is seen in the script matrices of Clyde and Frances, another couple in our group treatment. Figures 7 and 8 show how both at times assumed the Parent and Adult role in this symbiosis. Clyde, when in his playful Child ego state, would "roughhouse" on the floor with the children until they were extremely agitated and upset. Meanwhile, Frances would assume the role of Parent, trying to control both Clyde and the children. When angered, Clyde would beat the children, especially their 4-year-old daughter, while Frances stood by in a helpless Child stance. Clyde expressed both the playful and the rageful feelings for both parents, but rarely in a way that was appropriate or acceptable. Both spouses were scripted not to be dependent or adequate in expressing their needs and feelings. Neither Frances nor Clyde, as is so characteristic of partners locked in a symbiotic relationship, was thinking about feelings in a way that would allow a satisfactory expression of them.

4

Epidemiological Features of Child Abuse

Since epidemiology is concerned with the magnitude and distribution of health problems, along with their antecedents and consequences, a systems approach is particularly useful for exploring features of the host, environment, agent, and vector involved.[1] This chapter elaborates on the characteristics of parents who abuse, on the child who is abused, on the cultural scripts that influence interaction between them, and on the setting in which abuse occurs. Since historical practices and tradition are part of the antecedents to abuse, we will take a brief look at the past as it bears on the problem.

HISTORICAL PREVIEW

Child abuse is as old as the history of man. Even in mythology, children were murdered, sacrificed, beaten, abandoned, or mutilated.[2] There have been many justifications for abuse: religious beliefs, birth control, cultural rituals, superstitions, discipline, and monetary gain. The early Greeks' attitude toward children was expressed by Aristotle as follows: "The justice of a master or a father is a different thing from that of a citizen, for a son or slave is property, and there can be no injustice to one's own property."[3] The 1633 *Bibliotheca Scholastica* repeated the Old Testament Admonition not to "spare the rod and spoil the child."[4]

The Roman rule of Patria Postestas—which stated that a father owned his child and therefore had the right to treat the child as he saw fit[5]—is no longer legally sanctioned, but it still is unofficially in effect. In colonial America, a father had the right not only to kill his child but to call on colony officers to assist him.[6] It was "also common to flog children without provocation … to 'break them of their willfulness' and make them tractable, ostensibly for the good of their souls."[7] Until the 19th century, "dead or abandoned infants were almost commonplace on city streets. As late as 1892, 200 foundlings and 100 dead infants were found on the streets of New York City alone."[8]

Efforts to curb child abuse date back many centuries. Radbill cites 17th-century publications that pleaded for more lenient treatment of children. But it was not until the late 1800s that preventive action was taken in the United States. When 9-year-old Mary Ellen was found chained to her bed in a dingy tenement in New York City, the American Society for the Prevention of Cruelty to Animals intervened because no law for the protection of children existed. It was only after the case gained wide public attention that the first American organization concerned with children's rights—the New York Society for the Prevention of Cruelty to Children—was established.[9] New York passed the first state statute dealing with child abuse and neglect in 1874.[10]

Public and other private agencies began entering the field of child protection shortly after the turn of the century when the first White House Conference on Child Health and the

American Association for Study and Prevention of Infant Mortality convened in 1909.[11] Between 1963 and 1967, all states and the District of Columbia passed child abuse reporting laws, in one of the most rapid diffusions of a legislative innovation in this century.[12]

But it was 100 years after the New York law before there was federal legislation that protected children from physical, emotional, or sexual abuse by a parent or caretaker.[13] In 1974 the Child Abuse Prevention and Treatment Act was passed. The intent of the act was to provide for:

a broad and uniform definition of child abuse and neglect

nationwide coordination of efforts to identify, treat, and prevent child abuse and neglect

research leading to new knowledge and demonstration of effective ways to identify, treat, and prevent child abuse and neglect

compilation of existing knowledge and dissemination of information about successful methods and programs

training of professionals, paraprofessionals, and volunteers

encouragement to states, as well as private agencies and organizations, to improve their services for identifying, treating, and preventing child abuse and neglect

a complete and full study of the national incidence of child abuse and neglect.[14]

To carry out these objectives, the National Center on Child Abuse and Neglect (NCCAN) was established by the act. It has supported research and has set standards that serve as a model for child abuse and neglect treatment and prevention programs, as well as providing a uniform definition of maltreatment.[15]

As a nation, we have made enormous strides in recognizing and devoting resources to the problem of child maltreatment. Unfortunately, the statistics on incidence and prevalence that we will now address make it clear that the problem is far from solved.

INCIDENCE AND PREVALENCE OF CHILD ABUSE

The epidemiology of child abuse underscores the fact that such violence is a public health problem—communitywide in scope, not only in the United States but overseas.[16] Bishop reports that "the number of children at risk appears to be increasing ... to the point where it would appear that their plight and number constitute the largest single public health problem awaiting solution."[17] Whether child abuse is the largest health problem yet to be solved is debatable, but the evidence tends to confirm prediction of a rapid increase in the incidence—if not prevalence—of child abuse.

The exact scope of child abuse is the subject of wide debate, particularly since interviews with random samples of households project higher incidence and prevalence than does formal reporting.[18] Gil, in 1968, conducted one of the earliest and most rigorous studies on the annual incidence of child abuse. From that study, he estimated that between 2.5 and 4 million families either failed to act or used physical force with the intent of hurting, injuring, or destroying their children.[19]

In 1975 Straus and his colleagues, in the survey of families referred to in Chapter 1, revealed that 3.1 to 4 million children are kicked, bitten, or punched by their parents at some point in childhood. One in every 25 children ages 3 to 17 in two-parent households were seriously beaten by a parent or threatened with a gun or knife. The researchers projected that over 46,000 children are actually shot or stabbed by their parents in childhood and that over 1000 died as a result of these attacks.[20]

While their 1985 replication of the survey found a 47.5% reduction in the level of the most serious forms of physical violence toward children, they found relatively consistent levels in pushing and slapping. Even with the decline of the beatings, they estimate a minimum of 1 million children ages 3 to 17 in dual-parent households were subjected to serious physical abuse in 1985.[21] This estimate would increase into the millions if the surveys had included emotional and sexual abuse and single-parent families.

A central registry established by Gil for all reported cases of child abuse that occurred in 1967 and 1968 revealed 5993 cases for the first year and 6617 cases for the second. These figures represent an incidence rate per 100,000 children under the age of 18 of 8.4 and 9.3, respectively, for the 2 years. Kempe estimated that between 30,000 and 50,000 cases of child abuse (or 6 per every 1000 live births) occur each year in the United States, on the basis of reported cases in Denver and New York in 1971.[22] Helfer, in light of a comprehensive literature survey, calculated an overall annual incidence of children who are abused and/or neglected at an approximate rate of 10-15/1,000 children per year.[23]

Straus and his colleagues (1975) may have greatly underestimated the number of fatalities from child maltreatment. The National Center for Prevention of Child Abuse noted that in 1986 at least 1200 fatalities from child abuse were reported in the United States, and that one study, which reviewed official death certificates and clinical records, suggested that the actual number may be as high as 5000 deaths annually.[24]

As for the prevalence of abuse, the estimates of Kempe and Gil are based on reported cases and therefore do not include children who (1) were not treated by a physician, (2) were treated by a physician but were not identified as abused, or (3) were identified as abused but were not reported. These factors lend credence to the statement that there are at least 100 unreported cases for every reported case.[25] In 1973 Lynch estimated that reported cases represent only 1 to 10% of the total.[26] In addition, Kempe estimated that roughly 25% of all fractures seen in children under the age of 2 are caused by child abuse, and that 10 to 15% of all children under 3 years of age treated for trauma in hospitals have been abused, regardless of what their parents say or what social class they belong to.[27]

A federally funded National Incidence Study conducted in 1981 found that only 33% of child maltreatment cases identified by a representative sample of professionals across the country were formally reported.[28] The researchers projected an annual incidence rate of 652,000 cases, of which only 212,400 were known to local protective service workers.

While we probably never know the exact prevalence of child maltreatment, it is clear that the absolute number of reported cases continues to climb, even though the number of children in the country is declining.[29] The American Association for Protecting the Child (AAPC) found that in 1984 1,726,649 children were reported for abuse, an increase of 158% since 1976. The number of maltreatment cases reported nationwide has steadily increased since 1976, although the size of the increase has fluctuated.[30] The percentage of cases requiring child protective services intervention increased from 30% in 1979 to 36% in 1980 to 49% in 1983. The number of children officially categorized as having suffered physical abuse, neglect, emotional maltreatment, or sexual abuse increased 145% between 1977 and 1983.[31] The national survey by the NCPCA in the fall of 1986 suggests that child abuse fatalities are also on the rise. Between 1985 and 1986, the reported deaths due to maltreatment rose an average of 23% in 34 states. While this may be due in part to a more accurate identification system, the surveyors believe that the size and frequency of the increase in several states suggest an actual rise in prevalence.[32] The best data on the extent of the child abuse problem probably come from the national representative samplings done by Straus and co-workers. These figures do not rely on reported cases but reflect what families acknowledge—in interviews—as occurring within their households.

Regardless of the actual incidence or prevalence of child abuse, the numbers are staggering and make it clear that we are facing a public health problem of enormous proportions. Also, as Helfer notes, "The reader must not lose sight of the importance of the phrase 'per year.' Since abuse and neglect harm the child's developmental state, which does not 'heal' in the same manner as do many physical injuries, these figures are cumulative."[33]

CHARACTERISTICS OF ABUSIVE PARENTS

Relationship to Victim

Some of the most extensive early data on epidemiological characteristics of child abusers was collected by Gil,[34] who found that most child maltreatment is by parents. In his sample, 86.8% of the perpetrators of child abuse were parents or parent surrogates. The mother or mother substitute inflicted the abuse in 47.6% of the cases; the father or father figure did so in 39.2%. In 12.1% of the cases the abuser was another relative, and in 1.1% the perpetrator was unknown. Most of these parents were the biological parents of the children (71.1%). Stepparents constituted only 13.6% of the abusers, while 0.4% were adoptive parents, and the remaining 14.9% of the abuse was by foster parents, siblings, relatives, nonrelatives, or persons whose relationship to the victim was unknown.

In our therapy groups, which will be described in more detail in Chapter 5, the statistics on the abuser's relationship to the child differ from Gil's in that our sample included only parents. Among the abusing parents or parent surrogates in our group, the mother was the perpetrator in 50% of the cases, while the father or father substitute inflicted the abuse in 45% of the families. Both parents abused the children in 5% of the cases.

Sex of the Abuser

While Gil's findings indicated that the perpetrator of the abuse was more likely to be female than male,[35] there was no father present in 29.5% of the homes he studied.[36] In the homes where there was a male parent, he was the perpetrator in approximately two-thirds of the abuse incidents. In 50 out of 57 cases investigated by Steele and Pollock, the child's mother was the abuser.[37] The division between the female and male parents was more evenly divided in our sample, but the mother still inflicted the abuse slightly more often than the father or stepfather.

Age of the Abuser

Most abusers are, understandably, in the typical childbearing/childrearing age range of 20 to 40 years. In Gil's sample, 71.2% of the mothers and 65.9% of the fathers were in this age bracket.[38] However, more fatalities from maltreatment occur in homes with very young parents (16 to 20 years).[39] Seventy-five percent of the parents in our group were between 20 and 40 years old at the time of the reported incident, and 25% were under 20. Less than 10% of the mothers and less than 3% of the fathers were younger than 20 in Gil's sample.

Socioeconomic Factors

While there is an overrepresentation of minority, single-parent, and poor families among those reported for child abuse, this may be a function of their being subject to greater scrutiny by a variety of public welfare and health professionals rather than due to a higher incidence rate of maltreatment among these populations.[40]

The increased surveillance of these groups is in part due to the fact that "upper-class persons are able to get help from private doctors who are sometimes willing to let the abuse go unreported, while lower-class persons must go to the public hospital, which is required to make a report."[41] Also, practitioners may be more inclined to report poor, single mothers than they are white middle-class families.

The data from the National Incidence Study indicate that although hospital personnel reported cases of abuse and neglect to authorities more frequently than did other professionals, they failed to report almost half the cases they believed to involve abuse. Moreover, there were alarming racial and socioeconomic differences between those cases that medical personnel did report and those that they did not. Emotional abuse by higher-income white mothers was disproportionately unreported.[42]

In Gil's study, most of the fathers (77%) were skilled or semi-skilled workers, while only 9.5% were white-collar workers or professionals. (The occupations of the remaining 13.5% were unknown.) In the same sample, only 39% of the mothers were employed, and most of those (68.3%) were in skilled or semi-skilled jobs. Nearly 60% received or had received public assistance.[43]

The same socioeconomic pattern was reflected in our group population. Although our clinical group was much smaller, it did reflect a number of the demographic features found in larger surveys. Eighty-five percent of the men held skilled or semi-skilled jobs, while 15% were in white-collar or professional occupations. Forty percent of the women in our group were working outside the home, 88% of those having skilled or semi-skilled jobs. Two of the families were receiving AFDC financial aid when the abuse occurred, and an additional 10% received other public assistance.

Jason and her colleagues found in their study an absence of a disproportionate number of current AFDC recipients among the sample of those who had abused their children, leading them to conclude that the welfare benefits might actually be helping the family to reduce the level of stress and thereby mitigate maltreatment.[44]

As to education, our group members tended to be better educated than those in Gil's survey. The majority of his sample were not high school graduates: 57.7% of the women and 48.5% of the men had between 9 and 13 years of education; only 4.8% of the women and 8.5% of the men were college graduates or had graduate training. Approximately 24% of both the women and men in his sample had less than 9 years of education.[45] In our group, 20% of the men and women had undergraduate or graduate training or degrees. Seventy percent were high school graduates, and 10% had 6 years or less of schooling.

The racial makeup of our group closely paralleled that of our urban population. Seventy-five percent of the members were white, 15% black, and 10% Hispanic. The city's racial composition at the time was 62% white, 26% black, and 12% Hispanic.

Emotional History and Personality Characteristics

In previous chapters, we have discussed at length the psychosocial background of abusing parents, in particular their own histories of physical and/or emotional abuse. Beginning with Kempe's pioneering work and continuing through to recent studies, researchers have found a large number of the these parents to have themselves been victims of child abuse and neglect.[46]

Gil reported that the parents in his sample had histories that included foster home placements, hospitalization for mental illness, juvenile court experience, criminal records, deviant intellectual functioning, and an overall experience of childhood deprivation and maltreatment.[47] Eighty-five percent of those in our sample reported similar deprivation.

Severely mentally disturbed and psychotic individuals generally constitute no more than 10% of all the cases handled by protective services.[48] In our group, 5% were borderline psychotic. The mentally retarded have also been overrepresented in child abuse and neglect samples.[49] However, as Daro comments, "while mentally retarded individuals may begin with fewer resources in these areas, it is not necessarily true that their children always will receive less attention or good parenting than the children of nonretarded parents. In a certain respect, one might argue that mild to moderate mentally retarded parents may be an easier population to target for services in that their needs, at least some of them, are clearly defined and amenable to intervention."[50]

Even though most abusing parents are not psychotic or retarded, the majority of them represent a range of personality and emotional disorders. In studying the personality profiles of physically abusive parents, Olson found an unusually high percentage of rigid or authoritarian personalities, drug or alcohol dependency, neurosis, mental deficiency, and/or emotional immaturity.[51] Milner and Wimberly, using the Child Abuse Potential Inventory developed by Milner, found four strong discriminant factors that identified abusers. They were loneliness; rigidity; problems with self-image, family, and friends; and lack of social skills and self-control. Rigidity and problems with self-image were the strongest indicators of potential abuse among these four factors.[52] Most of the parents in our group fell into the category of "Intermittent Explosive Disorder," under the *Diagnostic and Statistical Manual* (3rd edition) classification system of the American Psychiatric Association, but they were all dealing primarily with the psychological issues of symbiosis, fusion, and dependency.

CHARACTERISTICS OF THE ABUSED CHILD

Child abuse received early attention by being referred to as the "battered baby syndrome," suggesting that it is a problem involving infants and very young children. Kempe stated that abuse was most common among children under 3½ years of age; Galdston found the problem most frequently among children aged 3 months to 3 years. According to Bennie and Sclare, 2- to 4-month-old infants are the primary target of abuse; Resnick reported that child murder is most common in the first year of life.[53]

But when Gil studied the problem from an epidemiological rather than a clinical viewpoint, he found that only about one-third of the victims of abuse were under the age of 3, while almost half were 6 or older. However, the first year of life remained at the highest risk—approximately 13% of the cases occurred during the first 12 months.[54] The youngest children clearly seem to be at greatest risk of dying from physical abuse. Surveys in Los Angeles County and in Illinois found that 75% of the fatalities from abuse were children 1 year of age or younger.[55]

Other investigators after Gil also found that abuse occurs more frequently after early childhood. One survey[56] noted that children reported for physical abuse are younger than those reported for neglect (5.3 years of age vs. 6.4), but on the average they are not infants or babies. Additional evidence that supports the observation that most physically abused children are not infants was presented by Lynch, who found that 51% of child abuse cases occurred among children ages 6 to 17 years. "Recognition of child abuse as a phenomenon of the older child—the school child—has been slow."[57] It may be that "although the most dramatic abuse occurs in the younger child, the most frequent abuse occurs in the school-age child. These children have been battered but manage to survive the high-risk years."[58] Whether the abuse began early in these children's lives but was only detected or became severe enough for protective intervention when the child was in school or was older will probably not be known in most instances.

In a study of 376 abused children in Buffalo, New York, Thompson and colleagues compared the percentages of abused children in various age brackets with the percentages of children

Table 4. Abuse of Children (by Age Group)

Age groups	Percentage of total child population	Percentage of abused children
5 years or under	35	49
6–9	25	22
10–17	40	29

in each age bracket in the total population.[59] The findings are shown in Table 4.

There is little doubt that abuse is a problem among school-age children as well as infants and babies. Our findings, however, agree with those of investigators who have found that the very young are at the highest risk. Among the children abused by parents in our group, 67% were between 4 months and 3 years of age. When 4-year-olds are included, the percentage jumps to 79%. Our data match those of Gil in his finding that 2- and 3-year-olds are at the same risk as children in the first year of life.

As to sex of the abused child, Gil reports that more than half of the abused children in his studies were male (73% in 1967 and 51% in 1968).[60] Forty-one percent of the abused children in our sample were male, with the remaining 59% of course being female.

Although high-risk groups of children will be discussed further in Chapter 9, we will note here that Bishop identified six groups of children that are at special risk of abuse: (1) infants born out of wedlock, (2) premature babies, (3) congenitally malformed babies, (4) twins, (5) children conceived during the mother's depressive illness, and (6) children of mothers with frequent pregnancies and excessive work loads.[61] In summarizing the research on child maltreatment with regard to the characteristics of the children who are abused, Daro comes up with this list of factors that have been found to contribute to a child's being at risk: behavioral problems/hyperactivity; unwanted during pregnancy; premature birth; physical illness; physical/developmental disabilities; mismatch to parent's personality; similarity of child to an adult disliked by parent.[62]

While Zalba reported that 50% of the abused children in Massachusetts were conceived out of wedlock,[63] in our group 17% were so conceived. Of course, in considering this variable, it is important to remember that many of the "illegitimate" births are to young teenage mothers, another factor that has been associated with higher risk for child abuse. One-fourth of the children of the parents in our group were born to depressed mothers.

Bennie and Sclare found that abused children are usually the youngest or only child in the family, but Gil reported that abused children were twice as likely to come from families with four or more children.[64] Several studies in the United States, England, and New Zealand indicate that "the average size for abusing families substantially exceeds the national average."[65] In Daro's survey of the literature, she also found a large number of children as being a characteristic of the household.[66] In our group, none of the families had four or more children. The largest percentage (38) had two children.

Thompson observed that one specific child appears to be the target of the abuse in an overwhelming percentage of abusing families. In 88% of the 376 cases he studied, only one child in the family was abused.[67] This was also the case in 80% of the families we treated.

As to seriousness of injuries, in 90% of Gil's sample and 95% of ours, no lasting physical impairment was expected. Although over half of the incidents in both samples were not judged to be physically serious injuries, 3.4% of Gil's sample involved a fatality.[68] One infant in our group died as a result of the actions of the mother.

As we discussed in Chapter 3 (see also Chapter 9) and as researchers have observed, difficult babies and children are at increased risk. It is easy to see why any child that puts excessive demands on parents who are already marginally prepared to nurture would be more likely to tip the fragile scales. Research has shown that when potentially abusive parents "have premature infants, infants with low birth weights, or infants who exhibit certain behavioral problems such as poor eating or sleeping habits, the risk for maltreatment becomes even higher."[69] In this sense, the child's behavior becomes a contributing factor to the abuse.

Harrington comments, "How far these features are a direct result of parental attitudes and how far they contribute to abuse is impossible to say, but there is a strong presumption that irritable babies are more likely to fall victims than placid ones."[70] Even nurses and social workers will admit to understanding how a parent of an infant with a particularly grating cry might be driven to striking out,[71] and there is literature implying that even nonabusive parents might abuse a particularly irritating or difficult child.[72] Martin, for one, observes that the aggressive child "perpetuates the notion that many of these children would invite abuse from the most normal of parents," and Flynn comments that "the obnoxious child" is a likely target of abuse.[73]

The implication is that some children are constitutionally and temperamentally so difficult that the average parent may be moved to use excessive measures of management. The opposite position is that "children are neither good nor bad.... If they are usually irritable, fearful, obstinate or sly, their parents have helped to make them that way."[74] The contribution of the child's personality is not an either/or situation. It is one variable that plays a role in the causal model described in the previous chapter.

SETTING, CIRCUMSTANCE, AND TYPE OF ABUSE

Most child abuse occurs in the home. More than 90% of the cases of abuse in Gil's study occurred in the child's home,[75] and all the incidents of abuse in our sample took place in the child's home. The conditions in the home do play a role. 'Abuse is more likely to occur in a crowded home, in one in which the family is large, or in one in which unemployment is a problem. Excessive change, which we discussed earlier, is also characteristic of the abusive home. The constant readjustment the change requires leaves the family without the emotional or social resources to bail itself out.

> Many mothers, and some fathers, in today's crowded and often shifting home environments, without the advantages of the extended family or the understanding neighbor, simply reach a breaking point. Someone to take over for an hour—even someone to talk to for a few minutes—can make the difference. That person may be less likely to be there today than in the past.[76]

Certainly the isolation of the abusive parents cannot be attributed solely to our being a more mobile nation and the consequent unavailability of the extended family and community for support. But mobility is a contributing factor. The factor of mobility was more pronounced in our group than in Gil's sample. Nearly all (85%) of the couples in our group had lived in their present homes for less than 1 year at the time of the reported abuse. This contrasts with Gil's finding that more than half of the families he studied had been living in their homes over 1 year.[77] Forty percent of our families owned their own homes, compared with only 13% of Gil's population. Twenty percent of the homes owned by our group were trailer homes. The percentage renting was about the same for both groups (55% for our group and 51% for Gil's). Only 5% of our couples lived with relatives, whereas 13% of Gil's shared their living quarters with another family. None of the families we worked with lived in public housing, in contrast with nearly 12% of Gil's families.

Certain times of day pose an understandably higher risk for abuse. Most every parent dreads "arsenic hour," the time around dinner when both kids and parents are tired and hungry. Not surprisingly, dinnertime is when most physical abuse takes place. According to Gil's study, 19% of the abusive incidents took place between 3:00 and 6:00 p.m., 20% between 6:00 and 9:00 p.m., and 9% between 9:00 p.m. and midnight. During the remaining 3-hour periods, the incidence of abuse varied from 1 to 9%.[78] Our findings were similar to Gil's: 30% of the incidents occurred between 3:00 and 6:00 p.m., 50% between 6:00 and 9:00 p.m., and 20% in the morning between 7:00 and 10:00. The peaks at late night and early morning can be attributed to the added stress of trying to get children to bed or up in the morning and to added fatigue on the part of the parents. Alcohol or drug use at night might also contribute to the rise in incidence at night. Thompson and his colleagues found that in 13% of the cases the perpetrator was drunk.[79]

There is usually some focal incident that sets off the abuse. Thompson found that 57% of abusive incidents were an "immediate or delayed response to a specific act of the child … [such as] crying, failure to eat, wetting the bed, normal developmental problems."[80] The abuse in that sample followed serious misconduct—such as stealing, running away, playing on railroad tracks—in only 10% of cases.

As we mentioned above, most injuries do not cause permanent physical damage. In Gil's study the most common injuries were bruises and welts, which were usually inflicted by a hand or with an instrument.[81] Bruises and welts made up 85% of the injuries in our sample. Five percent involved skull fractures (compared with 4% for Gil), 5% were other types of fractures (vs. 10% for Gil), and 5% involved burns. Most of the injuries in our group were inflicted by striking with a hand (65% vs. Gil's 39%). When an instrument was used by one of the parents in our group, it was usually a belt. Forty-four percent of the cases in Gil's population involved abuse with an instrument.

SUMMARY OF FACTORS CONTRIBUTING TO CHILD MALTREATMENT

In reviewing the research and literature on child maltreatment (which includes physical abuse, sexual abuse, emotional abuse, and neglect), Daro presents this summary of "the specific characteristics of parents, children, and households that place a given family at risk of maltreatment and lists those aspects of the society that place entire classes or all families at risk."[82] While we have focused primarily on physical abuse of children in this book, the summary reflects the many factors that have been associated with physical abuse as well as with the other types.

Risk Factors[83]

Characteristics of Parents
  Mental illness
  Difficulty dealing with aggressive impulses
  Tendency to be rigid and domineering
  Lack of social skills
  Low self-esteem
  Depression
  Substance abuse
  Poor self-understanding
  History of abuse as a child
  Observation of physical violence as a child
  Lack of attachment to the child
  Adolescent parenthood
  Social isolation
  Inadequate household and child management skills
  Lack of parenting skills
  Inconsistent use of discipline
  Lack of knowledge regarding child development
  Sole responsibility for all parenting tasks
  Inability to control anger
Characteristics of Children
  Behavioral problems/hyperactivity
  Unwanted during pregnancy
  Premature birth
  Physical illness

Physical/developmental disabilities
Mismatched to parent's personality
Similarity of child to an adult disliked by parent
Household Characteristics
Poverty/low income
Blended/reconstituted family
Single parenthood
Large number of children
Children less than one year apart
Chaotic family
Overcrowded or inadequate housing
Stress Factors
Birth of a new baby
Loss of job
Divorce/separation
Death of a close friend/family member
Sudden illness/chronic health problem
Loss of housing
Sudden financial burden
Social/Cultural Factors
Culture of poverty
Tolerance for physical punishment
Sexual stereotypes in child-rearing
Community isolation (i.e., lack of quality local
community services and limited access to other
neighborhoods' service systems)
Violence in the media
Extreme notions of individual rights and family privacy

The extent of this list supports our position that to understand child abuse it is necessary to consider a complete psychosocial model. We agree with Daro when she comments that each risk factor "is but one dimension of the total picture and that it is the combination of factors at a given point in time that can provide the only true predictor of incidence."[84] Some of the dimensions are more central to the problem of abuse than others, and it is these that need to be emphasized in treatment and prevention.

5

Therapy and Evaluation

The optimal goal in dealing with the problem of child abuse is to keep the abuse from ever happening—to prevent the explosive elements in a potentially abusive family system from ever developing or coming together. This is primary prevention, which will be discussed in Chapter 9. Once child abuse has occurred, however, the goal then becomes to prevent its recurrence—to alter the elements in the family system so that the abuse does not continue. We consider that preventing further incidences of abuse is a form of secondary prevention. While primary prevention is the ideal solution, secondary prevention is essential. Without intervention, more than 50% of the children who are abused will be abused again,[1] and many are likely to grow up to inflict abuse themselves.

There are a number of secondary prevention strategies for intervening in the abusive family system (see Chapter 10). The approach we adopted in the early 1970s and still endorse features a combination of group and family therapy, using a technique of setting goals and measuring change called Goal Attainment Scaling.[2] In dealing with the potentially life-threatening problem of child abuse, it is essential that there be some reliable measure of the effectiveness of the psychotherapeutic techniques being used in order to be able to answer the question "Will the children be abused again?" We place considerable emphasis on this compelling question and use an approach that enables the therapists and authorities to answer that question with a reasonable degree of certainty. In this chapter and in Chapter 6 we will discuss our intervention approach and the techniques we have found successful in working with abusive parents and their children.

COUPLES GROUP TREATMENT

In our work with abusive families, we chose to work primarily with couples—the man and woman in the household functioning as father and mother. Both were not necessarily the biological parents or even married, but they functioned in the parenting roles in the family. As we noted earlier, the family functions as a system and the parents or spouses represent the principal subsystem. Because the spouses are basically alike and tied to each other in a symbiotic relationship like Siamese twins, it is essential to work with both of them if the system is to be changed.

We experimented with allowing one partner in the marriage to come alone to group therapy, but our experience was that if only one spouse entered therapy, the other did all he or she could to sabotage the changes made by the one attending the group. In any family system, it is impossible for one person to change without affecting others in the family. In the case of abusive parents, the one not in therapy will stoutly resist those changes that threaten the basic symbiotic relationship. Thus, we held firm to the position that both partners need to be in treatment, not just the one who inflicts the injuries on the child. Other therapists also insist on this policy and conclude: "Both parents are the same. They should be treated. It doesn't matter which one actually did the battering."[3]

If the abuse occurs in a single-parent home, it certainly would be necessary to work with that parent. But we found that mixing couples and singles in the same group did not work well for the single parent. The single parent felt even more isolation knowing that everyone else in the group had a partner who was at least willing to attend the group sessions. They tended to drop out of therapy after only a few weeks. The more workable solution for treatment when there is only one parent would be to have a group composed principally of single parents.

The basic problems we will discuss below apply to one- or two-parent abusive families, but there are some additional problems that must be taken into consideration with the single parent, such as child-care and economic stresses. Also, when an abusive parent has no partner, it is necessary to look at the symbiotic relationship that parent is likely maintaining with his or her own mother or father. The focus of interventions then becomes more multigenerational than might be necessary when working with a couple, although dealing with issues in the family of origin is essential with couples too.

All the couples in our group for abusive parents were originally referred by the local Children's Protective Services (Harris County CPS in Houston). In 75% of the cases, the child had been removed from the home by order of the court.[4] The couples were told that their chances of getting the child back were likely to be greatly enhanced if they underwent therapy. Thus, most couples were resentful when they entered group because they were, in effect, coerced into coming to therapy. We will say more in Chapter 6 about the effectiveness of "coercive therapy."

The behavioral manifestations of the resentment were expressed passively by coming late, making excuses for not coming, and not participating. But by taking whatever the parents said was of concern to them and working with that problem, we could sidestep some of the resistance and at the same time engage the parents. As a result, the resistant phase lasted only 3 to 5 weeks for most group members. If it was clear from the beginning that a parent was unwilling to participate at all in the treatment process, we confronted that position quickly and asked the person to leave the group. Faced with the consequence of potentially losing the custody of a child, most parents reevaluated their defiant stances. A few, however, chose to give up the child rather than face the prospect of having to open themselves up to others and to change.

With time, the problem happily shifted from how to get people to come to group to how to get them to leave. Group cohesion, a sense of belonging, and being able to come to a place where they were accepted and affirmed for growth and change developed to the point that many couples would find reasons to continue therapy after the point where we had told them they could terminate. We recommended termination when the Goal Attainment Scaling scores showed that significant changes had been made by each of the parents in all of the identified problem areas. We will elaborate on this later in the chapter.

When the GAS scores and our own clinical assessment indicated that the parents were ready to leave and that there was little likelihood of repeated abuse, we informed the Children's Protective Services worker, who in turn informed the courts. If the child had been removed, he was returned home a minimum of 1 month before the parents terminated group so that problems of reintegrating the child could be addressed. The child was coming back to parents who had changed and who would be trying to relate to and parent the child differently. These changes require adjustments on the child's part as well as the parents', and we found it essential to be available during the transition. Both the therapists and the parents needed to be reassured that the new techniques of child management that the parents had been learning for months were being put into effect to everyone's satisfaction, and that the parents could have a place to deal with any feelings that surfaced with the child's return.

The average length of our group treatment was 5 to 6 months. While Helfer works with abusing parents 6 to 9 months, Kempe reported considerable improvement after only 3 to 6 months and rarely continued intensive treatment longer than 8 months.[5] A survey conducted by the National Committee for the Prevention of Child Abuse concluded that the optimal treatment period for abusive parents may be between 7 and 18 months.[6]

At the end of treatment, our clients certainly had not undergone a psychological overhaul, nor were they people without emotional struggles. But they had learned how to parent their children without physically abusing them, and to relate to their spouses in a more positive and supportive manner. They had also learned enough about their own emotional needs to be able to meet them without crisis or violence. Certain changes were not likely to happen in this brief time. The parents are dealing with deep wounds from childhood. Healing those wounds is a slow and painful process. It cannot happen in a few months.

One consequence of an abusive past is addictive behaviors. As therapist John Bradshaw observed in his book *Bradshaw On: The Family*, "When we are abused in families, we learn to defend ourselves with ego defenses ... we dissociate so that we no longer feel anything at all; we numb out. Our addictions and compulsivities are our mood alterers. They are what we develop when we numb out."[7] Drugs, alcohol, work, food, or codependent, symbiotic relationships are all efforts at numbing the rage and pain from childhood. A few months in therapy can do little to resolve those addictions other than open up avenues for understanding and present options for further treatment.

A maximum of five couples made up the group at any one time. Group sessions were once a week for 1½ hours. Couples joined the group after we interviewed them in depth individually, having been given the CPS report on the family ahead of time. Originally, the group met at the Texas Research Institute of Mental Sciences, and the psychiatrist at the institute who was the chief of adult services consulted with us on each case. Later, the group sessions were moved to a private office, and the psychiatric consult was discontinued unless one of the family members was in need of some medication. Fees were on a sliding scale based on ability to pay. Many paid nothing.

To encourage the couples to begin reaching out to others in time of crisis or need, we gave out our office and home telephone numbers. At the same time, we set boundaries by telling the clients that if they planned on having a crisis and wanted us involved, they should have their crises between 7:00 AM and 10:00 PM. In giving this instruction we were sending the clients two messages: (1) that we do what is necessary to take care of our needs, and (2) that they can and do have some control over the dramas in their lives. Only once did we receive a crisis call other than during those hours.

The couples were also asked to let us know ahead of time if they would be missing a session, which made it clear that they were expected and would be missed if they failed to show up. In part because the parents were mandated to come to therapy and in part because they found the experience in group reinforcing and helpful, attendance was quite high. Few couples missed more than three sessions in a 5-month period. As the couples began to develop trust, they began to call—first the therapists and then each other—more frequently.

Group therapy has proven to be more advantageous than individual therapy for persons who are abusing their children because the group setting more quickly breaks down the barriers of isolation that have grown up from a lifetime of distrust. In group, each parent finds others who are facing or have faced the same problems in handling the shame, fear, legal difficulties, and parenting failures. On the foundation of shared pain, trust slowly builds. The parents find themselves letting go of long-buried feelings and fears that they have never discussed with anyone. Their sharing is met with acceptance and understanding, not just by the therapists but by the other group members as well. Acceptance, friendship, trust, validation—all these are new experiences for the abusive parent that take time to incorporate. But as the parents let the new experiences sink in, their self-images slowly begin to shift. Undoing a lifetime of shaming and abuse certainly cannot be accomplished in 5 to 6 months, but "possibilities of being" are opened up.

We had three objectives for the group for abusive parents. The first and paramount objective was to promote changes in the parents and the dysfunctional family environment that would ensure the children's future safety—that is, to keep the physical abuse from recurring. The second objective was to enhance the problem-solving and parenting skills of these parents. Our third objective was to promote the couples' satisfaction with life and their emotional well-being.

To achieve these objectives, we began by considering the entire psychosocial system, as described in Chapter 3. We identified the dysfunctional behavioral and belief patterns of the parents and broke those down into problem areas that could be addressed in group. Next, we looked at deficits in the couple's knowledge of child development and management. Finally, we assessed the role played by the environment that might have been contributing to the family's crisis. We also considered the child's role, and whether the child would be difficult to manage regardless of family setting.

The tools we used to tackle the myriad problems of these families were all those we knew. The following therapeutic approaches proved most useful: transactional analysis, which is a theory of personality organization as well as a therapeutic tool for change; cognitive-behavior therapy, using techniques developed by Ellis, Lazarus, Wolpe,[8] and others; relaxation training; gestalt therapy; child management techniques and information on the needs of children during specific developmental stages; group process, which enabled the group members to learn from their experiences with others in group while being supported in making changes; and last, but certainly not least, humor.

To assess the effectiveness of our methods, we used the evaluative technique mentioned above, Goal Attainment Scaling (GAS), which measures outcome not only while the couples were in group treatment but at 6-month intervals after they have terminated.[9] GAS is also used as a therapeutic tool. We used it to clarify the main areas of concern of the abusive parents and to set contractual goals with them in each area. To identify these problem areas, we (1) gave the parents a checklist that asked them to rank-order what they considered problems (Figure 9), (2) interviewed all the parents in depth individually before they began in group, (3) borrowed from our own experiences with other abusive parents and their typical problems, and (4) took into account what the growing literature was reporting on others' experiences in successfully changing abusive family systems.

GOAL ATTAINMENT SCALING WITH SIX TYPICAL PROBLEM AREAS

Abusive families often have so many problems that it can be staggering to a therapist to know where to begin. While we began with what the parents said was of most concern to them, we kept in mind what we had found to be the six typical major problem areas for these parents. In setting contacts for change with the parents, we focused on these six areas and found that the parents' concerns generally fell into those categories. The six areas of concern are (1) symbiosis, (2) isolation, (3) talking and sharing with mate, (4) impatience/temper, (5) child development and management, and (6) employment. A GAS Follow-Up Guide was constructed for each group member, based on the mutually agreed-upon goals to be reached in each problem area within a 3-month period. Making a contract in all six areas usually took

Which of the following are areas of concern to you? (Check here)

_____ Low self-image: Low opinion of self, think you're no good, can't do anything right.
_____ Don't have friends: Stay to self a lot, isolated from others, feel alone.
_____ Temper and/or impatience: Have a "short fuse," blow up easily, or get impatient with nearly everyone.
_____ Dependent: Depend heavily on spouse, can't make decisions yourself, can't make it without spouse or some other relative, often irresponsible.
_____ Little support from spouse: Have to do most of decision making yourself, can't depend on spouse to help with kids or to give "moral support," or to say nice things.
_____ Stress: Feel under much pressure all the time from job, kids, house, finances, or other reasons.
_____ Child development and needs: Don't know much about the needs of babies and children at various ages and what to expect.
_____ Sex: Little or no sexual satisfaction in marriage, frustration, arguments over sex.
_____ Trust: Don't trust anyone, always being let down, look at people with suspicion.
_____ Depression: Feel down and hopeless, having trouble getting things done and making decisions, life looks bleak.
_____ Child is disappointment: Child isn't loving or doesn't do what you expect or seems different from other children.
_____ Child care and management: Need to know much more about what to do for and with baby or child at various ages, and how to get child to "behave."

Make sure you have checked all the problems that are of concern to you.

Now look at the list of problems again and RANK them in terms of which are bigger problems and which are smaller problems.

For example, if Temper/Impatience is your biggest problem, put the number 1 by it in the list below. Then go down the list and see what is your second biggest problem. If trust is the second biggest problem, put a 2 by it.

Put numbers by all the problems that are of concern to you so you will rank them according to importance. If two are of EQUAL weight or importance, put the same number by each of the problems.

(Rank problems by putting number by each concern)

_____ Low self-image
_____ Don't have friends
_____ Temper and/or impatience
_____ Dependent
_____ Little support from spouse
_____ Stress
_____ Child development and needs
_____ Sex
_____ Trust
_____ Depression
_____ Child is disappointment
_____ Child care and management

Figure 9. Checklist.

several weeks, depending on the client's readiness to talk about an issue. The same guide was used during follow-up interviews after a couple left the group.

Figure 10 presents a Goal Attainment Follow-Up Guide, showing the six typical problem areas and the five goal attainment levels. The contract sets an "expected level of success," and the GAS allows both the parents and the therapists to determine if that level or goal has been met or exceeded in the agreed-upon time period. The weight assigned to each scale varies, depending on a clinical judgment of the seriousness and extent of the problem for each couple. The weights are used to designate the relative importance of each area of concern. They do not necessarily add up to any fixed total.

Since symbiosis is central to the dysfunctional relationship between the family members, we usually assigned that problem more weight than the other areas of concern. Weighting for the other areas varied according to each couple's difficulties.

Generally, isolation received considerable weight, often second only to symbiosis, because it is such a severe problem for most abusing families. Straus compared abusive and nonabusive parents and found that those who were socially isolated (in the sense of not participating in clubs, unions, or other organizations) had higher rates of child abuse. Those parents who were involved in supportive social networks did not have higher than average rates of abuse, despite being under high stress.[10] Daniel and his colleagues found that black parents who abused their children suffered from poverty, social isolation, and stressful relationships with and among their kin.[11]

When Lenoski compared 674 abusing parents with a control group of 500 nonabusers, he found that 81% of the abusers, compared with 43% of the nonabusers, preferred to resolve crises alone. Forty-three percent of the abusers compared with 20% of the nonabusers preferred to be alone. Almost 90% of the abusers did not have listed telephone numbers, whereas 88% of the nonabusers did.[12] Gabarino asserts that "isolation from potent support systems" is one of two "necessary conditions for the occurrence of child abuse."[13]

Marital communication was usually assigned less weight than symbiosis because problems in this area begin to clear up once the symbiotic dependence is lessened. We put it down as an area of treatment focus, though, because it is one of the most common complaints of the couples entering our group. "We don't communicate" or "He/She never talks/listens to me" are oft-heard laments.

Handling anger is a problem for all abusive parents. Either they repress their anger and respond with depression or physical illness or they are explosive. The parents we have worked with agreed, in that 85% of them list temper/impatience as a problem for them.

Employment was listed as an area of concern for several reasons. Unemployment or stresses on the job often play a part in abuse because it is frequently a source of day-to-day pressure, which contributes to the abusive climate in the home.[14] Gelles, in constructing a profile of violence toward children in the United States, found that in families where the husband was unemployed, the rate of child abuse was 62% greater than for other families. In homes where the husband was employed part time, the rate of child abuse was nearly double the rate where the husband was employed full time.[15]

Clearly, being out of work does not inevitably mean that a parent will abuse his child. But the additional strain of financial fears and the self-blame and shame that accompany being out of work serve as contributing factors to the already potentially explosive situation. We also focus on employment problems because work is an arena where difficulties in relating to people show up quickly. Researchers in Australia found that mothers of battered children were more likely to have suspicious, assertive, and demanding personality characteristics, which would handicap them in social interactions.[16] When the parents in our group were out of work, kept having trouble at work, or could

Level at intake: √

Level at follow-up: ☆   Goal Attainment Follow-Up Guide

Scale attainment levels	Scale 1: Symbiosis (weight$_1$=)	Scale 2: Isolation (weight$_2$=)	Scale 3: Talking and sharing with mate (weight$_3$=)
Most unfavorable outcome thought likely (-2)			
Less than expected success (-1)			
Expected level of success (0)			
More than expected success (+1)			
Most favorable outcome thought likely (+2)			

Figure 10. Goal attainment follow-up guide.

Level at intake:

Goal attainment score
(Level at follow-up):

Scale 4: Impatience/temper ($weight_4 =$)	Scale 5: Child management ($weight_5 =$)	Scale 6: Employment ($weight_6 =$)

not get a job, we saw these difficulties as presenting an opportunity for looking at dysfunctional behaviors and beliefs that might be handicapping the parents in other areas of their lives as well.

We placed great emphasis on teaching child development information and management skills because abusive parents are woefully lacking in this knowledge. In general, people draw on their own parenting, consciously or unconsciously, as a model for parenting their offspring. Since many abusive parents were themselves abused as children, they draw on a coercive and violent model for imposing discipline. Abusive parents are more likely to see violence as an acceptable form of conflict resolution.[17] Not surprisingly, they also are simply not very good at getting their children to behave, and they find parenting far from satisfying. Mash and colleagues found that mothers who abused their children reported more stress from parenting and were less successful in getting their children to do what they wanted them to do than were nonabusive mothers.[18] Fortunately, parenting is a skill that can be learned.[19]

While these six problem areas are the typical ones for the abusive parents we worked with in group, GAS does allow for the addition of new goals as the need arises. We have found, however, that many general problems of the parents cleared up when they made changes in each of these areas. For instance, depression is a common problem with these parents, as it is with the population in general. But when the parents become less isolated and receive more positive recognition from others outside the family, from their mates, and from their own growing sense of self-worth and confidence, the depression lifts. Similarly, sexual difficulties and marital conflict are alleviated as communication between the spouses improves and each learns to be more effective in getting needs met.

Whenever a new problem was listed on the GAS, 3-month goals were set; these were evaluated at the end of that period, and new goals were set for the next 3 months. Figure 10 illustrates the five levels of predicted success or attainment that are agreed upon for each period. Goals should be specific enough to enable a follow-up worker to determine whether or not they have been met. For example, a 3-month goal for the problem of isolation might be that the "most unfavorable outcome" would be that the couple had no phone, no friends, and did not go out socially during that period. The "expected level of success" might be that they got a phone, made a friend, and went to church once a month. The "most favorable outcome" expected for the period could be having a telephone, making two friends, and going out with the friends or to church once a week.

For us to endorse the couple's leaving therapy, they had to reach at least the "expected level of success" in each of the six major problem areas. The GAS lends itself to a composite Goal Attainment T score that uses the numerical values attached to each level of outcome (from -2 to +2) and takes into consideration the weights designated for each scale.[20] The composite GAS score for each spouse in our group had to be at least 55 before we recommended termination.

Using these criteria, of the 34 couples who completed therapy with us since May 1973, 13 were reinvestigated by CPS for suspicion of repeated abuse. About half of those were investigated during treatment. According to Judy Hay, a veteran CPS worker for Harris County and their director of community relations, these figures reflect more that the supervisory system is effective in monitoring the families rather than a failure of treatment. The National Clinical Evaluation Study of child abuse treatment programs concluded that "reincidence during treatment is not, in and of itself, a very good predictor of the propensity for future maltreatment."[21] Parents who did receive group counseling, however, were 27% less likely than those who did not to demonstrate a continued tendency to abuse, the same survey noted.[22]

The Kempes,[23] in their work with abusing families estimated that 20% of the parents would be treatment failures in that the children would not be returned home, no matter what treatment intervention was used. They found that another 40% would improve to the point of no longer maltreating, and the remaining 40% would cease physical abuse but continue to be emotionally abusive.

While our results approximate the Kempes' estimate, what has to be taken into consideration is that most of the families referred to us were "hard core." They were the families that the caseworkers felt they could not handle successfully or that had been referred repeatedly in the past. So any estimates of treatability must take into consideration that most maltreating families never receive counseling beyond that offered by their caseworker. If all these families were taken into consideration, the "success rate" might be considerably different.

When Is It Safe for the Child in the Home?

A GAS score of 55 or more is the quantitative method we used to assess whether or not a couple had changed sufficiently for us to be reasonably confident that their children would not be reinjured if returned to the family or if the parents terminated treatment. What kind of changes are reflected in that quantitative score? Helfer suggests the following criteria to determine when a home is safe for a child: (1) A helpful neighbor or relative is available, (2) the spouse is understanding and helpful, (3) the family has a telephone and someone to call, (4) the mother views herself as helpful, (5) the couple has friends, (6) the amount of role reversal has been reduced, (7) the parents are willing to let the child be a child, (8) there is no scapegoating, and (9) there are few family crises.[24]

Kempe listed the following indicators of a safe home: (1) The self-image of the parents has improved, as seen in dress and social life, (2) the child is viewed more positively, (3) the parents reach out to others in moments of stress, and (4) the parents demonstrate they can handle the child emotionally.[25] In 11 3-year demonstration projects funded by two federal agencies in 1974, "the client's progress is measured against indicators thought to be associated with the potential to abuse or neglect— lack of awareness of child development, the way in which anger is expressed, for example—as well as against the individual treatment goals established for the client."[26]

Although these indicators of progress and Helfer's criteria are helpful, we wanted a more objective means of determining what amount of change parents must make to provide a safe home for their children. Clinical impressions are necessarily subjective, and one therapist's impressions may not agree with those of another. Goal Attainment Scaling allowed us to set goals that the clients themselves could observe and confirm so that their progress was not a matter of opinion alone. Follow-up interviews on our group members since 1973 and a search of the Harris County Children's Protective Services records have confirmed that when clients obtained a GAS score of 55 or more, it was safe for the child to be in the home in all but four cases.

Although our first objective was to ensure that the child would not be physically abused again, the changes the parents made while accomplishing this goal resulted in other important benefits for the child. For instance, we devoted considerable attention to whether the parents adopted a different way of disciplining their children and lessened their excessive expectations of them. Much work was done with parents on child development and management. Martin and Beezley express a concern

> that although most abusive parents can benefit from therapy, in terms of their own personality, their self-esteem, their capability to adapt to stress, and their ability to utilize people and agencies for their own needs, ... [there is little change in] the attitudes and behavior of these parents toward their children.... [In other words,] the child remains in a home where he is viewed in a distorted way, where

punitive and corporal punishment remains the mode, and where unduly high expectations remain and little positive reinforcement takes place.[27]

Our experience has been that when the parents change their behavior with respect to all six of the major areas of concern, the child returns to parents who not only are no longer physically abusive but also are more understanding and emotionally giving. The training in child development and management contributes greatly to specific changes in parental attitudes about the child and how he or she should be treated.

By the time couples leave treatment, the overall changes they have made take the following form: (1) Their symbiotic relationship has changed to the point where each spouse feels more competent in getting his or her needs and is able to provide emotional support to other family members. (2) The parents' isolation has been lessened to the extent that they socialize at least occasionally and reach out to others for support. (3) Marital communication has improved and stroking is more positive. (4) They have learned techniques for managing anger in a nonassaultive way. (5) They have learned and are using appropriate child management techniques. Also, they better understand and are meeting the developmental needs of their children. (6) Employment is less of a source of stress in that they have found work and/or have learned to function better on the job.

CASE EXAMPLES

The specific changes that the parents made in each area depended on the individual goals set for each person. An example of the GAS Guides for one couple, Diane and Al, is seen in Figures 11 and 12. A brief description of their struggles in each of the six typical problem areas will give some idea of how the guide is used.

Symbiosis. Most of the time, Diane assumed the Parent and Adult role, doing virtually all the thinking and even talking for her husband, Al. Al, in the Child role, allowed himself to be "taken care of" by being told what to do by Diane, who parented him just as she parented their two small daughters. When Diane became overwhelmed with the responsibilities and her own neediness, the symbiosis would rapidly shift. She would become hysterical and out of control, forcing Al to take over. But usually he was too late and did not act until Diane had taken out her rage on the girls, beating both of them with a belt.

Isolation. Diane and Al had no friends with whom they socialized. Their only social contact was their relatives, with whom they were often at odds. In an extreme crisis, they would turn to the relatives but were usually disappointed with the response they received.

Marital Communication. Al spent his time at home in front of the television set. If the children tried to get him to play with them, he told them he was too tired. He had little to say to Diane. She did most of the talking, which consisted primarily of complaining about Al, the children, and her life in general.

Anger. Diane was the standard bearer for rageful feelings in the family. She not only lost her temper easily with her children and Al, but her outbursts also had cost her a job on more than one occasion. Al never expressed his anger directly at Diane but instead was chronically irritated and impatient with their daughters.

Child Development and Management. Both Diane and Al were sorely lacking in accurate information on what their daughters were needing emotionally or developmentally. They also had no idea how they might "make them mind" without using physical punishment.

Husband
Goal Attainment Follow-Up Guide

√ Intake level
☆ Level 3 months later

Levels of predicted attainments	Scale 1: Symbiosis (weight$_1$ = 25)	Scale 2: Isolation (weight$_2$ = 15)	Scale 3: Talking and sharing with mate (weight$_3$ = 15)
Most unfavorable outcome thought likely (−2)	Make no decisions on own; do virtually no thinking or talking for self at home √	Make no friends; meet no neighbors; call no one in time of crises √	Neither talk to wife nor share feelings except to complain √
Less than expected success (−1)			
Expected level of success (0)	Make own decisions about job and other major areas; do own talking, thinking and acting	Make 1 "outside" friend; meet neighbors; call either in time of crisis	For at least 10 min. daily, talk about good things that happened during day, share feelings with wife ☆
More than expected success (+1)			
Most favorable outcome thought likely (+2)	Make own decisions in all areas and offer suggestions, when asked, to wife; take responsibility, when asked, for care of children ☆	Make at least 3 "outside" friends; meet neighbors; call them when needed; take wife dancing ☆	For at least 15 min. daily, talk about good things that happened; share feelings and support wife

Figure 11. Goal attainment follow-up guide for Al.

Level at intake = 19.36
GA score 3 months later = 62.25

Scale 4: Impatience/temper (weight$_4$ = 10)	Scale 5: Child development and management (weight$_5$ = 15)	Scale 6: Employment (weight$_6$ = 20)
Continue to feel uptight and take it out on children and wife √	Learn no child development or management techniques; continue present disciplining √	Continue present job-long hours, low pay; much pressure √
Learn relaxation techniques so won't express tension in dealing with children ☆	Learn development needs; use "I messages" and reinforcement techniques; assume responsibility for any "swatting" on rear of kids ☆	Seek and get better job with less pressure ☆
Learn relaxation techniques so won't express tension toward children, wife, or on job	Use "I messages" and reinforcement techniques; leave off all physical discipline	Seek and get better job with less pressure, shorter hours, and more pay

√ Intake level
☆ Level 3 months later

Wife
Goal Attainment Follow-Up Guide

Levels of predicted attainments	Scale 1: Symbiosis (weight$_1$ = 25)	Scale 2: Isolation (weight$_2$ = 15)	Scale 3: Talking and sharing with mate (weight$_3$ = 10)
Most unfavorable outcome thought likely (−2)	Talk, think, act for spouse; turn to children to be cared for √	Stay in house all day; visit no one; call on no one for help √	Criticize and nag spouse; give no positive strokes √
Less than expected success (−1)			
Expected level of success (0)	Do no talking, thinking, acting for spouse; seek no nurturing from children ☆	Get out of house each day; visit neighbors; call on them or friends in crisis	Give positive strokes instead of nagging and criticism to mate while talking and sharing for at least 10 min ☆
More than expected success (+1)			
Most favorable outcome thought likely (+2)	Meet own needs, give support when requested to spouse; support two children	Get out of house each day; go somewhere with a friend; go out with husband; call people in crisis ☆	Give positive strokes to mate while talking and sharing for at least 15 min

Figure 12. Goal attainment follow-up guide for Diane.

Level at intake = 19.36
GA score 3 months later = 54.59

Scale 4: Impatience/temper (weight$_4$ = 20)	Scale 5: Child development and management (weight$_5$ = 15)	Scale 6: Employment (weight$_6$ = 15)
Outbursts of temper and impatience at husband, children, and persons outside the home √	Continue present disciplining; learn no child development or management techniques; children not allowed to be children √	Continue to remain idle at home and demonstrate "job phobia" √
No outburst of temper or impatience at children or husband ☆	Learn developmental needs; use "I messages" and reinforcement techniques; let husband do any physical disciplining; children allowed to be children ☆	Overcome "job phobia" by getting and keeping job at least 3 months ☆
No outbursts of temper or impatience in home or elsewhere	Learn developmental needs; use "I messages" and reinforcement techniques; leave off yelling at kids	Overcome "job phobia" by getting and keeping job at least 6 months

Employment. Al was stressed by the pressure of long and late hours on his job as a security guard and by what he felt was unfair treatment by his supervisor. Diane, on the other hand, was idle most of the time after CPS temporarily removed her children. She became extremely bored and restless but was unwilling to seek work out of fear she would explode on the job.

As illustrated in the GAS Follow-Up Guides for Al and Diane, goals were set for each problem area. The most unfavorable outcome thought likely would be no change or improvement in their level of functioning. Where they are at the time the goals are set, the entry level, is designated on the GAS Guide with check marks. The goals Diane and Al reached after 3 months in group are indicated by asterisks.

Examples of the changes they made in that period are that Al began making some of his own decisions (starting with what he would wear when), offered suggestions to Diane when asked, and began taking some responsibility for the care of the children. Diane learned to curb herself from talking, thinking, and acting on Al's behalf and to make clear requests of him. As she became more effective in getting the support she was seeking from her husband, she began to stop turning to her daughters for nurturance. Diane learned relaxation exercises that enabled her to be in control of her temper both at home and at work. Al found a different job that enabled him to be more available to the family, and Diane took part-time work.

In each problem area there are behavioral criteria built into each goal. For example, in addressing the problem of isolation, Al and Diane agreed to meet their neighbors and to call on them for some kind of assistance, which they did within the 3-month contract period. The contract for the problem of symbiosis included Diane's agreeing not to answer for Al when he was asked a question, and he agreed to think of solutions to problems the family faced. Three months after they began in group, we filled out GAS Follow-Up Guides with Al and Diane to assess what changes they had made and if they had reached their goals. The therapists' clinical assessment of behavioral and emotional changes observed over the period serves as backup information for self-reported changes.

As Figure 11 indicates, Al attained the "expected level of success" on four scales: Marital Communication, Anger, Child Development and Management, and Employment. On the Symbiosis and Isolation scales, he reached the "most favorable outcome thought likely." Figure 12 shows that Diane reached the expected level of success in five areas and attained the most favorable outcome on the Isolation scale.

As we noted earlier, each goal level bears a numerical designation: −2 for the most unfavorable outcome thought likely, 0 for the expected level of success, and +2 for the most favorable outcome thought likely. Each problem area also carries a relative numerical weight, as we have described. The numerical goal levels and scale weights, and the changes the parents make between entry into therapy and the follow-up period, are plugged into the following formula to compute the composite goal attainment score[28]:

$$T = 50 + \frac{10\Sigma w_i x_i}{\sqrt{(1 - \rho)\Sigma w_i^2 + \rho(\Sigma w_i)^2}}$$

Given this formula, Al's goal attainment score after 3 months was 62 and Diane's was 55. In light of our previous experience with other couples, we felt it was safe to recommend that the children be returned to the home. They were returned, and there were no further incidences of physical abuse. Diane and Al remained in group 3 more months after the children's return because they believed they could learn even more about getting along with their children and with each other, which they did. At the end of 6 months in group, both had reached "the most favorable outcome thought likely" in all six problem areas.

ARE SOME FAMILIES UNTREATABLE?

While we are optimistic about the changes that abusive parents can make, we realize that not every family in which a child is abused can change sufficiently for the child to be safe. The Kempes found seven groups of parents that they felt commonly proved untreatable. They are the aggressive sociopaths, parents with delusions that involve the child, cruel sadistic parents who premeditatedly abuse their children, extreme fanatics, drug and substance abusers, mentally handicapped parents, and those with a history of prior serious injury or child abuse death.[29]

In a thorough review of the literature on abusive families that fail to respond to treatment, Jones concluded that:

> [a] picture emerges which emphasizes the poor prognosis for parents who have major personality disorders, psychoses that involve the child, addiction problems, or mental retardation. Untreatable parents are commonly those who were seriously damaged as children and who appear to have little or no capacity to love, relate to others, or empathize with a child. Additionally they are hostile, refuse help or treatment, and persistently deny the need for such.... Many abusive families have elements of the above features. However, the studies suggest that extreme degrees of the above situations, as well as their occurrence in combination, are common in untreatable families.[30]

Jones also found that certain types of injury were more indicative of a poor prognosis. These include severe forms of abuse (fractures, burns, scalds, vaginal intercourse, or sexual sadism), Munchausen by proxy, nonaccidental poisoning, and severe forms of nonorganic failure to thrive. Munchausen syndrome by proxy is a psychiatric disorder and form of child abuse that was first recognized in 1977.[31] A parent, usually the mother, gives spurious information about the child to physicians, with the apparent intention of leading them to incorrect diagnoses and treatment, or about who caused the injury, in order to appear heroic when she saves the child.

We have worked with parents who had burned or broken the bodies of their children and even caused the death of the child. But many of them have made remarkable and significant changes. The criterion seems to be whether or not they acknowledge the need for help in their lives and will commit to treatment. Even with a court-ordered threat of loss of parental rights if they do not enter treatment, some parents will not comply. In that respect, they are indeed untreatable. The same is true if they simply do not have the intellectual or emotional functioning sufficient to understand what is required of them as parents.

We accept consistent participation in group as a statement by the parents that they are willing to change. One indication of commitment that we have the first night the parents attend group is the checklist. If a parent gives it back with no items marked, saying, "We don't have any of those problems," we know they are unwilling to risk opening up sufficiently to change. Those parents rarely return after the first night, even if the consequence is loss of the child or criminal prosecution. We do not find it necessary for the parents to admit right away that they abused the child. That admission, even if tacit, must come at some point in treatment, but we do not see the admission as a necessary battleground for forcing "the truth." Rather we start with the problems the parents admit to having and build from there.

Jones found that rates of recidivism of child abuse in the studies he surveyed ranged from 16 to 60%.[32] The proportion of families unchanged or worse after treatment varied from 20 to 87%. A survey of 89 different demonstration child abuse treatment programs, involving 3253 families, showed that 30 to 47% of the families continued to be abusive.[33] Those families who received treatment tended to be judged the most severe cases, as were ours. The treatment they received varied. Some included a lay health visitor's seeing the family in the home once a week, or once-a-week contact with the caseworker, along with individual or group therapy.

Approximately 30% of the families referred to us by CPS workers either never came or dropped out prior to our recommendation for termination. Unfortunately, some people's life tragedies seem unsolvable by anyone other than themselves. In those instances, the best we can do is to protect the children and work at giving them an opportunity to live life less painfully.

6

Treatment Issues with Abusive Parents

Getting the family into therapy is obviously the first step in treatment. Most abusive parents are unwilling to seek help unless they perceive their lives to be in crisis and that they have no other option. To people who have grown up in violent homes, violence is not a crisis, but threatened dissolution of the family or imprisonment is. The other factor working against these families' being open to treatment is their basic distrust of people, stemming from their abusive childhood experience. Other people came to be seen as a source of pain, not comfort and sustenance. Isolation was a survival adaptation, and one not easily relinquished.

The combination of a high tolerance for violence and fear of reaching out for help means that abusing families are not likely to seek therapy even if the life or health of their children is at risk. This makes "coercive therapy" essential if there is to be successful intervention with these families. The concept of coercive therapy is applied when the client is under pressure to seek therapy. The consequences for not doing so play a large role in the person's decision. With abusive families, it is often necessary to impose consequences that are unacceptable to the parents. For many, only the threat or actual removal of the children from the family or the threat of imprisonment are sufficient coercion for abusive parents to seek therapy.

Even these coercions are not sufficient to induce all abusive families to leave the protective walls of their isolation and seek therapy, but many will. The fact that some families will relinquish their children rather than seek help points to how the concept of coercion in psychotherapy is somewhat misleading. No matter what the external pressure, the individuals make the choice to present themselves for therapy. Continued participation, under whatever conditions, is evidence of willingness to make some life change. Of the 40 couples we treated over a 6-year period, 75% had a child removed from the home and were told that being in therapy was one condition for the return of custody. In the other 25% of the families, the children's remaining in the home was conditional upon the parents' seeking psychological help.

The coercion was not enough to sustain the motivation for all the families. Six of the couples dropped out of therapy and subsequently lost custody of their children. In the remaining 34 families, there were 13 who were reported again for a recurrence of abuse. Those who completed therapy attended an average of 15 sessions over an 8-month period.

Once we do have at least an implicit commitment from the parents, the job becomes one of sorting through the maze of financial, social, physical, and emotional problems burdening these families. Using the Goal Attainment Scale makes it easier to keep a clear focus on what problems the clients and therapists have agreed to address, as well as offering a tool for setting contracts and measuring change. Staying focused is essential when dealing with these families that seem to be facing a never-ending wave of problems. We described in Chapter 5 the six basic problem areas we focus on when treating the couples in group. In this chapter, our treatment approach to each problem and some of the techniques we and others have found effective will be presented.

SYMBIOSIS

In addressing the problem of symbiosis in abusive families, the goal is teaching new coping skills for getting emotional needs met. Rather than struggling for nurturance through passivity or violence, the husbands and wives are taught communication tools that enable them to be both more responsible and more effective in getting what they want from each other. By using these tools, they relinquish—to some extent—the fantasy that their partners can or will magically know and meet all their emotional needs, as a good mother does for her infant. These parents must come to terms with their own ability and responsibility to meet their needs.

Our first job as therapists is to assess which roles each partner is playing in the family. Sometimes that is obvious, as in the case of Diane and Al. The first time we asked Al a question and Diane answered, it was clear that Diane had claimed the Parent slot, at least in social situations. To strengthen Diane's awareness of her own Child needs, we coached her in asking Al for what she needed. This meant she had to check in with her Child feelings and make a clear request, rather than complaining about Al's not doing something he had not been asked to do. Al, on the other hand, was encouraged to answer his own questions and feel freer to state his opinions, which enabled him to begin developing his own Parent and Adult and not have to rely on Diane's.

Formerly abused children, as most of the parents we worked with were, understandably have a great deal of difficulty in directly asking for what they want. They have to learn a new set of social interaction "stroking rules," which seem very foreign to them and which they distrust initially. They are so accustomed to exchanging only negative strokes or withholding all strokes that it is necessary to let them know they have other options for relating to people. The "rules"[1] we present to them are as follows: (1) All the strokes you need are available. This counteracts the "scarce supply" myth. (2) You have to ask for the strokes you need. It is amazing how many people, not just abusive parents, believe the myth that "it doesn't count if I have to ask. If you loved me, you'd know what I need." (3) When asked for a stroke, you can comply or decline. Having lived in families where compliance was part of survival, abusing parents operate with a myth of "I have to do it if they ask." (4) When offered a stroke, you can accept or decline. This rule counteracts two myths: "I don't deserve good things" (positive strokes), and "I have to take what's given me" (negative strokes). The parents are often disbelieving that this much choice is available to them.

When the symbiotic arrangement is not as obvious as it was with Diane and Al, we look for small indicators. Is the wife handling all the bills because the husband messes up the checking account any time he tries to keep track of the money? Is one spouse responsible for getting the other one out of bed in the morning because "he/she just won't get up unless I bring in coffee?" Does one partner pick out the clothes the other is to wear each day? We asked that question in group one night and were startled to learn that all but one wife said she told her husband what to wear. The remaining woman admitted that, while she did not instruct her husband on his wardrobe, "I put the right shirt with the right pants on the hanger together so he knows." Any of these indicators can form the basis of change contracts to be put on the GAS.

The transportation arrangement can be one helpful indicator of symbiosis. Ethyl maintained the Child position in the relationship by refusing to get a driver's license, which was indeed a handicap in the sprawling metropolitan area in which she lived. She reasoned—by discounting the existence of the problem—that she did not need a license because she could drive in an emergency if she had to and that (discounting the solvability of the problem) it was impossible for her to leave work to take the driver's test, and, besides, their car was not safe enough to take the test in. Breaking up the symbiosis between Ethyl and her husband began with her contracting, after much persistent confrontation of her discounting by the group, to get her driver's license. Once she did get it, Ethyl began to take on more responsibility for chauffeuring their child, running errands, and driving herself to work.

Whereas Ethyl was needing to use her Parent and Adult more, Robert, the computer analyst, was oblivious to his Child much of the time. In group, Robert always showed up immaculately dressed in a coat and tie, even though he had been home for dinner and had time to change into more comfortable clothes. He sat rigidly, even if he was leaning against cushions, with his arms and legs tightly crossed. Our invitation to Robert to become more aware of his feelings was by teaching him a little about body language. We asked him to experiment with sitting with his arms and legs uncrossed, taking off his tie, and practicing breathing more deeply. Robert was such a perfectionist that he worked hard at "being open" physically. Much to his surprise and alarm, his feelings began to surface. He realized that what he was holding onto so tightly was his fear and anger. When Robert began to experience his own pent-up emotions, Della was freed from having to express the fear, anger, and neediness for both of them.

ISOLATION

As a result of having experienced people as hurtful, abusive parents are usually cut off from others both socially and emotionally. Even if they do decide to turn to others in times of distress, it is unlikely that they will have anyone other than family to call on, or that they will know how to effectively use community resources that are available to them.

Participation in group therapy is one important first step in breaking up the isolation of these parents. As noted previously, a national survey of child abuse treatment programs found that "adults who received group counseling were 27% less likely than those who did not receive this particular service to demonstrate a continued propensity for future maltreatment."[2]

We believe that one of the reasons for the heightened success of group treatment is that once a week, for 1½ hours, the group members experience others as helpful and caring, rather than punitive, giving instead of exploitive. For some, this is the first time they have ever been treated with this kind of respect. Their concept of what is possible in human relationships begins to expand, and trust slowly builds. Friendships form.

Using the positive group experience as a starting point, the members begin to take risks that further break down the walls of isolation. The group meetings are not sufficient to break up a lifelong pattern of isolation, so we use behavioral contracts to get the parents to take further risks in reaching out. The risks may seem small—meeting a neighbor, applying for a job, getting a telephone—but each step out of the isolation builds a road to greater openness. Diane and Al's contract to meet their neighbors is an example of the kind of behavioral contract we encourage.

Getting a telephone was the symbolic focal point in addressing the isolation in Sheryl and Jimmy's life. Sheryl was 18 and Jimmy was 19 when they came to group. Their 8-month-old son had been removed by CPS after Sheryl took him to the hospital emergency room for treatment of chronic diarrhea. The physicians found him to be extremely dehydrated and malnourished, and he had multiple bruises on his body. Although both had been sociable in high school, Jimmy and Sheryl had no mutual friends. Sheryl's social contacts outside the home had dwindled to visiting her mother on weekends. She bitterly resented Jimmy's going out with his friends in the evenings, understandably, since she spent her days alone with the baby. We felt it essential that the young couple get a telephone so that Sheryl would at least be able to call someone in an emergency and, it was hoped, to begin to renew friendships with phone contact. She balked at the idea and proudly told the following story. Her father, who worked at an oil refinery for 40 years, had never once been called in for overtime. The reason, she explained, was that he had been clever enough never to get a telephone. She was telling us very clearly how she saw her isolation as a protection. Sheryl also explained, with some embarrassment, "I don't know anyone to phone and no one will phone me." They did get a telephone, with a listed number, and Sheryl was amazed to discover that she did have people to call and that there were people who wanted to talk to her.

Some socializing takes place among group members outside the sessions. We ask that people exchange phone numbers with each other, to have in case of an emergency or if they need a ride to group. One group rule is that any socializing with each other outside group is reported in the next session. It is an important rule. Sometimes the social interactions go well, and sometimes they do not. It went well when Gary, who knew little about automobiles, asked Chuck, an experienced mechanic, to give him some advice on repairing his car. Both men looked like delighted schoolboys when they told the group how they had fixed Gary's carburetor the previous Sunday. It went badly when Sonia, who had four young children and stepchildren of her own, agreed to keep Bob and Susan's three difficult-to-control children when Susan went into the hospital. Both the successes and the failures are useful learning experiences for the parents as long as they bring them back to group for more objective examination.

MARITAL COMMUNICATION

Improving communication in these families usually begins by getting the anger out in the open. The checklist we ask the couples to fill out their first night in group lets them tell us where they see the marital tension. If they check "little support from spouse" or "sex" as problems, we ask them to give us more information about those items when it is their turn in group. This nonverbal admission of problems breaks through the united front of denial that often comes from asking the couple aloud if they are having any marital problems. Sometimes the check mark on the questionnaire is the first acknowledgment one of the partners has ever given to anyone about his or her concerns.

A fairly standard marriage therapy technique we have used with success is asking each spouse to name three likes and dislikes about the other. This forces people to think of specific behaviors and traits of their mates that are both rewarding and upsetting. In order to do the exercise, they have to say three nice things about their mates, something that most of them have not done for a long time. It helps them to get past the black-and-white way they might have been viewing each other and opens the door for "bartering" for change.

An example of the bartering was the contract Robert and Della agreed to and kept. Della's main "dislike" was that Robert never talked to her when he first came home from work. Instead he turned on three television sets (one for each major network) and picked up the newspaper. Or he would immediately go outside to mow the lawn, which he did twice a week. For Robert, the one dislike he listed was that Della did not want to visit his friends. The contract the two of them came up with was that Robert would spend a least 15 minutes actually visiting with Della about their respective days before turning on television or mowing the grass. In return, Della would visit with his friends once a month. The agreement was meager in terms of the kind of sharing involved in a satisfying marriage, but it was a crack in the emotional wall between them.

Sometimes the bartering is physical. One woman asked for and got back rubs in exchange for sex. To her surprise, she started to enjoy sex more. To her husband's surprise, his wife began to initiate sex on occasion. The husband learned to be very generous in offering back rubs.

Because some of these parents are so explosive with their anger, their mates are afraid of saying anything that they think might trigger an outburst. When Greta joined the group, she reported, with terror in her voice, that she had taken her toddler to the physician that day for treatment of a bronchial asthma attack. This was the first her husband, Jerry, had heard about it. Greta said she had not told him before because she was afraid he would be angry that she spent the money. We coached Greta in asking Jerry directly how he did feel now that he knew. Jerry said that he was indeed angry, and hurt, but not because Greta had spent money. He was upset that she had not called him at work to discuss what she thought needed to be done. Greta had felt safe enough in the presence of other people to "confess" to what she had done. In so doing, she and Jerry both moved one step closer to trusting the other to hear them. Greta's secretive behavior and Jerry's response of feeling betrayed are common in these families. Because each assumes the other will be upset with what he or she has done (as their own parents were so often), each acts independently rather than checking out those assumptions. This virtually guarantees the mate's anger or hurt, since they feel discounted in not having been included in the decision. The wall of secrecy and self-protective deception comes down only when the spouses risk being honest.

ANGER

It is understandable that people who were emotionally and/or physically abused as children would have problems in handling their own and others' anger. The rage from childhood either explodes or is turned into depression. Typically in abusive families, one or both partners are "rage-aholics." As in an alcoholic family system, the addictive behavior is reinforced by either submissiveness or negative attention. Rageful acting-out and the family's adaptation to it was witnessed by these individuals as children, and they repeat the pattern with their own families.

A variety of approaches to handling the anger is necessary. The strategies range from "no-hitting" contracts to relaxation training. It is necessary to define clear limits for rage-aholics since no one may have ever done that before in their lives. Limit-setting and contracting for expressing anger appropriately enhances the parents' growing awareness of their ability to manage emotions effectively.

No-hitting contracts mean the parents agree not to hit their children or each other. Since it is often the case that only one of the parents inflicted the physical injuries on the child, we contract with that parent not to physically discipline the child under any circumstances. The contract serves as an important psychological protection for the parents, who feel a sense of relief at having had this limit set for them. The parent who injured the child has much less difficulty with the contract than the spouse who had been passively shirking the responsibility of punishing the children. Anger management training, which we will describe below, helps the rageful parent know what to do instead of attacking the children.

Since one of the spouses may be expressing all the anger for both of them, our goal is to teach both how to use anger effectively and how to calm themselves to keep from exploding in rage.

Newton Hightower, a social worker experienced in working with violent clients in group settings both in and out of institutions, found that the "hydraulic theory" of managing violence (i.e., letting built-up pressure explode) is less effective than the model of turning down the flame under a pot that is boiling over. Hightower recommends the following actions with violent clients to help them de-escalate: (1) breaking eye contact, (2) lowering your voice, (3) making a request in a quiet voice and repeating the request until it is carried out, such as "Leave the room, please."[3] In our work with violent clients, we found these techniques effective in helping them calm down and regain control. The approach was also helpful to the couples in dealing with each other when one was out of control.

Each session ended with a 15-minute relaxation tape. It consisted of a standard relaxation exercise—taking deep breaths and imagining being in a calming spot in a natural setting, for example. Ending each session with the exercise seemed to help the group members carry some of the relaxation over into the week, and the exercise seemed to have a reinforcing effect on the work done in group that night. By doing the exercise over and over, they became more proficient at calming their bodies and also became aware of an emotional control most of them never knew they had. We urged the parents to use the relaxation exercise or some abbreviated version of it at home, particularly when they found their tension mounting around the children.

With spouses that are afraid of anger, including their own, we use assertiveness training. Ethyl, who did not want to get a driver's license, was quiet, reserved, and terrified of her husband, Gary's, violent outbursts of temper, as most anyone would have been. After hearing over and over in group that anger is a natural emotion, Ethyl finally mustered the courage to express her anger—at the therapists. She told us with anger no one had ever seen how neglected she had felt by all the attention we had been giving to a new couple. Before Ethyl was able to let loose with her anger, Gary had to get his under control. When he first started in group, he was using medication to try to calm himself. Once he learned relaxation training, he became so adept that his violent outbursts ceased. He still shouted some, but Ethyl was learning to shout back.

The main point we make to the parents about anger is that it is an attempt to try to get needs met, and that they have to know what they want in order to get it. We want them to understand the difference between violence and anger, and to use a different model from the one most of them witnessed in childhood.

CHILD DEVELOPMENT AND CHILD MANAGEMENT

Abusive parents are woefully ignorant of what babies and children need at different ages and stages and how to respond to those needs. Just like most of us, these mothers and fathers draw on their own experiences of being parented when parenting their children. Since those experiences were frequently abusive for these parents, they have few healthy guidelines to follow naturally. Also, the emotional demands of their children serve as chronic, unconscious reminders of their own unmet demands when they themselves were children. Not knowing what to do, knowing the wrong thing to do, and not wanting to do any of it make for an explosive combination.

A good portion of each group session must be devoted to teaching information about developmental stages of children, appropriate parental responses, nonviolent behavioral management, and other basic skills essential to even minimal success in parenting. The teaching is typically in response to the parents' immediate concerns about their children's behavior, such as bed-wetting, lying, or school problems. The information given in group is supplemented with assigned readings appropriate to the educational level of the parent.

Schmitt emphasizes the importance of teaching all parents techniques for managing the seven most difficult developmental phases of childhood. He observes: "Normal parents appreciate help with raising their children. Most abusive parents and high-risk parents also want this kind of help, especially at a time when their children are frustrating them."[4] Those seven "deadly sins of childhood"[5] are colic, awakening at night, separation anxiety, normal exploratory behavior, normal negativism, normal poor appetite, and toilet-training resistance.

We give the parents a simplified chart that explains developmental needs of children at different ages and appropriate parental responses (see Table 5). Much of the teaching is in response to the parents' questions and concerns. Donna and Dean were alarmed when they found their 2-year-old son masturbating. Sue and James were at a loss of what to do to reassure 4-year-old Tommy that there were no monsters in his room when they turned out the lights. Greta was exhausted and frustrated in her futile attempts to make her 18-month-old daughter stop playing with dangerous objects.

The overall goal in addressing the problem of child development and management is to give the parents information they need in order to do a better job as parents. The irony is that to be licensed to drive a car, we have to demonstrate competence, but almost anyone who has the necessary reproductive equipment is entitled to have a try at parenting.

EMPLOYMENT

Problems with employment often reflect dysfunctional relationships with the world as a whole. A young mother who stays

Table 5. Developmental Stages and Needs

Age	Stage	What the child needs	What parent needs to do	What parent shouldn't do
0–6 months (or crawling)	Existential	To establish symbiosis Food and physical stroking To find that he/she has impact on the environment Talk	Feed, fondle, talk to baby When baby cries, check to see what is wrong Try out different things to soothe child	Don't withhold strokes Don't feed on schedule Don't spank Don't hover over baby when there's no discomfort
6 months–1½ or 2 years	Exploratory	Move around Get into things Drop things Self-feed	Continue giving unconditional positive strokes "Baby-proof" the house Provide protection	Don't restrict mobility Don't force toilet training Don't spoon- or force-feed Don't spank
1½ or 2–3 years	Separation	To test and oppose To be negative Break symbiosis Learn to consider needs and feelings of others	Expect child to start considering others Expect child to use cause-and-effect thinking and problem solving Institute disciplining Begin toilet training	Don't fail to discipline (not punish) and give reason to convey expectations Don't make expectations too high or be too demanding Don't be inconsistent toward child

Age				
3–6 years (can be 2½–5)	Imaginative	Identify differences in self and others: sex, color hair, eyes Ask questions Move away more from parents physically Invent monsters	Answer all questions with reasons Encourage problem solving Teach how to get strokes	Don't answer questions with "because I said so" Don't get uptight over masturbation Don't tease
6–12 years	Creative	Argue, compete, achieve Do things, have companions Join community activity	Discuss values and state rules Listen to child's reasons Encourage task completion and setting priorities	Don't make rules and values too rigid Don't fail to discuss rules and values
12–18 years (puberty through teens)	Recycling	Be contradictory Be part child, part adult Say, in effect, "Go away closer" and "Tell me what to do—I dare you." Recycle previous stages	Stick by rules and values Encourage independence but still offer "protection" and guidance	Don't give up Don't be overprotective or underprotective

at home alone, watching soap operas and waiting for protective service workers to return her children, refuses to look for a job because of fear of rejection. A man gets fired from his fourth construction job in a year because he blows up at the foreman or starts a fight with another worker. A couple works opposite shifts because they find they fight less only if they see little of each other.

All employment problems are addressed both from a practical and a psychological perspective. While it is helpful to give information about where the community employment agency is located, it is of even greater value to give the group members an opportunity to learn new skills in handling work relationships. Using a paradoxical therapy approach of contracting with Sheryl to apply for three jobs she will not accept gives her much-needed confidence in looking for a job without risking rejection. Inviting Bob, the explosive construction worker, to look at the triggers for his outbursts gives him an opportunity to think about what he can do to use more effective, nonviolent coping behaviors in handling conflicts.

Providing information on community resources is part of addressing the employment problem. Dean was unemployed and doubtful of his ability to get a job because of an old eye injury. We referred him to a vocational rehabilitation agency that tested his job aptitude and gave him a stipend while he was enrolled in a training program. The other group members also served as an informal network for job information.

Addressing problems related to employment often have the added benefit of helping to change the symbiotic relationship or lessen isolation. Mickey was able to give up his second job when Pam decided, with the group's support, that she could get a job. Jimmy was able to find a less dangerous and stressful job when Sheryl went to work. Positive changes the parents make in any of the problem areas lessen the pressure in the others.

IRRATIONAL BELIEFS IN THE ABUSIVE
FAMILY SYSTEM

Behind all these six major problem areas (symbiosis, isolation, marital dysfunction, temper, child development/management, isolation) and many of the other concerns that abusive families have in daily life is a belief system that sustain the tension, conflict, and disharmony. Albert Ellis described these beliefs as erroneous thinking.[6] In working with abusive families, these erroneous beliefs must be worked on for changes in behavior and feeling to occur. The following seven beliefs are the ones most commonly held by abusive parents that contribute to the abusive system.

1. If my child cries, misbehaves, or does not do what I want, he/she does not love me, and I'm a bad parent.
2. My child should know what I want and want to do it.
3. My child should take care of me the way I took care of my parents.
4. My husband/wife should know what I want and meet all my needs.
5. If I have to ask, it does not count, and I am a failure.
6. You cannot trust anyone.
7. People are only out for what they can get.

Much of the treatment of abusive parents is either directly or indirectly aimed at shaking their certainty in these beliefs. When they have an experience in group therapy of being supported and even nurtured, the parents' belief about all people being untrustworthy and selfish is shaken a little. Learning that asking directly for what one wants is the most effective way of getting needs met goes against these parents' belief that it shows weakness to ask. Bit by bit, their armored view of the world shifts, letting in the light and warmth of human caring and compassion.

THERAPEUTIC CONSIDERATIONS

In working with abusive families, there are certain issues that the therapist must be alerted to in order to be effective and not to make some very unfortunate clinical errors. These considerations have to do with what abusing parents need from the therapist, how the therapist and client see each other, competition with the abused child, and the reporting of abuse.

"Mothering" of Abusive Parents

Kempe and Lascari hold the position that the therapist must provide abusing parents with mothering because they never experienced sufficient mothering in their own childhoods.[7] While the parents' backgrounds have certainly been characterized by deprivation, both the therapist and the client have to come to terms with the reality that there really is no way to make up for what was missed at critical developmental stages. The most either can hope for is a consistent, compassionate, and appropriate interchange.

It has worked best for us to think of "mothering" in terms of extending unconditional positive regard. If we can accept these persons with empathy and understanding, regardless of what damages they have done, we have given them a kind of acceptance they lacked from their own parents. We agree with Ellis that it is important to separate the "doing" from the "being" part of the person.[8] Abusive parents do not understand that distinction and certainly judge themselves and others in terms of "doing." The message we hope to convey is "You are OK. You count. You have a right to exist. Even though you have done bad things, you are important as a person and can change."

A certain amount of dependency on the therapist is inevitable and even appropriate, given the neediness of these people. Clear limits are essential, however, if the therapist is not to be swallowed up by that neediness. Therapists who have problems in setting limits for themselves or their clients—such as ending sessions on time or accepting calls at all hours—will have a very difficult emotional and behavioral struggle with abusive parents. There is no real undoing of the damage done in childhood. We view our job as helping these parents to understand their needs and giving them some tools to meet those needs realistically and responsibly. This is not to say that long-term therapy would not be beneficial, but most of these parents will not have that resource available to them. Our goal is to enable the families to function in such a manner that the children are no longer being abused and the parents are turning to each other or to other adults for support. Self-understanding, communication skills, and parenting effectiveness are tools that facilitate competence in self-responsibility for these parents.

Therapist as an Authority Figure

The therapist is invariably going to be seen as having power over the lives and fate of the abusing family. Despite the fact that therapists do not have the authority to order removal or return of the child, the parents think that they do. For treatment to be effective, the therapist must be free of any authority to remove the child.[9] We try to make it as clear as possible to the parents that the action of the judge will be a function of what changes they bring about in their lives and that our role is to facilitate and report those changes. We explain and remind them repeatedly that we had no role in the removal of the child, that we are not involved in any court action other than reporting on what the parents do in therapy, and that we are not employed by CPS.

The emphasis is placed on their role in getting the children returned and CPS out of their lives. We acknowledge that they may feel wronged by the CPS's intrusion into their lives but remind them that it remains their responsibility to do what is necessary so that the courts can feel confident the children will be safe in their homes.

The therapist can do little to keep from being seen as either the good parent or the bad parent, or both at different times. That kind of projection goes along with any therapeutic relationship. Continuing to present the facts, putting the responsibility for the outcome back on the parents, and not pulling any power plays helps the therapist stay out of a godlike role.

Being seen as an authority in the sense of "an accepted source of information or advice"[10] is both appropriate and necessary. The parents need to see the therapist as knowing things they do not know and having useful advice for them, but not as someone who has "the right and power to command, enforce laws, exact obedience, determine, or judge."

Using Two Therapists

Investigators at the University of California at Los Angeles take the position that it is important to provide a male and a female therapist for a parents' group to facilitate the members' identifying with a father and a mother figure.[11] It is helpful for the parents to have both male and female role models and for the couples to watch how a nonabusing, nonsymbiotic relationship between a man and a woman can work. Both sexes bring up issues that they might be reluctant to discuss without a same-sex therapist present. For example, one man in our group wanted a private session to discuss a homosexual encounter he had had as a teenager that he felt was interfering with his sexual relationship with his wife. Had he not been able to share that with a male therapist privately, it is unlikely the issue would ever have been brought out.

There are other advantages of having two therapists. As Helfer has noted, if parents are angry at one therapist, they can let off steam to the other.[12] They learn in the process that an upset between two people does not have to involve other relationships.

The clients are actually shocked sometimes to see that the other therapist does not get involved in disagreements between the therapist and a client. Those kinds of boundaries are foreign to people who grew up in enmeshed families.

"Two heads are better than one" holds true in working with these multifamily, multiproblem groups. What one misses, the other is likely to see. When one has gotten bogged down, the other may see a way out. Having different points of view is helpful to both the therapist and the clients. The couples witness something they believed to be impossible—two people disagreeing and still having positive regard and respect for each other. They are presented with a different model for solving differences.

Finally, and perhaps most important, it is comforting to have an ally when working with people who are filled with such fear, anger, and neediness. It is comforting beyond measure at the end of a really tough session to know that there is someone who really understands what you just went through. There are moments when it feels as if the battle lines are drawn—us against them. No matter how skillful the therapist or how motivated the clients, this is tough work. It helps to know that someone else is in there fighting the battle with you for a cause you both believe in—stopping child abuse.

There are circumstances in which the above adage about two heads does not hold true. One is when the "two heads" have vastly differing ideas about how to treat abusing families. If the two cotherapists are not basically in agreement about the treatment approach and modalities to be used, it is preferable to do the group alone. The advantages of having two therapists would be lost if the therapists were not in harmony. It is more rewarding to see one person dance beautifully alone than two dancers tripping over each other. The other circumstance when one is better than two is if the resources for two therapists are not available. There is such an enormous need for treatment of these families that a single-therapist group is the easy choice over no group at all. In that situation, the therapist needs to take care to find outside support and consultation.

Handling the Therapist's Feelings about Abuse

Sanders states that "before any person becomes involved with battering parents he should try to recognize his own feelings about the problem."[13] Pollock notes that one of the first hurdles therapists have to overcome is their feelings about a parent who has hurt a small baby. "There is disbelief and denial, horror, a surge of anger towards the abuser."[14] The other extreme is a certain emotional numbness that can come from seeing too much of the horror and suffering. To experience anger, pain, or sorrow when we witness suffering is what it is to be a compassionate human being. Continued outrage or indifference are defenses people use to protect themselves from the emotional pain of dealing with suffering.

The outrage may have its foundation in denying the very real feelings of rage any parent has toward a child in the most trying times. Children are exasperating and trying, even the "good ones." No parents want to see themselves capable of hating or even wanting to kill their children, but even good "parents also have hostile and negative feelings. These feelings, however, are often totally unconscious."[15]

One way to deny these hostile and negative feelings is to regard abusive parents as completely different from oneself. To define them all as sick, crazy, or maniacs is to refuse to see that we have feelings that are just as negative. The difference is that, if we have been fortunate not to have those rageful feelings unleashed on us as children, we are able to separate our destructive feelings from our actions. It is true that some people who abuse children, some of the "untreatable families" described earlier, do fit those pejoratives. But most parents who hurt their children are like everyone else: a mixture of good and bad, cruel and

caring. Sadly, the balance of the scales too often tips to the negative in their lives.

Therapists who work with abusing families must also avoid
the other extreme of absolving abusive parents from any responsibility for their actions. No matter how the cards are stacked
against us, all of us are ultimately accountable for how we play
the game. Pitying the parents and encouraging them to blame
society or their parents is as unproductive as raging against
them. It is important to acknowledge the role played by society
and their own abusive parenting, but the therapist must do that
while steering away from encouraging the client to blame or play
"Wooden Leg" (as in "what do you expect of someone with a
wooden leg?").[16] Holmes observes that if a therapist has "a
warm, ongoing relationship with the parent, [he will want to
deny] the abusive act and see only the pleasant side of the parent
... forgetting that, in order to help, he must be able to accept
the rage as well as the love in the client."[17]

Having said all that, we do take steps not to intentionally
stir up our emotions. We read the initial intake interview and
familiarize ourselves with what the abuse was, but we seldom
go back to that again. We do not look at pictures of what parents
did to their children's bodies. By reminding ourselves that these
parents are abused children in big bodies and that what they
did was an expression of their own pain and suffering, it is easier
to reconnect with our feelings of care, concern, and compassion.

We also, for the most part, have not treated the abused children of the parents we have in group except in family therapy
sessions. The symbiotic competition with the child is so intense
when the parents first begin treatment that they see us as being
more interested in the child than in them. And indeed they may
be right. Despite our best intentions to the contrary, it would
be hard not to be more drawn emotionally to a small, injured
child than to the hard, tough man or angry woman who inflicted
the damage. Davoren found that when the therapist also treats
the child, the parents feel rejected and pushed aside, as they

have so many times before.[18] Clearly the children need treatment, but the whole family is likely to make faster progress if the parents and children each have their own therapist.

Reporting Abuse

In our work with the couples, we were not faced with the issue of reporting. The families had already been reported, court action had been taken, and they were offering themselves for treatment. That is not the situation for therapists in private practice, such as physicians, clergy, attorneys, or other professionals who discover that someone they are working with is abusing a child.

Despite the very clear laws in all 50 states mandating the reporting of suspected or known instances of child abuse, many people, including professionals, are reluctant to report. "Reporting is uncomfortable for most clinicians and may cause unexpected feelings to surface ... feelings of betrayal of a mother who clearly cared for her child, of fear that she would be treated harshly by 'the authorities' and fear she would stop treatment," observes Lyon of her own experience.[19] A psychologist admits, "I would not have immediately reported the incident, if not required to do so" and proposes a "limited reporting requirement."[20] Professionals other than therapists share some of these feelings, along with a reluctance "to get involved."

Regardless of our personal assessment of whether or not reporting abuse to the authorities would be in the family's or our best interest, we are mandated by law to do so and must. The evidence is clear that abusing families are more likely to get the help they need if they are coerced into doing so. As much as we might wish otherwise, their walls of isolation usually have to be battered down by legal intervention. When we remember that there are children and adults suffering intensely behind those walls, it is imperative that we do what we can to help free them from the abusive system. That means reporting all suspected or known cases of child abuse.

7

Overcoming Consequences of Abuse

In the previous chapters, we have discussed many of the individual and intergenerational consequences of child abuse. Using a variation on the concept of adult children of alcoholics (adults who suffer emotional and social consequences from having been reared in alcoholic homes), therapist John Bradshaw offers the following list of symptoms in adults who were physically abused as children.[1]

ADULT CHILDREN OF PHYSICAL VIOLENCE

A Abuse feels normal
D Delusion and denial
U Unreality
L Loss of the ability to initiate or solve problems
T Trust issues

C   Criminal behavior
H   Hostility and internalized rage
I   Intense jealousy and possessiveness
L   Loneliness, alienation, isolation
D   Dissociated and depersonalized
R   Rigidity
E   Eating disorders
N   Numbed out and apathetic

O   Objectification of self and others
F   Fixated personality development

P   Prostitution and sexualized rage
H   Hypervigilant and fear of losing control
Y   Yearning for parental approval
S   Shame-based
I   Illness-real or imagined
C   Co-dependent
A   Acting-out behaviors
L   Loss of boundaries

V   Victim role
I   Incensed at parents
O   Offender status
L   Low grade chronic depression
E   Externalizer
N   Nightmares or dream repression
C   Compulsive/addictive behavior
E   Extremely split

Not all children who are abused have all of these symptoms in adulthood, but it is likely that they will suffer from at least some of these consequences. Research studies conducted in the last few years document impressions that clinicians have held for years as to how physical abuse affects development.

Reidy compared 20 abused children with 20 nonabused children and found that those who had been abused were more aggressive in their free play and fantasy play and on psychological tests.[2] George and Main, in investigating preschool children, compared 10 abused children with children from families experiencing stress. The abused children more often assaulted other children at school, were verbally aggressive to the preschool staff, and were less likely to respond positively to friendly overtures from their teachers.[3] Jacobson and Straker did not find the abused children more hostile, but they were less socially active.[4]

In a review of the research on the effects of maltreatment on the child, Aber and Cicchetti[5] found that the research indicated that child abuse consequences included "a variety of emotional, societal, and cognitive disturbances including lack of responsivity, inappropriate affect, inhibition, anhedonia, extreme withdrawal, aggressivity, lack of impulse control, low frustration tolerance, school learning problems, and impaired interpersonal interactions."[6]

Several important follow-up studies have helped contribute to our understanding of why abuse affects children differently.[7] Egeland and Sroufe, in a prospective study, identified over 200 children whom they thought to be at risk for developmental problems because of poverty, limitations in parental knowledge about child care, lack of education, or the mothers' young age. They divided these children into four groups based on their mothers' behaviors and attitudes: physical abuse, hostile/verbal, psychological unavailability, and neglect. What they found was that the children had different developmental problems depending upon their age and the type of maltreatment they suffered. For example, at 18 months of age, few of the physically abused children were securely attached to their mothers compared to children of a group of mothers who were not considered maltreating. At 24 months, those same maltreated children showed more anger, frustration, and noncompliance when their mothers tried to teach them something. None of the babies who had psychologically unavailable mothers were securely attached to their mothers at age 18 months, even if they had been at age 12 months.

The Harvard Child Maltreatment Project (HCMP) was started in 1979 by Cicchetti and his colleagues as a longitudinal study of child maltreatment in the Greater Boston area. Its purpose is to research how abuse affects children differently depending on the interruption in normal developmental stages. Research at the HCMP is based on the theory of organizational perspective.[8]

> Within the organizational perspective, development is depicted as a series of behavioral reorganizations around a set of developmental tasks or issues.... These issues are not to be viewed as hurdles associated with any one age; each task remains important to the child's continuing adaptation, although it decreases in salience relative to other newly emerging tasks. For example, while the formation of a secure attachment relationship is the stage-salient task of the first year of life, emotional connections to others remain important across the life span.[9]

Table 6 presents the stage-salient developmental tasks according to organizational perspective.

Since its inception in 1979, the project has recruited over 300 families and given developmental assessments to 400 children in those families. Approximately 130 of those families were involved with CPS for having abused or neglected their children. The maltreating families were matched with about the same number of controls. Both groups had parents with relatively low education and income levels; most were receiving AFDC and were single parents. There was a second, smaller control group (35) composed of parents with middle income levels, higher education, and more resources. A group of 12 other families was used in a pilot study of mothers who were abused as children but did not go on to maltreat their own children. The HCMP is investigating, among other questions, how it is that some abused children are so badly damaged and others seem to be able to function well and do not become abusive to their children.

ATTACHMENT AND FAILURE

One possible answer to this question relates to Bowlby's attachment theory.[10] According to this theory, the most important task in the first year of a baby's life is to form a secure attachment with its primary caregiver. Forming that attachment is necessary both for physical survival and for giving a sense of "felt security that will enable the child to later explore both the social and physical world."[11]

Spitz, in the late 1940s and early 1950s studied a group of institutionalized normal but unmarried mothers and their babies. He noticed that the babies had a higher than normal incidence of infantile eczema, and that their mothers had a particular way of touching them that seemed to excite rather than calm the babies when they were anxious and upset. He also noted that as they grew older, the children had poor social adjustment, difficulty in handling aggression, and poor impulse control.[12]

Research has shown that the mother–child relationship is crucial to normal development in many ways, including the modulating of many vital functions, such as sleep, heart rate, respiration, temperature, vestibular function, and growth hormone secretion by touch on the skin.[13] The way in which a mother strokes her infant also influences the baby's sense of boundaries, helping it to define itself as an individual. Perhaps most important, the mother's attitudes about the infant are incorporated into its body image and self-esteem. Tender touch conveys the message to the child, "You have value and worth. You are lovable." Lack of touch or rough handling send the opposite message.

When there is a healthy attachment between the infant and the mother or caregiver, the infant explores the world while periodically maintaining contact through a touch, smile, or sounds. In a healthy mother–child dyad, when the baby becomes upset, it accepts comfort from the "attachment figure." In order to build

Table 6. Stage-Salient Issues According to the Organizational Perspective[a]

General developmental issue	Approximate age			
	0–12 months	12–30 months	30 months–2 years	7–12 years
	Modulation of arousal Physiological regulation	Differentiation of persons Awareness of self as distinct entity		
Attachment	Formation of secure attachment relationship with primary caregiver	Exploration of environment		
	Differentiation and integration of emotional reactions	Regulation and control of emotional reactions	Development of sense of efficacy and pride	
Autonomy		Problem-solving, pride, and mastery motivation Capacity to delay gratification and to tolerate frustration Awareness of standards	Awareness of social roles Ego-resiliency and ego control Sex-role development Integration into peer groups and social support networks	

	Development of language and communicative skills	Development of emotional bonds with peers	Hierarchization of social networks and multiple attachment figures
Establishing peer relationships		Role-taking	Formation of feelings of volition and agency of the self
		Empathy and pro-social behavior	Awareness of and ability to express multiple emotions
		Capacity to take initiative	Internalization of standards of right and wrong and development of morality
		Self-regulation	Capacity to assume responsibilities and to accomplish tasks
Hierarchical integration of attachment, autonomy and peer relationships		Development of criteria for evaluating one's performance	Awareness of internal psychological processes
		Hierarchization of plans	

[a] Adapted from "Sequelae of Child Maltreatment," by Dante Cicchetti, Richard J. Gelles, and Jane B. Lancasters (eds.), *Child Abuse and Neglect: Biosocial Dimensions*. New York: Aldine de Gruyter. Copyright 1987 by the Social Science Research Council.

this secure attachment, the infant's needs must be met in a consistent, loving, and predictable fashion. If not, the attachment tends to be anxious, and anxiously attached children have been found to hover near their caregivers rather than explore their environment.[14] Researchers have found that abused children tend to be anxiously attached.[15]

The most important aspect of forming a secure attachment is that the child who has successfully done so is "likely to possess a representational model of attachment figures as being available, responsive and helpful, and a complimentary model of him/herself as at least a potentially loveable and valuable person."[16] This means that children who have had their needs consistently met in the first year of life start out with a radically different view of the world from that of those who have been abused.

> The securely attached child with positive expectations of him/herself and others is more likely to enter into other loving and trusting relationships. In contrast, infants whose needs have not been met consistently, infants whose attachment figure responded inadequately or inappropriately to their behavior, come to expect that care is not available or dependable. Their representational model, of the attachment figure as being unavailable, unresponsive or unloveable, is what they bring to the caregiving relationship when they become parents.[17]

At the HCMP, they studied 37 infants from poor and less-educated families. Eighteen of these babies had been abused or neglected, and the remaining 19 were used as a comparison group. It was found that 67% of the maltreated infants had insecure attachments, in contrast to 26% of the comparison group.[18] The gap widened even more as the children got older, with those maltreated infants who had initially shown secure attachments later becoming anxiously attached.

In a school setting, children ages 4 to 8 who had been maltreated were found to be more dependent and imitative of adults who were new to them, showed less motivation to deal competently with the environment for the intrinsic pleasure of mastery, and were less cognitively mature.[19] The maltreated children appeared to be "more preoccupied with security issues in their relationships with novel adults,... therefore, less free to be motivated by competency concerns."[20] The data indicate that by the time the maltreated children enter school, they are already viewing the world as a dangerous place and are vigilant for cues as to how to protect themselves.

The World of Abnormal Rearing cycle that Helfer described begins with this failure to form a secure attachment, and the evidence is clear that most abused children go on to complete the cycle by becoming abusive parents. The continuity of this intergenerational cycle has now been studied empirically.

Beginning in 1975, at the Minneapolis Public Health Clinic, Egeland and his colleagues[21] enrolled 267 mothers in their last trimester of pregnancy who were at high risk for abuse or neglect. Within the sample, they identified 44 cases where maltreatment had already taken place from physical abuse ($n = 24$), neglect ($n = 19$), hostile/rejecting ($n = 19$), and psychologically unavailable ($n = 19$). There was overlap between the groups. For example, only 4 of the children in the hostile/rejecting category had not been physically abused.

The mothers were then identified, independent of the care of their children, as to the type of parenting they themselves received as children. They were divided into two groups: abused and not abused. The not abused group was then divided into those who were emotionally supported as children (describing their families as loving, concerned, and encouraging, giving them a sense of emotional security). The rest formed the control group.

The data gave strong evidence of intergenerational continuity of abuse. Seventy percent of 47 mothers who were abused were maltreating their own children. Only 1 of the mothers who had emotionally supportive parents was currently maltreating her child, but 40% were borderline abusers. The researchers speculated that the high percentage of borderline abusers in the group of mothers judged to be emotionally supportive might be due to those mothers having been abused as children but being unable or unwilling to report it to the interviewer. They also theorized that "the life stress, chaos, and disruption the mothers experience is a major cause of abuse."[22] It is possible that both explanations affected the results.

The study also found a very high relationship between a mother's having been sexually abused by a parent and her mal-treating her children. Of 13 mothers who reported having been sexually abused by a family member, only 1 provided adequate care for her child. The same pattern held with the mothers who had been neglected as children. Eight mothers were identified as having been neglected as children, and only 2 of them were providing adequate care for their children.

While it is evident that the cycle of abuse perpetuates itself, is it inevitable that an abused child will become an abusive parent? What is it about those few mothers in this study and others that make them the exception? How is it that they are able to take care of their children without abusing them while most are not?

It is now known, both from clinical observation and from empirical research, that children and adults do not respond iden-tically or suffer the same consequences from stressful life events and circumstances.[23] Although the exact way in which the effects of these stressors are modified is not known, there are factors that can be identified that play a part in the process. One such cluster of factors involves personal characteristics, such as age, sex, and sociodemographic background. A second group invol-ves an individual's personal qualities and earlier experiences, in-cluding coping styles, problem-solving skills, prior adjustment level and success in mastery, cognitive appraisal systems, and a sense of control versus powerlessness. External factors, such as the strength of a child's support system, also have been shown to have a moderating influence on children facing a variety of stressful life events.[24] We will look now at the factors that enable some abused children to break the cycle.

ABUSED CHILDREN WHO DO NOT ABUSE

Until fairly recently, it was considered inevitable that the cycle of abuse in families would perpetuate itself. Now researchers are finding exceptions to that assumption and examining factors that contribute to some individuals' being able to break out of the cycle. When Egeland and her colleagues interviewed in depth the 30% of the mothers who had themselves been abused but were adequately parenting their children, they concluded that a major variable seemed to be the severity of the abuse the mother experienced as a child.[25] The mothers who were maltreating their children were the ones who reported the most serious abuse as children. A case was considered "mild abuse" when the child's basic physical needs had been met and the incidences of severe physical punishment were infrequent.

But in the instances where severely abused mothers were able to parent their children adequately, Egeland found that the women had several factors in common: (1) They had one parent (or foster parent) who provided a loving and supportive model, (2) they were currently living in more stable home situations than the maltreating mothers, (3) they had emotionally supportive husbands who were helpful with the children, (4) they were aware of what happened to them as children and saw their treatment as having been abusive, (5) many of them received psychotherapy as adolescents or young adults.[26]

There were other characteristics that these mothers had in common. All five of the women were married to the fathers of their babies, which made them exceptions in this particular population. Four of the five stayed married through the child's preschool years, and all of them reported that the father helped in taking care of the children. They lived in homes they owned, and the fathers were the primary wage earners, although some of the mothers worked too. They also came from more stable backgrounds in that four of the five mothers in this group came from intact families.

These observations parallel those of other researchers who have looked into exceptions to the abuse cycle. In integrating the findings from more than 50 studies of extremely maltreated parents, Yale psychologists Zigler and Kaufman[27] derived an estimate that 30% of abused children go on to become abusive parents—an estimate that is considered lower than findings from recent research. They also pinpointed several "protective factors" that they think may explain how the vast majority avoid becoming abusive. Says Kaufman, "Parents who did not repeat the cycle of abuse tended to have more extensive support from family and friends and were more openly angry about the abuse they experienced as children. Not only could they describe that abuse in great detail, but they were determined not to abuse their own children."[28]

The nonabusers also reported that at least one parent did not abuse them or was supportive when they were children, or they now had a spouse or lover who was that way. Zigler and Kaufman found, as did Egeland and his colleagues, that counseling and therapy was a very important "protective factor."

Despite their finding that the majority of abused children do not maltreat their own children, Kaufman adds, "It is important that we not give the impression that abuse doesn't have bad effects. It does. Abuse can be devastating to one's sense of self. In fact, abused children are six times more likely to become abusive parents than parents in the general population (30% compared to 5%)."

RESILIENT CHILDREN: CHARACTERISTICS
AND SKILLS

Patricia and David Mrazek, both teachers at the University of Colorado School of Medicine, observe that many factors seem to contribute to resilience in child maltreatment victims.[29] "Resilience," according to these authors, is a more accurate description than "invulnerable" or "invincible" for children who appear to survive a devastating childhood seemingly unscathed. Whereas invulnerable implies that some children are impervious to all stressors because of some constitutional makeup, the evidence is rather that they are resilient, in that the way they adapt to their maltreatment can change over time and is affected by both genetic and environmental factors. They note that the central question about the resilience of children is not whether it exists but rather what traits contribute to this attribute and what mechanisms facilitate its operation.[30]

Using research on children who have faced other stressors, such as war, divorce, or disadvantaged circumstances, the Mrazeks state several "protective factors" that appear to foster resilience. They suggest that the following protective factors may ameliorate the consequences of the abusive experience for maltreated children:

Rapid Responsivity to Danger. This is an ability to recognize and adapt to the immediate situation in order to avoid harm. Being able to do so "requires intense vigilance, intelligence, willful inhibition of affect, and often conscious forethought" (p. 359).

Precocious Maturity. Becoming "pseudoadults" by assuming a parenting role may both deprive children of needed nurturing and allow them to behave in a manner that lessens the abuse.

Dissociation of Affect. Developing the ability to distance oneself from one's feelings of helplessness controls the experience of pain and suffering. The disadvantage is that this coping skill also tends to numb victims of abuse from all feelings.

Information Seeking. By having a desire to learn as much as possible about the dangers in the situation, children have a body of knowledge to draw upon in a crisis, are better able to plan strategies, and sometimes are given insight that enables them to understand that they are not responsible for the abuse.

Formation and Utilization of Relationships for Survival. The ability to form helpful relationships gives children a source of support in crises and lessens the sense of isolation.

Positive Projective Anticipation. Being able to project into the future and fantasize about a better life when the abuse is over requires both dissociation from present pain and the intellectual capacity to imagine oneself in a different time and place. Abused children who can do this are able to keep hope alive and give themselves some pleasure in their situation. The ability also gives them a sense of control in a family where there is such a lack of control.

Decisive Risk Taking. Those children who are willing to take some risks in order to protect themselves counteract their sense of learned helplessness and may actually change what happens to them. An example would be the child who tells the teacher about being beaten.

The Conviction of Being Loved. It is a hard task for these children to maintain a sense of "lovableness" when their parents treat them as having so little value, but those children who can hold onto a sense of worth and do find someone whom they care for that reciprocates those feelings have added protection. Even the remembrance of a kind relationship may sustain them, as can believing in a person and loving God.

Idealization of an Aggressor's Competence. When children can see abusive parents as having competence in some areas, such as the ability to achieve financial success, they may feel more positive about such parents and respond in a way that decreases some of the abuse.

Cognitive Restructuring of Painful Experiences. Cognitive restructuring means looking at past negative events in a way that makes them more acceptable to one's current view. A negative illustration would be the child's deciding the beatings were "for my own good," which Egeland found led to a perpetuation of the abusive cycle. A more positive cognitive restructuring would be a child's coming to understand that a parent's alcoholism contributed to the abuse.

Altruism. The child who gives up on getting nurturance may find some sustenance in taking care of others, such as younger siblings.

Optimism and Hope. This orientation to life affects all aspects of the child's behavior and thoughts. It also affects relationships in that more positive children are likely to be happier and draw others to them. How some children are able to maintain their optimism and hope in the midst of maltreatment is a mystery we may never fully understand.

In addition to these personal protective factors, the Mrazeks identify several "generic protective factors in the environment of stressed children." These include (1) being in a middle to upper social class, (2) having educated parents, (3) having no family background of psychopathology, (4) having a supportive family milieu, (5) having access to good health, educational, and social welfare services, (6) having additional caretakers besides the mother, and (7) having relatives (especially grandparents) and neighbors available for emotional support.

OTHER PROTECTIVE FACTORS

While the Mrazeks base their observations on research with children who have undergone forms of trauma other than physical abuse, Recklin and Lavett recently reported on their findings with 10 women they treated who had been victims of child abuse but were nonabusive as parents.[31] One common factor they observed in the backgrounds of these women was that they "recalled incidents as early as in their first year of life when they rejected violent behavior as a means of expression." Other commonalities were that their abusers had been someone other than the mother or primary caregiver, that someone other than their parents nurtured them, and that they identified with that nurturing person rather than with the abusive parent. Early on, these women were able to identify the inconsistencies and inappropriate behaviors of the abuser and to reject that behavior (not identify with the abuser). Recklin and Lavett suggest that the abuse to nurturance ratio may have been lower for these mothers as children than for children who became abusers. For example, they had one parent who only nurtured and one who only abused.

It is important to note that even though these abused women did not abuse their children, they still exhibited a lack of trust of others, extreme concerns for physical safety, often a phobic reaction to violence, a fear of being like the adults who abused them, a degree of dissociation with the abuse they experienced, at least a partial feeling of responsibility for the abuse, and a deep fear of and sensitivity to rejection. On the positive side, they showed a pronounced independence of thought and a need for independent action. This points out that maltreated children are far from "invulnerable," even if they do not become abusers.

In a study of 700 children born in 1955 on the Hawaiian island of Kauai, 1 in 10 was able to withstand early difficulties of having one or more alcoholic or mentally ill parent and to develop exceptionally well. Werner, a psychologist at the University of California at Davis who directed the study, stated: "Without exception, all the children who thrived had at least one person that provided them with consistent emotional support—a grandmother, an older sister, a teacher or neighbor. These are kids who are good at recruiting a substitute parent who is a good model for them."[32] Many of these resilient children, who were interviewed when they were 30 years old, could recall a teacher from as early as the first grade who acted as a mentor and gave them a sense that they could achieve despite their difficulties in childhood.

Additionally, the children who excelled in spite of their abusive beginnings had a talent or special interest that absorbed them and gave them a feeling of confidence. "They were able to use whatever skills they had well, even if they were not terribly bright," observed Werner. "For some it was simply being good at swimming or dance, for others being able to raise prize-winning animals. But these activities offered them solace when things got rough." The resilient children went on to receive more education and reach higher economic levels than the other children in the study.[33] Garmezy, a psychologist at the University of Minnesota, is leading a network of research projects at different universities on factors that protect children or put them at risk. He has found that "the absence of a supporting adult in a child's life is seen over and over in a range of problems, from delinquency and drug abuse to teen suicide."[34]

In another study of children from deprived and troubled homes, psychiatrists Felsman and Valliant at the Dartmouth Medical School tracked 456 men from early adolescence into middle age. They found that the more successful adults were more industrious and organized in early adolescence. Some worked in a part-time job, took on major chores at home, or were intensely involved with a school club or team.

Psychologists Farber and Egeland, whose research is discussed above and presented in *The Invulnerable Child*,[35] found protective traits virtually from the beginning of life. At birth, they found, the resilient children were more alert and interested in their surroundings than others. However, these children had one very important environmental factor going for them: At the age of 1 year, they had a secure and warm relationship with their mothers. Despite later abuse, at age 2, the resilient toddlers were comparatively independent, easygoing, compliant, and enthusiastic, and had a high tolerance for frustration. At age 3½, the children were more cheerful, flexible, and persistent than others. With the nurturing beginning, it is hard to separate "genetic" traits from behaviors that come from having had needs met at a critical developmental stage. In all probability, the factors interact, but the evidence is clear that having a loving person in their lives gives some maltreated children an important advantage.

Putting all this research together gives a hopeful picture that childhood abuse does not inevitably condemn a child to a life as an abuser. It also points the way for assisting children in ameliorating the impact of abuse and shows the impact one loving person can make in the life of a child in an abusive family. As Cowen suggests, "These unusual copers may hold a Rosetta stone which, once decoded, can be applied gainfully to many profoundly stressed children steering an inexorable course to personally disastrous and socially costly outcomes. Thus, the study of invulnerable children is one legitimate way to strengthen primary prevention's generative base."[36]

In Chapter 9 we will discuss the many efforts that are being made in primary prevention, including those that focus on strengthening the child's understanding of human needs. But first we will look at what we and others have done to help children cope with their abusive experience.

8

Treating the Abused Child

Many treatment programs for abusing families have not included direct services for the children. All six of the intervention models initially proposed by the National Center for the Prevention of Child Abuse were parent programs.[1] The national survey of child abuse treatment programs described earlier found that in 31 programs involving over 2000 families between 1974 and 1981, very few children received direct treatment. Overall, there has been a paucity of direct treatment for abused children.[2] Of those few children who did get some form of therapy in the early demonstration programs, over 50% showed improvement developmentally, emotionally, or socially.[3] Later programs began incorporating more treatment for the abused children, and the rate of gains in all areas rose to 70%.[4]

While it is true that what the children in abusing families need foremost are nurturing, nonabusive parents, even when the parents do change, the children have suffered psychic damage that needs repair just as much as any physical damage to their bodies. In Chapter 7, we discussed the consequences to children from not having had their needs met at critical stages and what factors ameliorate those consequences. Some children, probably most, do not have built-in resilience factors that help them overcome the psychological damage from maltreatment without some outside intervention.

When we first began treating abusive families, we felt it was important not to try to be therapists to both the child and the parents. We believed, as did many other professionals, that the parents' competition with the child might be exacerbated by the competition for the therapist's attention and loyalty.[5] On some occasions, we recommended that the children be seen by another therapist, and we coordinated our efforts with the child's therapist. For the most part, though, the children of the parents we worked with did not receive therapy.

Eventually we decided to risk the competitiveness and loss of trust for the gain from having more information and being able to work with all the family members. We began offering the families a combination of group therapy for the parents, individual therapy for the children, and family therapy sessions. Most of our contact with the parents was in the group context and not all the children were seen individually by us, but we offered treatment to those who were willing to use it.

What we will share with you in this chapter is our experience and that of others who have treated abused children. We will focus on the issues that needed to be addressed with these children and the treatment approaches used with each of the issues. First, though, we will give a summary of early warning signs of abuse in children. Before the treatment begins, the identification must be made. These signs, along with the dynamics of the abusing family that we have been discussing, will enable the therapist, teacher, physician, or any adult to identify with some confidence that a child is being physically abused.

EARLY WARNING SIGNS OF ABUSE

The following signs of abuse are offered as clues to alert anyone, lay or professional, that a child may be being maltreated. The signs are intended to be considered in conjunction with the overall abusive family pattern described in Chapter 3.

Physical Factors

Cheek Bruises. "Hands and fists can be used as weapons. Be especially suspicious of cheek bruises. Children fall down and hit their head but they seldom hit their cheeks."[6]

Hidden Marks and Bruises. If a child returns to school after an absence of several days dressed in a long-sleeved shirt and long pants, even in warm weather, or is reluctant to change into gym clothes, he or she may have hidden marks and bruises.[7] If there are marks and bruises in areas other than where children usually injure themselves (knees, elbows, shins), the child should be checked.

Unusual Marks. Some parents use electrical cords to beat their children. These cords leave a characteristic mark on the skin. A few burn their children with cigarettes, which leave an oval scar, unlike the usually round scar commonly caused by an infected insect bite or impetigo.

Soreness. If a child hesitates to play at recess or moves unusually slowly or seemingly painfully, that child may have been beaten.

Distended Stomach. A certain percentage of physically abused children are also neglected. One sign that a child is not being fed properly is a protruding stomach. When questioned, the parents may claim that the child is a finicky eater or has a vitamin deficiency, or "the doctor doesn't know what's wrong with her."[8] These children often come to school without lunch.

Behavioral Patterns

Withdrawn, Passive Behavior. Some children respond to beatings by becoming quiet and showing little initiative. They try to guard against further abuse by acting as though they are not there: They ask for nothing, say as little as possible, and try to avoid attracting attention. Any abrupt behavioral change in this direction should make an observer suspect abuse.

Regressive Behavior. Some abused children revert to infantile behavior, as if bidding for the sympathy or mercy of adults by their very helplessness. The regressive behavior may include thumb sucking, wetting, soiling, or persistent crying.

Aggressive, Bullying Behavior. Other abused children pick fights or try to beat up their playmates. They may be acting out the anger and hostility from being beaten themselves, or they may be identifying or modeling those who abuse them. They also may steal small items to give to others in an attempt to buy friendship.

Inability to Make Friends. Children who are abused at home understandably often fail to make friends at school. They usually see themselves as unlovable and unacceptable to anyone. Because of their poor self-image, few of their peers want to be around them. If they do try to make friends, their parents are likely to discourage these efforts since such parents "have a vested interest in keeping themselves emotionally isolated."[9] If the parents' quest for isolation leads them to move often, the children's efforts at making friends are further thwarted.

Obviously one symptom alone does not necessarily indicate child abuse. But if several occur together or form a pattern over time, a suspicion of child abuse is likely to be justified. Direct questioning of the child may or may not bring confirming testimony. Abused children have had to learn to be wise beyond their years. A child in this situation is likely to assume "a protective attitude toward his parents. Even though his parents are torturing him at night, he will back them to the hilt in the light of day."[10] Not doing so may bring on worse beatings. Also, the parents represent the only security the child knows. For this reason, any questioning of the child as to the cause of marks or bruises needs to be done as casually as possible.[11] The importance of early detection cannot be overemphasized. As the American Humane Association states:

> If children are identified when they show the earliest impact of the families' troubles, help can be made available at a stage when their problems can be more readily resolved. Too often referrals to protective services are not made until the conditions of neglect or abuse become acute and intolerable. Such referrals may come too late to salvage the home.[12]

Physicians are well positioned to identify abuse at its very earliest stages. The physician can pick up cues from the parents as well as from the child that help to confirm an abusive pattern of parenting. Kempe offered this guideline to physicians for identifying an abused child:

> A potent case-finding lead is a discrepant history. The parent may tell us that the child fell down a flight of stairs, but on examination we find that he has spiral fractures on both arms. There is simply no way that that accident could have produced those injuries; the areas had to be twisted. In general, a history totally out of keeping with the clinical findings, or x-ray evidence of repeated fractures when a history is given of only one injury, is very revealing.[13]

Another clue is the parents' description of the children and their behavior that does not match the physician's observations. A mother may say that her child is clumsy and always bruises easily or insist that he/she is irritable or retarded. The physician, however, finds the child agile and not bruising easily, or amiable and bright. "These contradictions tell us that the mother or father is seeing the child unrealistically. In general, we have come to believe that any inappropriate viewing of the child can be a valuable aid in diagnosis and prognosis."[14]

The parents' behavior when they bring an injured child to a physician or a hospital may give indication of an abusive pattern. Morris and colleagues found that nonabusive parents report the details of their children's injuries spontaneously, express concern about the injury, treatment, and prognosis, and ask questions about discharge date and follow-up care. They also exhibit a sense of guilt and visit the hospitalized children frequently, bringing gifts. Abusive parents, in contrast, do not volunteer information about their children's injuries and are evasive or contradictory. They do not ask about treatment or prognosis, discharge date, or follow-up care. They seem critical of their children and angry with them for being injured, seldom visiting or playing with them in the hospital. Their attitude is one of self-preoccupation, and they do not seem to feel guilt or remorse.[15] Not all abusive parents will seem this uninvolved, but they are likely to show atypical emotional responses to the injury situation.

The behavior of abused children also differs from the normal injured child's response. Typically, injured children cling to their parents when they are brought in for treatment, turn to them for assurance and comfort during and after examination and treatment, repeatedly express in words and actions that they want to go home, and seem reassured by the parents' visits to the hospital. Abused children, on the other hand, are likely to cry hopelessly during examination and treatment but very little other than during that period. They do not look to their parents for reassurance, are wary of being touched by them or anyone else, and may become apprehensive when an adult approaches another child who is crying. When admitted to the ward, they usually settle in quickly, but they are constantly on the alert for danger and assume a blank facial expression whenever discharge from the hospital is mentioned.[16]

Once the physician, hospital, teacher, social worker, neighbor, or relative reports the suspected abuse and the case is confirmed, the next step in secondary prevention is getting help for the children as well as for their parents.

TREATMENT ISSUES WITH ABUSED CHILDREN

Building Trust

Understandably, children who have been beaten by the very adults they count on to protect and nurture them are distrustful of any adult who approaches them. Mann and McDermott assert that "to abused children, adults are unpredictable and always potentially dangerous."[17] The first task in working with these children is convincing them that the therapist means no harm. That convincing takes time, patience, and consistency, along with genuine caring.

Stewart and her colleagues, who conducted nine therapy groups for abused children over a 4-year period at the Family and Child Psychiatry Outpatient Clinic of the University of California at Davis Medical School, found that the children felt safer in a group setting with two therapists (male and female) because "each child, based on his or her unique history of abuse, could initally relate to the less threatening therapist, and gradually develop a relationship with the second therapist."[18] Being in a peer group helped to dilute any threat and protect that one child from "the potentially awesome power of the adult therapists."[19] These children are often unruly and aggressive, but they also may be cowering and fearful. The therapist has to reach a balance between limit-setting for protection (the therapist's and the child's) and nurturing permissiveness. The process of trust-building cannot be rushed and may be tested as long as the relationship exists.

Establishing trust begins with the therapist's being available at the appointed time. If the clients fail to show up or are late, we tell the children in the following session that we were sorry not to have been able to spend the planned time with them and are glad to see them now. Consistency is an important element in building trust with any child, and particularly with these children, whose parents have so often been inconsistent. Meeting the clients in the same office, with the same toys available, and offering essentially the same greeting gives a calming reliability to the sessions.

Learning to Play

Mann and McDermott, Solnit, and Stewart[20] found that play therapy was very valuable in working with abused children. One difference in doing play therapy with these children and with nonabused children is that some of the abused children must first be taught how to play.[21] We let the child choose from a cabinet of toys and take the chosen toy or toys into the treatment room. The toys include games, dolls, guns, books, and art supplies. Two of the most popular choices are the board games Candyland and Operation. We think the children choose the first because they are often familiar with it and feel less threatened playing a game they have some experience in winning. The second game is a caricature of a man who has various "body parts" (such as "spareribs" exposed and ready to be removed with tweezers by the skillful "surgeon"). Operation seems to give the children a sense of mastery and control while they face memories of some trauma to their own bodies.

Whatever toy the children choose, we let them determine the length of time they play (within limits of the treatment session), allowing them to stop when bored or frustrated. The play itself offers more opportunity for trust-building, since the therapist plays by the rules each time and expresses appropriate emotional response to the children's winning or losing. The children begin to experience an adult as nonshaming and noncompetitive, someone who does not need them to lose in order to be happy. They also begin to see that not every adult gets angry at losing.

The play gives us as therapists valuable information on what psychological pain the children are holding and how their behavior may be causing problems at school or home. For example, if children show no pleasure at drawing good cards or winning the game, we know they are suffering from such despair or depression that they are living joylessly. On the other hand, children who erupt in anger at losing are probably both modeling a parent and setting themselves up for punishment and criticism from teachers and peers. Whatever the children's responses, we offer observations, saying how we think they must be feeling and how we feel when they behave a certain way, while being careful not to shame or blame them.

Nurturing

Abused children need above all else to know they have value to another human being. As the studies we discussed in Chapter 7 pointed out, abused children who did not go on to abuse their own children were helped in part by having had someone in their lives who was loving and supportive.

The form of nurturance we offer these children varies depending on the age and personality of the child. To some we read fairy tales or some book they bring in. Usually the child chooses to sit right next to us or even in our laps. Other children want to have tea parties, with juice in the teapot. All children and their parents are offered a soft drink or juice when they come to the appointment. The psychological nurturance from "feeding" them extends far beyond the physical sensation of having something to drink.

In the groups run by Stewart and her colleagues, food was an essential component of the group structure. Group sessions began with children and therapists convening around a table for a glass of juice, and the final 10 minutes of each 1-hour session were reserved for snack time, with juice and a nutritious snack again served at the table.[22]

Some of the children eventually open themselves up to being rocked. Touch, for all these children, is associated with pain more than pleasure. We initiate touch only so far as perhaps a pat on the back when they are leaving the session. But as the children start to position themselves closer to us physically, we respond with appropriate touches or hugs. We will say more about this shortly under the section on touching.

Release of Anger

Children who have been beaten either turn their rage inward or vent it on others, usually those smaller or weaker than themselves. Whether they are expessing their anger or not, they have learned that violence is an acceptable means for solving problems, and they carry that imprint with them in all relationships. As Stewart observed, most of the children have lived in homes where "actions speak louder than words."[23] They approach life either as a Persecutor or a Victim. The crucial job we have as therapists to these children is to enable them to release their pent-up rage and frustration from having been so helpless in the face of their parents' rage, and to teach them that violence is neither necessary nor acceptable.

The first step is setting limits on aggressive behavior in the therapeutic setting. We have a "no-hitting" rule. The children are not allowed to hit, kick, or push us or another child. When they do, they receive a "time-out," which means they have to sit out in the waiting room for 5 minutes of "no play" time. If the parents are waiting for them, we ask that they just sit with the child and not shame or criticize. If the child is too much out of control to calm down, the session is terminated. After a few time-outs, most children can control their behavior when they get a warning. The added benefit of this technique is that we are modeling nonphysical discipline for the parents, who see that it is possible for their children to be controlled without violence.

Teaching the children how to manage their anger without hurting themselves or anyone else is the second step. Our approach is to offer them several options that they can draw on when they feel their anger mounting. The more options they have, the more control they experience in a variety of settings.

"Hitting pillows" is what the kids call one technique. This consists of having the children lie on their backs on the floor with pillows under the body, including under the hands and feet. With the knees bent, they are instructed to start pounding the floor with fists and feet, moving their heads from side to side and screaming, "No! No! No!" We encourage the children to do this as hard and long as they can, up to 20 minutes. Immediately after the exercise, we cover the children with a light blanket and encourage them to rest with their eyes closed.

The exercise is a very powerful means of allowing the abused child to safely vent rage without risk of retaliation or harm to anyone else. Some children are so afraid of anger, including their own, that they are reluctant to do the exercise initially, but just knowing about it gives them a tool to use if they choose to do so. After the exercise, the children usually feel a calm that stays with them. Some of them are so impressed with the technique that they even tell their parents that they need to "hit pillows" when they sense the parents' anger building. Sometimes the parents do exactly that and are equally pleased with the results.

We also teach the children relaxation exercises, just as we do their parents. This often consists of leading them through a guided imagery to a calm, peaceful scene, but it may be as simple as giving them phrases to say, such as "Be cool. Take it easy. Slow down. No sweat." These phrases are part of what we call "water words" for the children. We use the metaphor that anger is like a fire that is getting out of control. What is needed is water to douse the fire, and these water words have the effect of putting water on the fire. In contrast, "gasoline words" make the fire explode and spread. Gasoline words are "I hate you! I can't stand it! You creep! You did it on purpose!" The children and their parents report remarkable success in controlling their anger by knowing the difference between the "flammable and inflammable" words and how to use them.

A final objective in helping the children deal with their anger and other feelings is to teach them to translate their thoughts and feelings into words. Steele observed that abused and neglected children are handicapped in their ability to handle language.[24] When the children are helped to label their feelings and express them with words, they are learning a skill that transforms their lives and relationships.

Changing Stroking Patterns

We mentioned above that abused children associate touch with pain. An important part of therapy is to teach them the difference between "good touch" and "bad touch." One way we do this is by introducing the concept of "strokes." We teach them that strokes consist of anything that people say or do to each other. Strokes, we explain, can be with words or touch, and they fall into two categories, depending on how we feel when we receive them. "Warm fuzzies" are words or touches that make us feel, of course, warm and fuzzy inside. "I love you" and "I'm so glad to see you" and hugs are great warm fuzzies. "Cold pricklies" make us feel just the opposite—cold and prickly inside.

Hitting and insults, the children understand right away, are cold pricklies. These two concepts enable us to discuss feelings with the children and help them to see why they feel bad when their parents do or say certain things.

In teaching them to be comfortable with and exchange positive strokes, we sometimes do a "warm fuzzy/good touching" exercise at the beginning of a session. This consists of letting the children choose a form of touch they would enjoy. The requests range from back rubs to hugs to wiggling toes together. Not infrequently, the children initiate these touching transactions with the parents in the waiting room, where they can test the new stroke possibility with some protection. Ever so slowly, the stroking pattern for the family begins to change, or at least expands to include new possibilities.

Peer Difficulties

Abused children often have poor social skills, just as do their parents. "Usually their social negotiating skills are ineffective, and they often elicit rejection or abuse from children as much as they do from adults," observed Stewart.[25] They may be aggressive or withdrawn, but they certainly are not the kind of children who have a good sense of self-esteem and draw other children to them with ease. Some are bullies. Others are loners or the class clown. Part of the work in therapy is helping the abused children understand why others treat them the way they do, what "hooks" their own aggressive behavior, and what they can do to improve their social lot.

A group setting provides abused children with an opportunity to learn about social transactions and how to change them. Research has demonstrated how monkeys who had been maternally deprived were helped developmentally by being with peers.[26] Both monkeys and human children need play to help them develop control over the intensity and target of aggression.

In a group with peers, the abused children learn from each other and from the therapist how and why to modify their behavior. When they act out or set themselves up to be the scapegoat or clown, the therapist can use the interactions to help the children understand what happened, how things could have gone differently, and how each child felt about what happened. In this way, the children begin to get insight into why they are treated as they are by other children, and why certain things happen in the family the way they do. An "impairment of empathy" is a problem for abused children, just as it is for their parents. Observed Stewart:

> Abused children often have little awareness of the impact of their own behavior on others.... For example, a child may accidentally spill paint on a therapist, step on another child's hand, or in an escalation of acting out, deliberately destroy another child's play construction. When challenged the child may have great difficulty engaging in an interchange permitting exploration of that behavior and its impact on the other person, and may instead escalate his or her defiant, acting out behavior (or withdrawal). Interrupting this pattern has obvious implications for prevention of future abuse both of, and by, the child.[27]

One way for the pattern to be interrupted is through repeated positive confrontations. A little boy we treated, who was constantly in trouble with the teacher as a result of his "class clown" antics, heard from the other children in the group and from the therapist why they would feel unhappy with him, even if they first laughed, for disrupting the class and continually needing to draw attention to himself. He eventually realized that he tried to get the uproar going when he was feeling either afraid or lonely.

Since it is not always possible to have a group for the children, seeing several of the children from the same family together can bring out important dynamics and offer the same opportunity for observation and interpretation. Also, the other children in the family can often offer valuable insights as to what is going on with a sibling.

Another possibility for helping abused children understand their impact on others is through role-playing the problem situation, with the therapist taking the role of an abused child. The role reversal forces the children to give instructions about their own behavior and allows for insight into the feelings of others by playing their roles.

Building Self-Esteem

All of the tasks above flow into one ultimate goal—helping the abused child have a greater sense of self-worth. Abused children often believe they are responsible for the maltreatment inflicted upon them. This belief has to be countered repeatedly with accurate information that challenges the misinterpretation.[28] The positive stroking, nurturing, affirming, and listening all add to their sense of self-worth and serve as drops of healing water on a parched soul. For new seeds of growth to sprout in the arid soil, the watering may take a long time. The therapist may not see any signs of growth and new life in the time the child is in treatment. But that is no certain indication that such children will go away the same as when they came. It is impossible to predict what effect the small but steady applications of love and positive regard will have on any individual child. The importance of taking the opportunity of possibly being the one loving person in the abused child's early life cannot be minimized. That one caring relationship may make the difference between that child's becoming an abusive parent or being one of the ones who break the cycle.

9

Primary Prevention of Child Abuse

We have identified child abuse as a public health problem, requiring public health approaches. Although it fully qualifies for such a designation, the public health profession largely ignored the problem until recently. One consequence has been that other professions must wrestle with the question of primary prevention—a problem for which public health has traditionally assumed responsibility.

Primary prevention consists of heading off a problem before it occurs. Unlike secondary prevention, it reduces not only the prevalence of the problem but also its incidence—the number of new cases. Secondary prevention, as we define it, encompasses all efforts directed at preventing any further acts of abuse once maltreatment has already occurred. The medical model of prevention sees primary prevention as targeting services to the general population with the objective of stopping any new reports of a given disease or condition. Secondary prevention involves targeting services to specific high-risk groups in order to avoid the continued spread of the disease or condition, and tertiary prevention is seen as targeting services to victims of the disease or condition with the intent of minimizing its impact or negative consequences.[1] Using these divisions as applied to child abuse, some have seen primary prevention as limited to those services or social policies aimed at ensuring that abuse never occurs, secondary prevention as those services offered to "high-risk" parents to try to head off abuse of their children, and tertiary prevention as any efforts aimed at preventing a recurrence of abuse or neglect.[2] Because of the nature of child abuse, it is difficult to distinguish between efforts that stop further abuse and those that minimize its negative consequences. Therefore, we divide prevention efforts into those that are aimed at preventing maltreatment from ever happening and those designed to lessen its impact and prevent future abusive incidents.

Prior to the last decade, medical, nursing, and social work professions were the disciplines that devoted most time and effort to the child abuse problem, and their work has been largely secondary prevention. The time has come for public health to join the team with more than public health nurses, to focus on the issue of primary prevention, and to do something about the epidemic proportions that child abuse has reached. In other words, research must be done by public health professionals, and city, county, and state public health departments must participate actively in the prevention of child abuse.

Some of the programs that will be discussed in this chapter have been instituted, but their implementation is far from widespread. Although the surgeon general has declared child abuse to be a public health problem and effectiveness in preventing abuse has been documented for some of the programs, child abuse is still being struggled with at the secondary level for the most part. One reason is that primary prevention touches on the sacrosanct question of whether parents have the right to raise their children as they see fit. As Daro concludes in her intensive survey of all levels of prevention aimed at maltreatment, "A commonly-recognized barrier to primary prevention is the right of people to be left alone."[3] Just about every far-reaching strategy that might be designed runs headlong into the issue of parental rights—the right to bear children (including out of wedlock), the right to have any number of children, the right to be left alone, and the right to be free of investigation as to how the children are doing. But the rights of children to a safe and healthy home and a mother and father with adequate parenting skills must be given equal priority. Parents do not "own" their children but are responsible for promoting their well-being, which means providing a home free of abuse.

A variety of commissions and national and international organizations have issued proclamations on children's rights, and slowly their statements are being given some attention. The Joint Commission on Mental Health of Children stated that children have the right to be wanted, to live in a healthy environment, to have their basic needs satisfied, and to receive loving care.[4] The General Assembly of the United Nations also specified the rights of childhood in its Universal Declaration of Human Rights. [5] Yet public sentiment—and the law—still favors parents' rights. Kempe stated that

> the rights of the child for reasonable care and protection must be balanced against the right of parents to be free to raise their children in their own image. But the child does no longer "belong" to his parents, he belongs to himself in the care of his parents unless he receives insufficient care or protection.... We do force all parents to present their 5-year-old child to society for an attempt at basic education under penalty of prison for the parents who refuse. Why would it not be right to force each parent to present their infant to society in the form of an understanding and properly trained health visitor for required basic supervision of physical and emotional health at regular intervals?[6]

To have health visitors check on the development and well-being of babies represents a primary prevention intervention strategy and is one that has been documented as having promise of effectiveness. We will now discuss that strategy and others designed at stopping abuse before it happens.

PRIMARY PREVENTION INTERVENTIONS: HIGH-RISK GROUPS

The primary prevention intervention strategies can be designed to reach as many parents and future parents as possible or to target high-risk groups and environments. The parent–infant programs are one example of the latter.

Parent–Infant Programs

While the nationwide screening program that Kempe envisioned has not become a reality in the United States, there have been successful primary prevention programs established as adaptations of his model. One is the program begun in Rochester, New York, evaluated by Olds. Known as the Prenatal/Early Infancy Project, the study sought out high-risk first-time parents, most of whom were teenaged, unmarried, and/or poor. During the mother's pregnancy a nurse began making visits to the home about twice a month. These visits continued through the second year of the infant's life, with fewer visits as the child grew older. Olds found that intervention during the first pregnancy was crucial.

> It fostered an effective, caring relationship with parents before any implication of inadequate care-giving might arise; encouraged the acceptance of support during the biological, psychological, and social changes of this period; supplied useful information and emotional support to the parents themselves (usually the mother); had the potential

for preventing low birth weight and prematurity; and prepared parents for the early care of the newborn.... First-time parents were more likely to be open to the offer of help from the nurse; and because this was their first experience in childbirth and childrearing, the parents had not established deeply ingrained methods of coping with pregnancy and early caregiving.... whatever improvement in caregiving the nurses and parents achieved was more likely to be carried over to later-born children. [7]

The results of this nurse home visitation program are impressive in demonstrating that primary prevention can be effective. The mothers who received the intervention had a significantly lower incidence of child abuse over the 2-year period following the birth of their children. The children also had fewer accidents, were less likely to require emergency room care, and the mothers reported less frequent need to punish or restrict their children.[8] Other home visitor programs have also reported improvements in parent–child interactions and the development of the child.[9] The home visitor need not be a nurse for the program to be effective, as long as the paraprofessional is trained.[10]

In 1984 the Greater Houston Committee for the Prevention of Child Abuse chose the Perinatal Positive Parenting program at Michigan State University as the recipient of its national "Outstanding Primary Prevention Program" award. PPP targets first-time adolescent parents and parents with infants in intensive care for intervention. While in the hospital, the participants are given written materials and shown videotapes on parenting. Volunteers visit the parents at home, giving them a copy of *Parenting: The Tender Touch*,[11] which describes age-appropriate touching/playing activities for the mothers or fathers to do with their babies. Through these home visits and telephone contacts, volunteers provide empathy, concern, and friendship, and act as role models for new parents. The program also has a peer-parent resource group to give the parents an opportunity for support, friendship, and information exchange.

Evaluation of the program indicates that participants have a significantly better maternal involvement and create a more nurturing environment for their babies than did the control group parents, who received no intervention. The mothers in the program also initiate interaction with their infants more often than do controls.[12]

Another primary prevention program to be honored by the Greater Houston Committee for the Prevention of Child Abuse is the AVANCE Parent-Child Education Program in San Antonio, Texas. AVANCE began as a demonstration project in 1979 to intervene with Mexican-American women with children under 3 years old. Their clients are low-income, poorly educated women who are likely to be AFDC recipients. The participants are recruited by door-to-door canvassing and offered a variety of services, including parenting education, children's services, infant stimulation, child care, nutrition classes, toy-making classes, home visits that are videotaped, transportation to the center, referrals to other services, and group counseling. It is a bilingual program.

AVANCE is set up to coincide with the school-year calendar, so that parents can attend while older children are in school. A home visitor sees the family once a month. At that time, parent-child interaction is videotaped and critiqued with the parents, thus giving them immediate feedback and monitoring progress. Once a week, parents attend a 3-hour class at the center. The first hour consists of a toy-making class with emphasis on learning through playing, including a discussion of what the child will learn by playing with the toy the parent just made. During the second hour, parenting instruction is given, using a curriculum developed by the project. There are guest speakers or field trips during the last hour.

At the end of 9 months, parents completing the program attend a graduation ceremony (complete with diplomas, rings, pictures, and invitations). Approximately 60 out of the initial 100 recruited will graduate.

An analysis of pretest/posttest scores of participants revealed significant improvement in attitudes toward punishment, knowledge of children's social, emotional, and cognitive needs, and actual severity of punishment used. Compared with the control group, program participants initially had more severe attitudes toward punishment and were less hopeful (p = .02). After program completion, however, they were more hopeful about the future, were more knowledgeable about children's social, emotional, and cognitive needs, and had less severe attitudes regarding punishment. AVANCE participants also reported less severe punishment actually used than did the controls (p = .06) An equally impressive statistic is that AVANCE costs only $229.62 per client annually.[13]

The Pre-School Intervention Program (PIP) in Bloomfield, Connecticut, is a primary prevention program that trains parents in a preschool setting to be advocates for their children. PIP participants are mothers between the ages of 19 and 29 who are having problems parenting their kids. Most of the mothers are single and receiving state welfare assistance. The objective of the program is to teach the mothers problem-solving and parenting skills.

Both the mothers and children are actually in school. When the child is enrolled in a therapeutic preschool, the mother agrees to work in one of the preschool classrooms. The mothers also attend daily parenting classes. Every day, each mother-child dyad has a 20-minute observed play therapy session, followed by 10 minutes of feedback from the staff. The program goal is concrete behavioral change in both parent and child. When a mother has completed 5 to 6 months of training, she then enters a "payback" phase of 4 to 6 months. During this time she plays an active role in training new mothers and acting as a role model to them. The program also has an option of a 10-week (twice weekly) in-home parent training course.

Over a 5-year period, graduates of PIP used $128,000 worth of services, and 95% of these expenses were incurred in the

1-year program. A comparison group, on the other hand, used $450,000 worth of services, and the cost was equally divided over the 5 years. The conclusion was that the latter group would continue to incur high costs to society while the PIP graduates would be self-sustaining for the most part.[14]

Nationwide Home Visitors?

Although the idea of expanding the Prenatal/Early Infancy Project, PPP, or AVANCE nationwide may seem far fetched, we would like to point out that the United Kingdom has both a national health screening program and a health visitors program.[15] The health visitors program, adopted in some cities more than 65 years ago and in a few a century ago, requires public health nurses to visit the home of every newborn and follow the child's physical, emotional, and mental development on a periodic basis. Although the law states that these visits must be made, it does not require parents to admit the health visitor to their home. But because these health visitors have earned a reputation for helpfulness and are trained to deal effectively with recalcitrant families, few if any newborns escape examination. Parents are given friendly tips and useful information on the baby's needs and how to meet them.

> All ... [health visitors are] able nurses who go to every house, rich, poor, middle class, knock on the door and say, "How are you, Mrs. Jones?" They are always courteous to the mother. Eventually they have some tea in the kitchen and eventually they see the child and then they do what amounts to an advocacy job for the child.[16]

A large corps of health visitors would be needed for a similar program in the United States. But if the United Kingdom has been able to bear the expense since the early 1900s, this country can certainly do so. Successful primary prevention programs more than pay their way in terms of savings to the community.

Although opposition to health visitors is likely—even if families are not required by law to admit them to their homes—a truly comprehensive primary prevention program may well require this extensive measure. The home is the only place where all the critical points of the triad of host, agent, and environment can be observed. If children are followed up beyond infancy, early warning signs of other problems can also be detected, including those we have identified elsewhere as warning signals of later violent behavior.[17] The fact that parents are hungry for information on effective childrearing became apparent to us when we produced 80,000 copies of an easy-to-read, illustrated booklet titled *Your Child's Behavior* and held 150 workshops on family problems for parents and teachers.[18] These booklets are now in use in schools and neighborhood centers as well as in many homes. We will now describe other intervention strategies that intervene at the level of high-risk parents, high-risk children, high-risk environments, or a combination of the three.

High-Risk Parents: Other Programs

Because the profile of the potential abusing parent is fairly well established, steps can be taken ahead of time to assist potential abusers. The Child Abuse Potential (CAP) Inventory, based on those behavioral and situational predictors most frequently cited in the literature, has been successful in correctly classifying physical abusers.[19] The CAP Inventory has proven to be particularly useful as a preliminary screening tool in situations where the parent has been identified as at risk on the basis of other measures, such as clinical interviews and observations. Even so, Milner, the author of the CAP Inventory, cautions professionals that not enough testing of the instrument has been done to use it as the only source of making a decision to remove a child or label a family as abusive.

The Family Stress Checklist, however, developed at the University of Colorado Health Sciences Center, has now been tested for reliability and validity as an instrument that can accurately predict serious parent problems with a sensitivity of 89%.[20] In a study of 587 women who were interviewed at between 3 and 6 months' gestation by a skilled social worker using this checklist, 7% of them scored as "high risk" for maltreating their babies. In a review of the medical charts 2 to 2½ years later of 100 of the children whose mothers had been considered "at risk" and 100 whose mothers were considered as "no risk," 25 of the children had experienced neglect, abuse, or failure to thrive. Twenty of these maltreated children were from the original high-risk mothers, giving an incidence of neglect/abuse in that group of 52%. The no-risk control group of 100 mothers showed a 2% incidence of abuse/neglect, while a low-risk group had a 4% incidence and a midscore group showed an abuse/neglect rate of 5%.

The predictive factors in this study were not whether the mothers were single or teenage. Rather, the critical determinants were the parents' history of abuse in their own childhood, criminal or mental illness record, suspicion of past child abuse, low self-esteem, social isolation, depression, multiple crises, violent temper outbursts, unrealistic expectation and harsh punishment of the child, a difficult child or one perceived to be so by the parents, and a child's being unwanted or at risk of poor bonding. What is so important about the Family Stress Checklist is that a tool is now available that has been proven to be an accurate assessor of the factors we and others have described as being contributors to child abuse. It gives therapists and CPS a more objective and quantitative way to assess at how high a risk a family is for abuse.

Use of any predictive instrument requires establishing careful policies, procedures, and safeguards. The idea is not to label parents who fall into a high-risk category but to offer them support and guide them to helpful services. Administering a screening questionnaire to parents who fall into the high-risk categories we discussed in previous chapters would aid in directing to support services those parents who scored at risk—services such as psychotherapy, parent education courses, parent aide/visiting nursing programs, or homemaker assistance.

While there is certainly a shortage of these resources now, much more could be offered using existing resources and volunteers. For example, parenting courses could be offered by city or county health departments at sites convenient for parents— either at the hospital or in neighborhood health centers. Physicians could urge all parents, but especially those they sense might be at high risk for abuse, to attend these courses. The hospitals and public health nurses could also make parents aware of the courses and the necessity of attending. The same professional groups could distribute information on community resources that could help the parents in times of need, such as crisis centers, well-baby clinics, emergency shelters, and unemployment agencies. If programs like these were more widespread, high-risk families could have a parent aide, homemaker, lay therapist, or public health nurse to call on in times of crisis.

What Physicians Can Do

Although hospitals are an ideal source of identifying high-risk parents, physicians in private practice can be equally helpful because they see more cases of child abuse than any other professional group. While medical personnel are responsible for 11% of all child abuse reports, three times as many (34%) are made by friends, neighbors, relatives, or the children themselves.[21] There are various reasons why physicians may fail to report cases of child abuse,[22] and no one will ever know how many cases of abuse physicians are preventing through early intervention. But much more needs to be done. What can physicians do? They can observe the early interaction between mother and child and pick up cues on the potential for abuse. For instance, the high-risk mother often views her infant as ugly or unattractive, is unconcerned about supporting the baby's head, handles the baby roughly, does not coo or talk to it, believes that the baby does not love her, makes adult judgments about the baby and its abilities, and cannot see any physical or psychological attribute in the infant that she values in herself.[23]

Even during pregnancy, the high-risk mother provides clues that the physician can use as a basis for intervention and assistance. She may express an unusual amount of doubt about her ability to cope, be overly concerned about fetal deformities, complain about her husband's lack of support,[24] have negative feelings regarding the pregnancy, or have several children close together.[25] In short, the high-risk mother says in one way or another that she wants someone to take care of her and that she may expect her baby to do so.

Kempe, who was himself a pediatrician as well as a pioneer in calling attention to the problem of child abuse in this country, believed there was much a physician could do to help prevent abuse.[26] He recommended that before the baby is born, the physician should make sure that high-risk parents get into classes on the care and behavior of babies. The physician may actually be in the best position to prepare new parents for the fact that some babies keep crying even when the parent has done everything to soothe them. "Discipline counseling" with the parents, emphasizing that spanking is inappropriate treatment of babies, can come from the physician, as can family planning discussions. Kempe felt it was also the domain of the physician to discourage high-risk parents from having additional children, encouraging early placement of the child in day care to avoid the parents' becoming overstressed, and promoting the mother's early return to work to encourage a sense of competence and autonomy.

Role of the Public Health Nurse

Although physicians are a vital part of the team for prevention as well as treatment of child abuse, we also emphasize the role of the public health nurse. As we noted earlier, the nurse can act as a health advocate for children, visit with families periodically, and supervise parent aides or homemakers who work with the parents. Like the physician, the nurse too can do much to identify high-risk mothers during pregnancy and the neonatal period. Being the one member of the public health profession who already works in the field of child abuse and has the respect of other health professionals, the public health nurse is ideally suited to take a leading role in primary prevention. Traditionally seen as the least threatening professional, the public health nurse "can gain entrance to homes where no one else is accepted ... [and] is also the most available professional and in small communities she may be the only resource."[27] Kempe and Hopkins believed that "in the long run it is possible that a well-organized preventive movement of this kind could do more to alleviate social and individual problems than any other effort one might conceive."[28]

The contacts the public health nurse has with pregnant women in their homes and in obstetric clinics provide an opportunity to help physicians screen mothers before their babies arrive. Some of the cues Kempe and Hopkins recommended the public health nurse watch for that indicate high risk for abuse are when the mother does any of the following: (1) denies her pregnancy by avoiding prenatal care until late in the third trimester or goes into labor insisting that she was unaware of her pregnancy, (2) seeks an abortion or has unsuccessfully attempted one, (3) agrees to give up the baby for adoption but changes her mind after it is born, (4) does not exhibit nesting behavior or neglects to prepare her home for the baby, (5) is addicted to drugs or alcohol and is unable to take care of herself or the baby, (6) has recently been abandoned by the baby's father or rejected by her family, (7) has already injured another child or has temporarily lost custody of another child because of neglect, or (8) has a baby whose father has a criminal record of assault or has been psychiatrically diagnosed as a sociopath.[29]

There is also much the public health nurse and the physician can do in the way of primary prevention once the baby is born. By observing how the mother responds to her new baby while it is still in the hospital, the nurse and the physician can detect the following signals that have been suggested as indicative of a high risk of abuse when the mother (1) does not exhibit "claiming" behavior—that is, she is not interested in naming the baby or in feeding or holding him; (2) indicates her rejection by remarking on how ugly, defective, or disappointing the child is; (3) is repelled by the child's odor, drooling, regurgitation, or stools; (4) exhibits extreme postpartum depression that may be related to feeling overwhelmed by a new baby she does not want rather than to a rapid drop in estrogen levels; (5) visits her premature baby less and less often after she has been discharged from the hospital; and (6) is unable to control her impulses, as seen in her spanking or becoming enraged at her newborn infant.[30]

In the weeks and months after the baby is born, the public health nurse and the pediatrician, Kempe suggested, should observe whether the mother increasingly enjoys her infant and the tasks she does for and with the baby, develops a greater understanding of its emotional states, learns to comfort the baby more appropriately, recognizes its needs for new stimuli, and senses the baby's fatigue more readily.[31] The suggestion that the public health nurse and the physician watch for all these cues is not for the purpose of placing an additional burden on these professionals but rather to urge them to further join in the effort to prevent children from ever becoming victims of abuse.

High-Risk Children

Just as strategies can be designed for intervention on the parent (host) level, primary prevention can also be based on intervention with the child at risk (agent). As we mentioned earlier, premature, illegitimate, difficult, congenitally malformed, and mentally retarded children are especially prone to abuse. Although we will discuss specific intervention programs for premature, illegitimate, and difficult children, similar approaches can be used with malformed and retarded children.

Premature or Low-Birth-Weight Babies. The fact that a disproportionate number of premature or low-birth-weight babies are found among abused children has been investigated by a number of researchers.[32] One explanation is that prematurity predisposes a baby to anoxia, which in turn causes irritability and fussiness. Another explanation is that babies who weigh less than 5½ pounds at birth may have subtle dysfunctions of the central nervous system, which results in restlessness and distractibility. In his study of 674 cases of abuse, Lenoski found that 22% involved children who had been premature babies, compared with 10% of 500 control cases. Thirty percent of the abused children had been delivered by Cesarean section (compared with 3.2% in the control group), and 9% had complicated deliveries (compared with 4.2% in the control group).

Low-birth-weight babies also are unlikely to be picked up as often as normal-weight infants, and this factor, the lack of touch, has been found to have an unfavorable influence on the neonate's development, resulting in unresponsive behavior.

Powell, Brasel, Raiti, and Blizzard found that severely growth-retarded children, from emotionally disturbed home atmospheres, had abnormally low growth hormone levels in their blood until they were removed from their families, at which time they grew rapidly to their normal heights without any special treatment.[33] In another study, low-birth-weight babies less than a month old were placed alternately each day on either lamb's wool or cotton bedding in their incubators. The babies gained 10 grams more weight each 24 hours that they were on the lamb's wool. The researchers concluded that the extra tactile stimulation from the lamb's wool helped increase the babies' growth hormone and an enzyme (ODC) related to protein synthesis and cell growth.[34]

The prenatal emotional condition of the mother may also contribute to these babies' having a poor start. Nuckols, Cassel, and Kaplan studied 170 mothers who gave birth at a large military hospital. Ninety-one percent of those who had high life-change scores and low social support had complications with their pregnancies. Other women who also had high life-change scores but good social support had no more complications than women with more stable lives.[35]

Premature infants may also be at high risk because they are separated from their parents for the first several weeks of life. The establishment of the child-caretaker bond is delayed, which in turn can adversely affect the interaction between baby and mother—especially the mother's response to the infant. One indicator that delayed bonding has affected the mother's claiming behavior and responses toward her child can be the amount of time the mother spends visiting and inquiring about her baby. One study concluded that mothers who infrequently visited or called the hospital subsequently neglected or abused the child.[36]

In a later study, Siegel did not find a relationship in improved attachment or rate of reported abuse or neglect between low-income mothers who had early and extended contact with their newborns combined with frequent paraprofessional home visits during the first 3 months postpartum.[37] In contrast to Siegel, O'Connor and her associates found that early intervention of rooming-in did correlate with fewer subsequent cases of parenting inadequacy. Referral to protective services was less frequent in the rooming-in group, but the difference did not reach statistical significance. Of note is the fact that more than 90% of the women who did not receive rooming-in failed to demonstrate any evidence of parenting inadequacy, which led the authors to conclude that although rooming-in may enhance the mother–child relationship to some degree, its absence is not usually associated with demonstrable harmful effects.[38]

To alleviate problems in parenting that might be due to poor bonding from separating a mother from her premature baby, hospitals can and do arrange for early contact between the parents and the preemie and encourage frequent visiting. Some mothers need to be allowed inside the nursery to handle and feed the baby as soon as possible, so that they not only begin to bond with the baby but also have the support and instruction from the hospital staff. Care-by-Parents units, such as those established in Kentucky hospitals in the 1970s, let the mothers of premature babies become accustomed to, and take complete responsibility for, their infants before leaving the hospital.[39]

The role of the public health nurse comes into play once again with these babies. The local health department could assign a public health nurse to visit all families of low-birth-weight babies. The nurse could educate the parents that underweight babies are going to be difficult to care for and urge the parents to seek help when they need it. Being given parenting tips in printed form, along with information on how to obtain the services of a parent aide, lay health visitor, or homemaker, would give the parents something to refer to in times of crisis.

Illegitimate Babies. A number of investigators, as we have noted previously, have identified illegitimate and unwanted children as being at high risk for being abused.[40] If a mother is ashamed of her baby or does not want it, she is likely to be rejecting, at least initially. Furthermore, the baby's behavior may contribute to her rejecting or abusive behavior. Illegitimate and unwanted babies are especially prone to be irritable and colicky. Some investigators suggest that the mother's emotional state during pregnancy influences the unborn child. For instance, Landis and Bolles suggested that if an expectant mother is under stress, her baby may be colicky and irritable.[41]

One understandable source of stress for a pregnant woman is concern that she is not married or does not want the child. A colicky or irritable baby may simply reinforce the mother's rejecting attitude. Even if the mother does want the baby, its difficult behavior can leave her feeling inadequate and resentful. If her stress continues or she looks to the baby for evidence that she is loved and adequate, the situation is ripe for abuse. If the mother feels (or indeed *is*) rejected by the child's father, she may view the baby as her last chance to obtain the love she never received from her own parents or from boyfriends. Abuse happens when the mother desperately tries to force that compliance and love. The parent–infant programs described above would be effective interventions for these high-risk babies and their mothers.

Difficult and "Mismatched" Children. According to Kagan, "the difficult child does not establish regular feeding or sleep patterns, reacts intensely to imposition or frustration, and withdraws passively from strange events or people. He seems to require a long time to adjust to anything new and is difficult to rear."[42] This kind of child is hard to manage and evokes frustration and resentment in even the most patient parents. Jenkins, acknowledging the role of temperament in a child's behavior, describes as difficult the "irritable youngster, the constantly crying baby, the hyperactive child, and the child who fails to maintain toilet habits."[43] Some of the reasons for a child's difficult behavior have already been discussed. Some children, though, just seem to be "born that way." It is known, however, that each neonate has a unique congenital and temperamental makeup, which in part is related to its prenatal and perinatal experiences. Thus, parent-child relationships are a two-way exchange.

However babies come to be the way they are, the match between baby and parent is important. While a difficult child can be a problem to almost any parent, this type of child is at risk of maltreatment if its mother or father, because of her or his temperament and characteristics, expects or demands docile, compliant behavior from the child. Martin and Beezley found that even if the child is not especially difficult or does not have an unpredictable temperament, there still may be "disparity between characteristics of the infant and the parent's capability and capacity to parent that type of child. The characteristics of the infants and child need not be abnormalities, but rather idiosyncratic traits within a spectrum of normalcy.... Assessing variations in infants' behavior repertoires may prove extremely helpful in preventing abuse by identifying those parent-child matches which need intervention."[44]

Hospital policies that facilitate close observation of interactions between parents and their newborn child offer such an opportunity for intervention. A living-in arrangement not only provides hospital staff with the best opportunities for these observations but offers mothers and fathers a chance to get acquainted with their infants in a protected environment. The difficult baby can be detected early, on the basis of reactions to the parents' handling and feeding. Mismatches between parent and child could also be spotted.

If the parents of a difficult baby do not have the profiles of potential abusers, then the intervention plan could consist of periodic visits by the public health nurse and counseling sessions to prepare them for handling the stress of dealing with a difficult child before the parents leave the hospital with the baby. If the baby is not difficult but is mismatched with its mother or father, the most useful intervention would be having the parents attend courses or do reading on child development in order to correct unrealistic expectations of the child. The courses would also offer them an opportunity to learn what a child—as opposed to the parent—needs at various developmental stages and how to respond to those needs appropriately.

High-Risk Environments

Unemployment. The environmental condition that is cited most often as placing a family at risk in terms of child abuse is unemployment. The stress created by idleness and the lack of a certain source of income has been shown to be a contributing factor to abuse. Our groups of abusing parents had both mothers and fathers who inflicted violence on their children during periods of unemployment. An especially explosive situation is created when the daily child-care duties are turned over to a father who is accustomed to being the breadwinner in the family. Both women and men understandably feel a loss of sense of worth when they are unemployed, and parents who have low self-esteem to start with may feel even more diminished than someone who has a pretty good self-image prior to being out of work. Other environmental factors, such as crowded conditions in the home, a large family, and lack of education, have already been discussed as contributing to the potential for child abuse. Light analyzed the effects of unemployment, overcrowding, family size, and lack of education on 1380 abusing families and reported the following findings:

1. Abusing families in which the father is unemployed are much more likely to live in an apartment and are less likely to share their quarters with other persons or families than are comparable nonabusing families.
2. Abusing families in which the father is unemployed tend to have many more children than do comparable nonabusing families.
3. In abusing families where the father is unemployed, a very young child is likely to be abused. If the father is employed, the target is likely to be an older child.[45]

One possible primary intervention strategy for guarding against child abuse among the unemployed would require the administration of predictive questionnaires (based on profiles of persons who abuse, such as the CAP Inventory) to individuals who register for jobs.

Although the central site of registration is usually the state or county employment agency, some of the unemployed look elsewhere for jobs. Thus, the unemployment insurance office could serve as a supplementary site for administering the questionnaire. Those with high abuse-potential scores could be visited by a public health nurse, who would observe the interactions among the spouses and children. The nurse could pay special attention to large families living in apartments, and to families with parents who lack high school educations. Given the nurse's findings during the initial visit, a schedule of home visits could be set up at fairly short intervals for families with the highest potential for abuse and at longer intervals for those with less potential. High-risk parents could receive counseling from the public health nurse and also be assigned a parent aide or homemaker. At the minimum, they could be given printed material about how to obtain financial and other assistance and be given telephone numbers to call in times of crisis.

While this specific strategy is directed toward defusing the potential for abuse among the unemployed, legislative efforts to guarantee jobs for everyone who is able and willing to work are extremely important. Although legislation would not ensure that there would be no idle adults at home with children, it could help alleviate one stressor that has been found to be associated with child maltreatment.

Change. Earlier we discussed the evidence that excessive change also contributes to child abuse. We noted that one distinguishing feature of the abusing family is the experience of too much change too fast; that is, so many changes occur in a given period that the family members are unable to adjust. Table 2 showed the sharp differences in life change scores between abusing and nonabusing parents.

Remedying this situation is not easy. Abusing families seem to live in a perpetual state of crisis. Much of the stress these families experience is self-induced and stems from seeking symbiotic relationships and having learned such poor coping skills. However, there is a societal feature to life crises and excessive change. Toffler provided a blueprint of excessive change in his book *Future Shock*.[46] The society he envisioned for the future was one in which people as well as things are disposable and transitory. Abusive families already lack a sense of emotional roots and relatedness. They move frequently and remain isolated. When excessive mobility is coupled with this alienation from others and the complex problems of urban living, it can be a predisposing factor to violence.[47] If societal attitudes reinforce the abusive family's sense of alienation, the problem is compounded.

Thus, the problem of child abuse must also be addressed on a societal level. Restoring a neighborhood sense of community would be a beginning. People need to know who their neighbors are, and that is not going to happen without a willingness to reach out and to become acquainted with others, to get involved in other people's lives in a meaningful and helpful way. There are signs that this may be starting to happen again in America. Volunteerism is increasing. People are starting to feel the importance of making a difference to someone other than themselves. Believing that each of us can and should do something to prevent child abuse is the most powerful primary prevention intervention strategy possible.

PRIMARY PREVENTION STRATEGIES: BROAD-BASED

Parent Education

The health visitor programs, which were described earlier, provide parent information as one of their functions. Another successful approach to educating parents has been to offer intensive parenting courses.[48] The Minnesota Early Learning Demonstration (MELD) is one of the most successful of these programs and was the 1983 recipient of the Greater Houston Committee for the Prevention of Child Abuse award for primary prevention. The MELD programs offer intensive 2-year parenting education and support. Since they began in 1975, six programs have been developed: MELD for New Parents, MELD for Young Moms, MELD Plus for growing families, La Familia/MELD for Hispanic families, MELD Special for parents of children with special needs, and HIPP/MELD for hearing-impaired parents. The goal of all these programs is primary prevention—to prevent abusive and neglectful patterns from ever beginning.

MELD programs are structured so that weekly meetings of 10 to 20 parents are led by extensively trained parent volunteers. The meetings last 2 to 3 hours. The 2-year programs are divided into four 6-month phases that include 30 meetings each. Participants are provided with transportation and child care if needed. Using a variety of techniques, such as small group discussions, role-playing, homework, and informal socializing, topics discussed include child development, health, child management, and personal growth.

While the MELD programs have not been evaluated specifically in terms of child abuse prevention, the Child Welfare League of America recently evaluated them and found that 80% of the participants had finished or were finishing high school, compared with an overall school completion rate of only 20% for the general adolescent parent population. The MELD teenage mothers in the Young Moms program also had fewer repeat pregnancies in the year after the birth of their first child (10 to 15% vs. 25% for all teenage mothers). Importantly, parents who went through the MELD programs also changed their disciplining patterns. The percentage who spanked their children decreased from 56% at the start of the program to only 12% at the end.[49]

The parent education programs have several advantages over the home visitor approach, as well as some disadvantages. At the centers, the parents have opportunities to share childrearing and personal problems with other young parents, which serve to break down their isolation. The MELD program includes an ongoing support group for parents in addition to the actual classes. It is also much less labor-intensive than the one-to-one model and therefore less costly. Offering the parenting information in classes outside the home means there are likely to be fewer distractions and that the classes will be held even if some of the mothers do not show up. Getting them to show up is indeed a problem, though, even with transportation and baby-sitting assistance. Dropout rates can be as high as 40 to 50%.[50] Organizing their lives sufficiently to be at the weekly meetings is more than many of these young mothers can manage, which is where the home visitors can be more beneficial. As Daro concludes, "Reaching the full spectrum of the at-risk" population clearly requires some combination of both methods.[51]

Parent Licensing and Training

If the home visitors program seems to be a bold measure (despite its long existence in the United Kingdom), an even bolder one would involve the licensing of parents. We do not necessarily endorse such a measure, but we continue to believe it does deserve more public attention. Margaret Mead pointed out that although society requires people to get licenses before they marry, no constraints are placed on childbearing, which is an even greater responsibility.[52] When parents are ill-equipped and uninformed, the consequences affect not only the child but society at large. Lord and Weisfeld, in support of licensing parents, asked, "For ... the protection and welfare of parents, children and society ... should there not be the requirement that potential parents have at least some rudimentary knowledge and skill in the field of effective parenthood?"[53] Toffler observes with irony:

> Raising children ... requires skills that are by no means universal. We don't let "just anyone" perform brain surgery or, for that matter, sell stocks and bonds. Even the lowest ranking civil servant is required to pass tests proving competence. Yet we allow virtually anyone, almost without regard for mental or moral qualifications, to try his or her

hand at raising young human beings, so long as these humans are biological offspring. Despite the increasing complexity of the task, parenthood remains the greatest single preserve of the amateur.[54]

Enough is now known about the principles and techniques of childrearing and management to dispel any arguments against the idea of requiring all potential parents to take courses that will teach them these skills. The empirical evidence is clear that parent education, whether offered through home visitors or in centers, is most effective when provided to first-time mothers.[55] Hawkins recommended that "a training program that will improve the quality of child-rearing and prevent the development of mental health problems should reach parents before their first child is born. Because there is no practical way to identify inept parents in advance, it would be necessary to have a compulsory parent-training course that would reach virtually all potential parents. The school is the logical place for such a program."[56]

A compulsory parent-training course either could be linked to mandatory licensing for parenthood or could stand separately. By itself it would be more likely to gain acceptance. As a prerequisite to licensing, however, it would carry more weight, in terms of being taken at least as seriously as driver's training. Kempe was convinced that if a licensing law for parenthood existed, there would be a dramatic reduction in the number of battered, abused, and unwanted children.[57] Despite the advantages for both children and society in the future, licensing of parents is unlikely to become a reality anytime soon. "Perhaps in the 21st or 22nd centuries such legislation and licensing programs may end—or diminish—child abuse, battering and neglect. In the meantime... ?"[58]

Required Courses in Schools

In the meantime, strong intervention strategies such as universal parenting training could be initiated. Courses that include information on child development already exist in schools, primarily at the high school level, but these are often part of homemaking or home economics classes and thus reach few male students. Also, the courses may focus on the mechanical aspects of child care, such as how to feed and change the babies. While those basics are certainly part of adequate parenting, more emphasis must be placed on the psychological and developmental aspects of parenting. Kempe urged that the schools teach students "something about mothering"—about nurturing, what a child needs at different ages and stages, and how parents should respond to those needs.[59]

The kind of classes needed would not only discuss childrearing but would actually require a substantial amount of practical experience in a day care center or nursery school affiliated with the high school.[60] This classroom and laboratory work would make up a 1-year course in childrearing and should be required of all students. Just as students who take driver training courses are required to learn by driving real cars, students in the childrearing classes would be required to take care of real children and confront some of the tasks that they will face as parents. Although this program would ensure that young people would be trained for parenthood before marriage, the education would need to be supplemented during pregnancy.

But do high school students want this kind of child development/management information? There is good evidence to suggest that they do. In areas where pilot programs on the prevention of child abuse are being conducted in schools, students have not only expressed an interest in the courses but recognized the need for them.

> Many [students] believe that a curriculum unit on "How to be a parent" should be required for all high school students.... Courses on parenthood should be offered to all students and the courses should emphasize how important nurturing—or the lack of it—is to a child's normal growth and development.[61]

An overwhelming proportion of the abusing parents we surveyed and worked with said they definitely needed to know more about child development and management. Many believed that if they had known more about how to deal with children, they would not have abused their own.

The lack of skills in child development and management is certainly not the sole cause of child abuse. But the evidence we have presented amply suggests that it is a contributing factor. This fact alone is enough to justify parent training. As Hawkins notes, however:

> A move to institute parent training in our schools will strain the system and generate resistance. Some persons will object to the instructing of adolescents in behavior-modification techniques. They will raise the old cry that we should not teach persons to manipulate their children. But these child-rearing methods are not new. People have always taught and learned complex behaviors through these methods.... It is only our ability to analyze, isolate, name and teach the components of the art of teaching that is new.[62]

Obviously, one does not need to be a specialist in behavior modification to understand the principles and techniques of childrearing and management. Many other practical approaches are available to help potential parents manage their children without resorting to an undue amount of physical discipline. For example, we teach token economy systems and the techniques of Parent Effectiveness Training.

Of course, knowledge of good parenting skills alone will not keep child abuse from occurring in a family since many factors contribute to the problem. Parents may be knowledgeable about parenting skills but have emotional responses to their children that prevent them from doing what they know should be done. Even so, findings clearly suggest that the overwhelming majority of abusing parents do not fail to use their knowledge of effective parenting behavior. They simply lack that knowledge in the first place.

Professional Parents?

Some individuals who become parents are so lacking in basic nurturing ability that teaching them the skills of parenting will not be enough to ensure the safe and healthy development of their children. Nor will providing them with lay or professional home visitors or placing their children temporarily outside the home be enough. For these parents, there must be an alternative. At one time in our history, the extended family provided an alternative. If the biological parents could not do the job of childrearing, a grandparent, an aunt, or an uncle would. Today we must create other alternatives, which leads to the idea of "professional parents"—persons who are equipped by upbringing and training to give children the nurturing, care, and nonphysical discipline they need. These parents could be certified for competency on the basis of their experience, training, and record.

With a proper change in public attitudes and policy, biological parents who lack the qualities and skills necessary for childrearing could feel free—and would be encouraged—to contract with professional parents to do the job for them. Toffler has suggested that the biological parents could fill the role of interested godparents and spend time with the child as interested outsiders.[63] They would be permitted to visit, telephone, and spend summer vacations with the child, and they would be assured that the child would be offered a good shot at growing up to be a successful, effective, and constructive member of society, not marred by the scars of abusive parenting. There probably would be few takers for this somewhat utopian arrangement since most people want to parent their children their own way, no matter how ineffective that way might be. Too, the emotional, mental, spiritual, and physical costs of parenting are so great that the fee professional parents would charge would likely be prohibitive to all but a few. Even so, it is an interesting possibility to consider.

Family Planning

For most present and future parents, training in child development and management would be enough, particularly if supportive services were available in the form of parent aides and homemakers. Knowledge and experience would provide them with the means of doing effective childrearing. But primary prevention of child abuse requires knowledge in yet another area—the area of family planning. In early studies by Elmer and by Gil, there seemed to be a definite relationship between the number of children in a family and child abuse.[64] The data from the 1988 Study of National Incidence and Prevalence of Child Abuse and Neglect[65] indicate that children in families with four or more children showed higher rates of maltreatment on a variety of measures. The researchers conclude that "there are qualitative differences in the experiences in children in the larger families which increase their perceived risk or endangerment from physical maltreatment in its various forms." Light observes that "family size data suggest that widespread family planning education might be more effective in preventing child maltreatment" than courses in child development and management.[66]

Both types of education are needed. But to make family planning widespread, there must be reliance on more than traditional agencies. We believe that just as parent training should be compulsory, there should also be a required high school course in family planning that would include a close look at the consequences of having unwanted children or children the parents are not equipped to support. It is imperative to reach a maximum number of young people before they begin their own families. Although voluntary use of family planning agencies is increasing, such programs cannot reach the large numbers that high schools can. Again, there is resistance to requiring family planning courses in high schools, but the potential benefits, in terms of a reduction in the number of unwanted children being born to unprepared young parents, are a strong argument in favor of such a policy.

Human Needs Education

A third and final course that must be instituted in American high schools to combat the problem, not only of child abuse but of mental and emotional dysfunction, involves the nature of human needs and how to meet them. While most abusive parents are not psychotic, they do have serious problems in managing their emotions and behavior in areas that extend beyond their relationships with their children. An illustration of this is seen in a survey conducted by Sever and colleagues of the most dominant characteristics of 48 sexually abusive families. They found that these families had many problems in addition to sexual abuse. Among the problems were alcohol abuse (61%), physical child abuse (56%), spousal abuse (42%), previous criminal behavior (33%), drug abuse (31%), and prior use of the foster care system, voluntarily or court-imposed.[67] Similar patterns of multiple emotional and behavioral problems in physically abusive families have been found by other researchers.[68]

There is ample evidence as to what basic human needs are and how they can be healthily met.[69] Symbiosis, which we have seen is a central problem in abuse, stems from an individual's failure to meet his or her own needs, which results in turning to others in an effort to be nurtured. If young people learn how to obtain strokes, find positive recognition, and structure their time without manipulating others, they can avoid or alleviate symbiotic and other fused relationships that result in either emotional problems or social dysfunction. And if they learn how to meet the human needs for responsibility, affection, control, and mastery, they will be more likely to avoid the pitfalls of delinquency, crime, alcoholism, and other social problems. Recent surveys conducted in the United States indicate that the first drinking experience today usually occurs around age 12.[70] About 30% of fourth-grade respondents to a 1983 *Weekly Reader* poll reported peer pressure to drink beer, wine, or liquor.[71] The Cooperative Commission on the Study of Alcoholism reported as far back as 1967 on the need to improve the public's general understanding of human emotions and interpersonal relations— not only as a means of combating alcoholism but of reducing other psychological and social problems as well.[72] Alcohol abuse accounts for approximately 98,000 deaths annually,[73] and approximately 10,000 of these are young people aged 16 to 24 who are killed in alcohol-related accidents of all kinds.[74]

We have found that most people are ignorant of the nature of human needs and how to meet them. Ideally, this learning would begin in elementary school since relationship patterns are already laid down by adolescence, but compulsory courses on human needs beginning in junior high school could offer information that would help the young people better understand their feelings and behavior and those of their families and others.

We do not mean to imply that cognitive understanding alone will protect people from all psychological and social problems. But it is also obvious that without that understanding, there is little hope of their acting in a way that will bring psychological satisfaction to themselves and others.

There are signs that school systems now recognize the need to teach more than traditional academic subjects and basic vocational skills. The most common reason that people fail to function adequately in their jobs, marriages, and communities is related to their lack of understanding of themselves and others, not to a lack of preparation in traditional school subjects. Courses in family life, values clarification, and "Patterns of Healthful Living" are now offered in some schools. But what must also be included, to address not only the problem of child abuse but a wide range of other psychological and social problems as well, is the kind of instruction that will provide students with a clear understanding of human needs and how to meet them. Again, courses on human needs must be a standard part of every schoolchild's curriculum.

Compulsory courses in high schools, licensing for parenthood, and the national health screening program are all examples of methods of primary prevention on a societal level. Each has a broad-based approach—the broadest being the national health screening program. They are nonspecific in that no specific high-risk group need be singled out. They are also nonspecific in that they would be beneficial in more than one way; that is, they would prevent not only child abuse but other problems arising from poor parenting as well. Massive numbers of people would be contacted on the theory that this is the best way to reach those who would commit abuse if the intervention program did not exist. But because these nonspecific programs would be costly and controversial, they find much opposition. There is growing evidence, though, that prevention can be cost-effective.

Cost Savings

Research shows that treatment efforts, at best, are successful with only half of the clients. Also, the poor and most dysfunctional families are least likely to achieve success. Providing a lay therapist to a family will cost around $2860 a year (in 1987), and a year of comprehensive therapeutic and support services for one family can run up to $28,000.[75] This adds up to between $2.8 billion and $28 billion annually for the estimated 1 million abusive families identified each year. In contrast, 2 years of weekly parenting education and supervised parent-child interactions for all adolescent mothers could be provided for $1.3 billion.[76] It does not take much math to see what an enormous saving in dollars, not to mention human suffering, could be brought about by prevention efforts.

We think that primary prevention, to be effective, need not require the utopian reforms that Gil proposes when he says that "primary prevention of child abuse, on all levels, would require ... a reconceptualization of childhood, of children's rights, and of child rearing. It would necessitate rejecting the use of force as a means for achieving societal ends, especially in dealing with children. It would require the elimination of poverty and of alienation conditions of production, major sources of stress and frustration which tend to trigger abusive acts toward children in adult–child interaction. And, finally, it would necessitate the elimination of psychological illness."[77]

Public Education

Public education programs on child abuse prevention are another example of efforts with a potential payoff in terms of primary prevention. The National Committee for the Prevention of Child Abuse (NCPCA) has been in the forefront of this effort since the 1970s. It has helped to establish 67 local chapters in 50 states, all of which have as their mission the prevention of child abuse. Many direct their efforts at primary prevention, such as the chapter in Houston. That chapter, now called the Child Abuse Prevention Council, has as its motto "It shouldn't hurt to be a child." Efforts of the Houston chapter range from holding a symposium each year that features the best-documented primary prevention program in the country to producing *Programs That Work*,[78] a listing of all child abuse prevention programs in the country. NCPCA has done a remarkable job in educating the public as to what child abuse is and what people can do to help stop and prevent it.

While the media has done a great deal to make the public increasingly aware of the problem of child abuse, there is always a danger that the emphasis will be placed on the most gory, gruesome, and atypical cases, such as the Steinberg case in New York. M. Fritz, a former spokesperson for Parents Anonymous, described this tendency as follows:

> Dead babies sell newspapers.... [The media] are so hell bent
> on exploiting [us] to the extent they can, the anxiety level
> around the problem of abuse is so damned high that most
> people can't deal with it all. And if they do they get so
> upset that they just can't think rationally. We need to get
> out of that dead-baby bag so that people can deal with the
> problem in a rational way instead of with this intense
> anxiety-fear reaction.[79]

The media may not actually have exploitation as their intent, but rather than blowing up pictures of badly battered babies, they would serve prevention efforts better by showing how "nice, ordinary people" can end up abusing their children and what can be done to head off the abuse.

It will only be through public education on a broad scale that intervention can be made at the cultural level—the vector level in the public health triad. Cultural scripts, in which children are regarded as property and parents have the right to treat children as they see fit, must be changed. So must cultural scripts that insist that all babies are cuddly and loving (the "Gerber baby" myth) and all mothers smile sweetly at all times (the "Madonna Mother" myth). Parents need education as to the warning signs of their own potential to abuse and information on how and where to reach out for help before they maltreat their children.

Cultural scripts on the issue of discipline will be the most difficult to overcome. Should all physical discipline be banned, or at least placed in the realm of socially unacceptable behavior? Over 97% of American children are physically punished. While it has not been established that the use of physical punishment per se is harmful to children, Straus found that higher rates of physical punishment are associated with increased levels of aggression toward siblings and increased rates of child abuse and spouse abuse in the next generation.[80] Corporal punishment in the schools is legal in 39 states.[81] The media will be a decisive factor in the changes that occur in public attitudes toward physical discipline and its relationship to child abuse. As attitudes change, so will cultural scripts on the issue.

RESOURCES FOR PRIMARY PREVENTION
PROGRAMS

In proposing intervention strategies in this chapter, we have referred to a number of different workers and community resources—parent aides, lay health visitors, homemakers, and public health nurses. Where will the funds come from to support these services? We agree with Kempe's view: "If we wait for the money, we will wait forever. I am satisfied that the resources of this country have never been gathered together in any reasonable way to excite people to do a proper job. I mean the old and the very young."[82]

The social service field has barely tapped into the significant help that volunteers could give. As Routh points out: "Many services can be provided through the use of volunteers. There are not enough professionally trained individuals in the helping and caring professions to do the job at hand. It behooves local community-oriented agencies to realize that many services not presently being provided to clients can be made available through volunteer help."[83]

There are enormous untapped supplies of volunteers in this country who could provide primary prevention services in the specific area of child abuse. What it takes to recruit volunteers and put programs into effect is commitment—and a willingness on the part of professionals to admit that laymen can be effective. "We haven't been willing as social workers, as physicians," said Kempe, "to hand over our sacred skills and our stethoscopes to lay people because we are afraid that somehow or other it is going to devalue our money, our skill."[84]

Psychiatrists Pollock and Steele observed that "sensitive, devoted persons without specific professional training can be extremely valuable, adjunctive 'lay therapists.'"[85] The skill required to go into the home and deal with high-risk parents and children is the ability to nurture. This ability cannot be learned in professional training. Individuals acquire it by having had nurturing parents and by nurturing children of their own. Even in programs that do use professionals, such as nurse home visitors, the nurses "were carefully selected according to three major criteria: (1) their warmth, compassion, and ability to work with families from different social backgrounds without condescending; (2) their prior professional experience in some aspect of maternal and child health; and (3) their being parents themselves."[86]

Every city has many people who have the ability to nurture (who have the mothering imprint) and would serve or are already serving in these roles. The efforts might be spread much further and faster if local health departments would assume the responsibility for carrying out the intervention strategies. Some health departments already use volunteers, but rarely for prevention of child abuse—an area in which the record of public health has been dismal. Juvenile probation departments, mental health agencies, and hospitals could all provide models for the effective recruitment and use of volunteers.

How many volunteers would be needed for the programs we have outlined? Clearly it would depend on the program and the number of people to be served. If a health visitors program became a national policy and the home of every newborn were visited, a regular corps of professional health visitors would have to be established with federal funds, although volunteers could probably do the bulk of the job. In Houston, which averages about 32,500 live births each year, more than 650 health visitors would be needed. Volunteers, serving as parent aides or mother surrogates, could be recruited to do the important job of helping families identified by health visitors as high-risk. This step was taken at one Houston hospital, Jefferson Davis, which has more than 14,000 births per year, more than any other hospital in the country. Their "Best Friend" program uses 10 volunteers to work with 60 mothers under the age of 16. There were many others, most of them teenagers, who were eligible had more volunteers been available.[87]

To a large extent, volunteers could also staff community resources such as crisis nurseries, which could be sponsored by churches. "In this country, churches are standing absolutely empty except for three or four hours a week. They could all be used as day care centers, as some of them are. They could be used as crisis nurseries. The manpower really is here."[88]

Where will all the volunteers come from? As Kempe noted, "We haven't begun to really get all people who are able to give time.... They have time and they have love. All you need are those two items."[89] When the Volunteer Center opened its doors in Houston in 1975, more than 500 volunteers were interviewed and referred for service during the first 2 months. In 1987–1988, they referred over 16,000 volunteers, many of whom donated their time to 1 of 12 agencies dealing with abusive families and abused children.[90] Many retired people are eager to be asked to do a job, as are a growing number of young people. Kempe described the use of grandparents in their program. "We are putting babies that need fostering into homes for the aged, where four or five elderly ladies take four-hour shifts nursing babies and give more mothering than most babies can stand as a matter of fact. The only problem we've had is that some babies don't get enough sleep."[91] Volunteers, then, are both available and an answer to providing some necessary programs at a relatively low cost.

Volunteers have not waited around for health departments or agencies to tell them how to fill a need. The National Committee for the Prevention of Child Abuse, with its volunteer network spanning the nation, is one example of what volunteers are doing in the areas of primary prevention. In the following chapter, we will look at many successful volunteer efforts that have been addressed toward secondary prevention.

Because of the outstanding record of what volunteers have already accomplished in the last decade, we think that it will be less difficult to find manpower and resources to prevent child abuse than to get institutions to change their policies so that high-risk parents and children can be identified. Administering predictive questionnaires to parents of new babies will require the cooperation of all hospitals, not just the few that are now instituting programs. Systematically identifying difficult babies and observing parent–child interactions will require the participation and perhaps additional training of the hospital staff. Screening the unemployed would require the cooperation of state employment agencies. Identification will have to be balanced with parental rights not to be stigmatized or singled out unfairly. In short, all these programs would require major changes in institutional policies and procedures.

Is it worth all this? It is if the rights of children to a safe home and healthy parenting are recognized as legitimate. If Americans have a genuine commitment to their young, the obstacles can be overcome and the necessary manpower and resources will be found. When we have the necessary commitment, institutions will cooperate, as successful prevention programs have found.

10

Nonprofessional Caregivers, Parent Services, and CPS

Secondary prevention, as we defined it in the previous chapter, encompasses all efforts directed at preventing any further acts of abuse once maltreatment has occurred. In Chapters 5 and 6 we described psychotherapy treatment models, including ours, that are aimed at secondary prevention—treating the parents and family so that the abuse stops. Most of these treatment models assume that professionals are doing the treating, but much of the treatment of abusing parents in this country is done by laypersons who are nonprofessional caregivers or volunteers. In addition to laypersons providing most of the treatment to abusive families, many, if not most, suspected cases of abuse are reported by laypersons. Therefore, it is important to look at the crucial role the nonprofessional can and does play in secondary as well as primary prevention.

There are several reasons why the layperson plays such a prominent role in secondary prevention. First, treatment of abusing parents by professionals is expensive, particularly on an individual basis with psychoanalysis or other psychotherapy. It may be impossible even to extend group therapy to enough people who abuse to help all those who need it. Relatively few professional therapists are interested in working with abusive parents, either because they feel unprepared to help these parents or because their caseloads will not allow them to take on many of these very emotionally demanding clients. The nonprofessional can deliver many treatment services at lower cost and greater availability.

In addition to delivering treatment services, laypersons are at the forefront in detecting suspected cases of abuse. Neighbors, relatives, friends, and teachers are much more likely to see the signs of maltreatment than are physicians. Abusive or neglectful parents may avoid taking the child to a doctor unless the injury is life-threatening, or they may "doctor shop," not allowing any one physician to see a pattern to the injuries. Neighbors and teachers, on the other hand, see the child and family day in and day out. They know when "something's wrong," and, with the added support of laws mandating the reporting of suspected child abuse, more and more people are stepping forward to say when they think a child is in danger.

In this chapter, we will discuss secondary prevention efforts that nonprofessionals are making, including lay therapy, self-help groups, and supportive services. Secondary prevention efforts being delivered by children's protective service workers will also be presented. Finally, we will also discuss how the various approaches to secondary prevention can be linked into an overall, multidisciplinary delivery system.

LAY THERAPY

It has long been held that the outcome of psychotherapy depends in large part on the warmth, empathy, and respect that one person shows while listening to another. Those are traits that cannot be learned through professional training. Persons who are naturally endowed with the gift of compassion or have learned it through life's experience may need no special training to be effective healers and are especially suited to working with abusive parents as lay therapists.[1] Unlike the professional psychotherapist, they may be more able to break into the isolation of the abusive family's life and offer a warm parenting model.

The lay therapist in the field of child abuse goes by many names—parent aide, community aide, mother surrogate, "best friend." Most receive training and are considered paraprofessionals. But their most important "training" consists of having been loved by their mothers and fathers and having been loving mothers or fathers themselves.[2] They offer their time and love for little or no pay and become meaningfully involved in the lives of the abusing families. The lay therapist's commitment proves to the parents "that she is available to reach out and offer comfort and concern even when it is not convenient to do so."[3] Because they are willing to do so, these lay therapists are often successful in helping these families turn their lives around.

At Colorado General Hospital, the federally funded foster grandparents program we discussed in the previous chapter was a secondary prevention project with parent aides that expanded from the hospital into the homes. The program began by assigning grandparents to cuddle, nurture, and give attention to hospitalized battered children. The grandparents found themselves mothering the parents as well as the babies. Some began making visits to the homes, and eventually a program of using parent aides in abuse cases emerged. The program organizers recruited men and women from a wide range of socioeconomic backgrounds and ages (24 to 60). The parent aides were assigned the task of taking care of emotionally deprived adults who had abused their children. The lay therapists and parents were matched by social class. They spent an average of 15 hours a week in the home during the first week of being assigned, 10 hours the second, and 4 hours every week thereafter for the next 6 to 8 months.

The requirements of the job were quite demanding. In addition to having had good parenting and being a successful parent, the parent aide had to be a "mild and loving individual who is not easily upset by an ungrateful, suspicious and often initially unwilling client."[4] Additionally, "the surrogate mother has to be available by phone, day and night. She is the recognized lifeline for that family. She tries to give these people, who are damaged, suspicious, unfriendly, and hurt, their first experience in mothering because these people, for better or worse, missed out with their parents. Later on they missed out with teachers and then friends."[5] By providing this kind of relationship to the maltreating parents, the parent aide or mother surrogate helps them to acquire some positive mothering qualities and abilities. If they internalize what they see, hear, and experience the parent aide doing, and most do to some extent, they begin to parent their children similarly.

In addition to offering emotional support and appropriate modeling, lay therapists are called on to help solve life crises, which are frequent in abusing families. At these points, being an empathetic listener and a good model is not enough. So a necessary part of the training of lay therapists is informing them about community resources and how to use them. As one client protested to her parent aide: "I'm cold and I'm hungry.... If you aren't going to bring me food, heat and light, why come? We've got to feed my kids first. Let's get rid of all this jazz of worrying about my feelings and how I'm doing and developing a friendship, when you don't even show me how to get food."[6]

Because working with abusive parents involves much emotional wear and tear, the professional staff of the Colorado General Hospital conducted regular group meetings. In these meetings the parent aides had an opportunity to vent their feelings of frustration, fear, and anger that inevitably arise when working with abusive parents. The professional staff also supervised the parent aides, did the psychological and psychiatric assessment of each case, and provided the aides with support and information in times of crisis and stress.

One of the pioneer programs in lay therapy is Family Outreach of America. Begun in 1973 by members of the National Council of Jewish Women, Family Outreach now has more than 30 centers and over 750 volunteers who work with distressed and abusive families. In 1988 Family Outreach volunteers contributed 112,325 hours to supporting families, teaching parenting classes, and administering the program. Of those hours, 6907 were in direct services. The families are referred to Family Outreach by relatives, friends, school counselors, teachers, and nurses, or by their own request for help. A primary prevention aspect of Family Outreach is that the volunteers work with families in crisis who may not have abused their children or yet been reported to CPS.[7]

An important new resource of lay help to abusive families are the ESCAPE centers across the country. The ESCAPE centers are a network of centers coordinated by the National Exchange Club Foundation for the Prevention of Child Abuse, headquartered in Toledo, Ohio. The Houston ESCAPE center, which began operation in 1983, provides both direct intervention and community education. Parent aide volunteers, supervised by a professional case worker, commit 1 year to working with a family where CPS has confirmed child abuse/neglect. The goal is to offer long-term support and guidance to the abusing parents and a trusting, nurturing relationship while role-modeling appropriate parenting skills. The center trains their volunteer parent aides and organizes in-service training sessions to provide them with additional information about issues related to child abuse, such as chemical dependency.[8]

How the lay therapist fits into an overall treatment program is illustrated by the case of Mr. and Mrs. R.[9] They were an attractive, ambitious, upper-middle-class Jewish couple referred to the Sinai Hospital Child Abuse Project because of kidney damage that their 7-year-old son, Paul, suffered when his father punished him for disobeying his mother. Mr. and Mrs. R were typical of abusive families in their backgrounds and pattern of relating. Mr. R had been born out of wedlock and was abandoned by his mother. He was reared by relatives who treated him with indifference or rage and left him to shift for himself. Mrs. R had loving parents and had suffered little childhood trauma but was locked into a symbiotic relationship with her father and turned to him rather than to her husband. She had few friends and experienced much distress in the marriage. Mr. R degraded her, had expectations of her that were impossible to meet, and demonstrated little affection or emotion. Mrs. R responded with manipulative behavior and somatic complaints. Their son, Paul, became a vehicle for their rage and manipulation. In contrast, they both idealized their daughter.

The treatment plan consisted of weekly marital counseling sessions for both parents, as well as frequent individual sessions. A community aide, as the lay therapists were called in the Sinai Hospital project, helped Mrs. R overcome her isolation and find more effective methods of disciplining the children. With the community aide, Mrs. R experienced a warm, trusting relationship while going through her daily tasks. In so doing, she also learned that her father was not the only person she could turn to in time of need. Paul was given medication and play therapy.

Although Mr. R continued to have difficulty controlling his temper, his outbursts occurred at less frequent intervals. He also began to develop more sense of personal satisfaction. Mrs. R. developed outside interests and made new friends. Paul learned to trust adults and to communicate his needs more constructively. The intervention by the lay therapist or community aide was successful in changing the family dynamics and demonstrates how professionals and laypeople can and do work together to treat the abusing family.

SUPPORT SERVICES

The term *support services* means all the resources that, even if not specifically designed to be therapeutic, are a vital part of the secondary prevention of child abuse. These resources include some we have already mentioned, such as homemaker services, co-op nurseries, day care centers, foster home care, and telephone hot line programs. Whether combined or offered separately, they are an important adjunct to stopping the continuation of abuse.

Homemaker Services

The professional homemaker, like the visiting nurses we discussed in the previous chapter, is sometimes welcome when other professionals are not. The role of the homemaker service in secondary prevention is to teach some of the principles of home management to parents who often grew up in homes with little order. In the process, the homemaker contributes to bringing some measure of order and structure to homes that are frequently chaotic.[10] The intervention also helps break up the lonely isolation of these parents and serves as a link between the family and the community.

The successful professional homemaker has to be aware of the deep-seated insecurities of the abusive parents. A model that is overly brisk and efficient may increase their feelings of unworthiness and inadequacy.[11] Gentle encouragement and reassurance goes far with these parents who need to know that someone cares about them and their family. In some programs, the homemaker assists in evaluating the family's strengths and weaknesses and provides information that assists in the determination of whether or not an abused child can remain in the home or must be removed.[12]

Although homemaker services can be expensive, the costs must be weighed against the alternative of removing the children and placing them in foster care. Certainly homemaker services are less expensive than most psychotherapy programs and offer an important adjunct in teaching the parents skills they would not be learning in treatment. Regrettably, the availability of homemaker services is limited in most cities and probably will continue to be unless this effort incorporates volunteers, as other prevention programs have done so successfully.

Child Care Services

Under the heading of child care services are programs that either partially or completely take over the care of abused children. They include crisis nurseries, co-op nurseries, day care programs, and foster care. All these programs are important for the prevention of repeated maltreatment, but, unfortunately, some exist more in theory than in reality.

Crisis Nurseries and Emergency Shelter Care. Underlying the concept of crisis nurseries is the idea that parents should have a place to take their children when they feel they can no longer cope. In theory, the crisis nursery would be available day and night, 365 days a year, and would be a place where preparation, planning, and expense for leaving a child would be minimal.[13] The purpose would be to give any parent some relief from the pressures of parenting.[14]

Critics of the concept of crisis nurseries protest that parents themselves should bear the burden of childrearing since they chose to have children in the first place. They also predict that if parents have the opportunity to let someone else take care of their children, they will misuse the privilege, although Kempe did not find that to be the case.[15]

With good day care facilities being in such critical shortage in this country for parents in general, it is not surprising that there are few crisis nurseries in existence. While such centers might seem a luxury, the role they could serve in preventing instances of abuse could be significant. Wide availability of these crisis nurseries would be necessary, though, for them to serve effectively in encouraging maltreating families to seek help.[16]

Even less available than crisis nurseries are emergency shelters. Emergency shelter care has several advantages, some of which are now being offered at centers for battered women.

> It can allow the parent to separate from the child for part or all of the day, whichever seems best, but it does not make complete separation necessary as a part of relief and treatment. A shelter staffed by treatment people can observe crisis behavior and either intervene when necessary, at an especially meaningful time, or, in less threatening situations, allow the crisis to run its course.[17]

Crisis shelters could be a useful alternative to removing a child from the abusive home and also serve as a setting for parents to receive appropriate parenting instruction with added safeguards for the children.

Co-op Nurseries. Another type of therapeutic program that does not separate parent and child is the co-op nursery. Usually staffed by volunteers, it is a place where the abusing parents can work with their children, visit, and observe how children can be handled without physical discipline. As one abusive parent admitted: "I didn't know you could get a kid to do something without hitting him."[18] In Boston and San Francisco, co-op nurseries were established using previously abusive parents as volunteers. Although these parent-run nurseries have been successful, similar nurseries operated by nonabusing parents who can serve as role models may be even more effective.

Teaching parents how to play with their children is one important function of a co-op nursery. Abusing parents whose own parents never played with them find it threatening to just play with children. Through play therapy and "philiotherapy" (as the co-op nursery program in Lansing, Michigan, originally called their "love therapy"), parents get in touch with their own need to have fun and in so doing learn to let their children act like children. The end result is that their expectations of their children become more realistic.

Day Care Centers. Although crisis nurseries, emergency shelter care, and co-op nurseries are not widely available, various kinds of day care centers are, although the quality ranges widely. The majority of these centers are not designed as therapeutic resources, but they can and do relieve parents from the burden of continuous care of children. One family in our group illustrates this point:

> Donna was a bright articulate woman with two small daughters and a husband who worked the night shift as a guard. She became so angry and frustrated about the misbehavior of her children that, in addition to spanking them herself, she insisted that her husband beat them with a belt when he got home from work.
>
> When these parents entered our therapy group, one of our first recommendations to Donna was that she seek employment and put the children in day care. She was elated and surprised because we considered it acceptable for her not to stay home all the time with the children. Once she began working, there were no further instances of physical abuse.
>
> A crisis developed when one child was sick for several weeks and Donna had to take a leave from her job to stay home. When the pressure from staying home began to mount again, we recommended that the family find someone to stay with the sick child. They did, and the tension subsided once Donna returned to work.

Realizing that they are not expected to stay home all day taking care of their children enables some parents to cope much better when they are at home. Donna is an example. In this sense, any adequate day care facility becomes therapeutic and may be preventing abuse.

Some treatment programs have day care centers built into the structure. One such model was the Parents' Center Project for the Study and Prevention of Child Abuse in Brighton, Massachusetts. There, not only were children cared for and protected from further abuse, but also the parents were provided with opportunities to interact with their children in a supervised setting and to watch models of good child care. While similar programs do exist in other parts of the country, there are far too few of them.[19]

Foster Care. The scarcity that marks therapeutic day care centers and adequate, affordable day care facilities in general also extends to foster care. Since foster care is not at this time either socially attractive or financially rewarding, there is a severe shortage of quality foster homes where a child not only receives adequate care but is healthier for having had the experience.[20] Yet there is a dire need for placement of children who cannot safely be left in their own homes. Foster parents receive a modest financial payment for taking in children who are often extremely difficult to manage.

If foster homes are to be a resource in the secondary prevention of child abuse, the compensation, either monetarily or emotionally, for undertaking this challenge must be increased. The cry that abused children should be taken away from the "bad parents" and put in "good homes" fails to take into account that there simply are not that many "good homes" open to troubled children. The saintly parents who do take on these children are to be greatly commended, but their role still needs to be an interim one in the lives of most abused children.

Courses on Child Development and Management

A number of treatment programs for abusing parents include a parent education or child management component. The reason for this is apparent from our discussion of the characteristics of abusing parents. Since most abusive parents are products of the "world of abnormal rearing," parent education is essential to overcome its effects.[21] So in addition to being a valuable tool for primary prevention of child abuse, education on child development and management is integral to secondary prevention efforts.

Much parent education is given in conjunction with other programs and interventions of a secondary prevention nature. For example, a program for abusive parents established at the Neuropsychiatric Institute of the University of California at Los Angeles incorporated a child management class, which was taught by the nursing staff.[22] The staff emphasized behavior modification techniques and used Patterson and Gullion's book entitled *Living With Children* to help parents modify their maladaptive behavior.[23]

In our work, we used Smith and Smith's *Child Management* and Gordon's *Parent Effectiveness Training*.[24] As noted in Chapter 5, we used the group therapy context to teach childrearing and management. Although we approached the subject in an instructional fashion, the parents were learning about appropriate parenting indirectly in our program and in many others we have discussed here. For example, they were learning about kindness from gentle interactions with lay therapists and parent aides. The visiting nurse programs and nursery settings are powerful sources of parent education that is not delivered didactically.

Whatever the approach for offering the educational material or modeling, the other critical problems of abusive parents—their dependency, feelings of inadequacy, marital strife—must be taken into account. Although educating the parents about the developmental needs of their children and techniques for child management is essential, the parents are unlikely to be able to manage their children's lives any better than they can their own.

Transportation

One of the biggest problems in implementing secondary prevention programs for abusing parents is transportation. If parents are to participate in group therapy, parenting classes, or nursery options, they must be able to get to the service. Many low-income abusive parents have chronic transportation problems. Either their cars break down and they cannot afford the repairs or they live in areas where public transportation is inadequate or nonexistent.

Although parent aides and caseworkers do more than their share of helping these parents get to the services, the problem is substantial enough to address separately. Virtually every successful prevention program has built into it a transportation aspect. Helfer has even argued that a "transportation group," consisting of resources for getting abusive parents to sources of help, needs to be organized as a supportive service in secondary prevention programs.[25] As is true of most efforts at solving community problems, one of the main hurdles to overcome is getting the clients to the services. The delivery of child abuse prevention and treatment services is compounded by the distrust and isolation of the parents. Some of the programs we have discussed solve this problem in part by coming into the homes of the parents. But those that do require the parents to come to a facility have to be willing to go that extra bit to ensure that they get there.

Telephone Reassurance Service

Providing abusive parents with someone to reach out to in times of stress and crisis is a vital link in both the primary and secondary prevention of child abuse. Telephone "cool" lines and reassurance services provide this link, particularly when parents have no contact with a parent aide, homemaker, social worker, therapist, or even a friend.[26] One of the first models of services designed specifically for potentially abusive parents was the Child Abuse Listening Mediation program (CALM), established in 1970 by a housewife in Santa Barbara, California. Operated by volunteers, CALM provided a link between those asking for help and those willing to provide. When clients called CALM, they were given counseling and reassurance and told that volunteers (who functioned much like parent aides) were available to help them. Most of their calls were self-referred and came from parents who feared they were going to abuse their children. Some of the calls, though, were from parents who had already abused their kids or from concerned third parties. Third-party calls were referred to children's protective services.

CALM stimulated the growth of similar programs across the United States: Home Emergency Lifeline for Parents (HELP) in Phoenix, Arizona; Suspected Child Abuse and Neglect (SCAN) in Little Rock, Arkansas; several in California, including the Child Abuse Listening Line (CALL) in Santa Monica, Quality of Life Hotline in Palo Alto, Child Abuse Prevention Services (CAPS) in Napa, Parental Stress Service (PSS) in Berkeley, and Help for Upset Mothers in Redding; the Crisis Clinic in Aurora, Colorado; Family Focus in Birmingham, and the Child Abuse Resource Exchange in Battle Creek, Michigan; the Citizens Committee on Child Abuse in Vestalk and the Heart Line in New York City; the Child Abuse Study Committee in Salem, Oregon; Child Abuse Prevention Effort (CAPE) in Philadelphia; SCAN in Spokane, Washington; and Child Abuse Restraint Effort (CARE) in Green Bay, Wisconsin. This long list is only a sampling of the telephone reassurance services that have been available in virtually every community.

The proliferation of telephone hot lines for parents makes it apparent that the need is there. How much abuse is prevented by these services will never be known for certain. But for many of those parents who do reach out in distress, finding a caring person who is willing to hear about their problems may indeed mean the difference between child abuse and coping.

Another type of child abuse prevention hot line has emerged that is designed to make it easy for anyone to report a suspected case of child abuse at any time. Usually sponsored by public agencies, such as the department of public welfare or children's protective services, the reporting line is set up in conjunction with a public information campaign. In Texas, the Lift-A-Finger program reminded citizens that "it doesn't take much—just a phone call. Lift a finger, report child abuse. You may save a child."[27] The telephone number of the toll-free statewide child abuse hot line was widely advertised in television, on radio, and in brochures. Connecticut offered a telephone service along similar lines with a "24-hour statewide toll-free child abuse prevention and information line" operated by the Connecticut Child Welfare Association, a private agency.[28]

There is no doubt that these campaigns work well in terms of increased reporting of child abuse. Following the campaigns, there is usually a dramatic surge in reports. The problem then becomes how to investigate the reports and deliver services to more families with a CPS staff that typically is seriously overloaded already. There appears to be some correlation between funding for CPS and public information campaigns. There is little point in undertaking efforts that result in an increase in reported cases when workers can barely keep up with the steady flow of new serious cases that come with no public awareness activity. This in no way implies that any CPS agency does not want to know about suspected cases. It is just that with funding so restricted, as it is in most states, many workers have more cases than they can handle. This is all the more reason why primary prevention efforts are so crucial if the steady rise of new child abuse cases is to be stopped.

Child Abuse Registries and Indexing

Statewide central registries that record all reported cases of abuse, regardless of where they occur in the state, have become an important tool in secondary prevention. The concept of a central register has existed for some time for health problems such as cancer, and registers for child abuse were set up in some states in the 1960s. The register provides local CPS agencies with a central source for determining whether an abusive parent brought to their attention has ever been involved in child abuse elsewhere in the state or nation.

At a time when so many families move from city to city, it was difficult to determine whether abusive parents have had similar problems elsewhere. Some abusing families move deliberately to escape detection. Now, with the registry system, it is easier to determine whether they have a past history of abuse. Because this kind of information can influence decisions about removing a child from the home or attempting to rehabilitate the parents, central registries are crucial in some secondary prevention efforts.

For rapid retrieval of information, register systems are now computerized. In Texas, a system called Child Abuse and Neglect Recording Information System (CANRIS) went into effect in 1974. At that time, the Office of Child Development of the U.S. Children's Bureau, which operated the National Center on Child Abuse and Neglect in Washington, D.C., identified an effective central register of child abuse as an essential element of a comprehensive secondary prevention program.[29] Such a system now exists, so that CPS agencies in any state can check a case for previous records elsewhere, although the interstate tracking is still far from coordinated.

Just as child abuse registries need to be interlinked among cities and states, hospitals need a cross-indexing system to identify suspected high-risk parents and children before injuries escalate. The Vulnerable Child Committee was set up in the

Brockton, Massachusetts, area to promote early identification of high-risk children, using cross-indexing as one means to alert hospitals and social agencies to the cases.

> The general goals of the VCC was to establish early identification of children vulnerable to abuse and neglect, to provide their families with preventive resources to help them maintain adequate care for the physical and psychological development of their children, and to offer public education and consultation to the professional and lay community in relation to child abuse and neglect.[30]

The VCC and six cooperating hospitals used the following guidelines to identify vulnerable children: Has the child been injured three times within 1 year? Do the child's parents refuse to follow medical advice? Do the parents demonstrate inappropriate concern or a lack of concern? Is the child's mother or the family situation inadequate? Does either parent abuse alcohol or other drugs? Is there a lack of parental supervision in the home?

The VCC set up a cross-indexing system to alert cooperating hospitals and social agencies to the vulnerable children it encountered. The following excerpt is an example of early identification and alerting:

> A 3-year-old boy was brought to a hospital by police ambulance. Reportedly, the child had fallen from his second floor window during his naptime. There was no injury. The parents' explanations of the accident were contradictory and suspicious. The mother, a very anxious woman, told the staff that she was "abused by her parents as a child"; then she became tearfully upset and said she could not cope with the pressures of her life. The case was indexed for the purpose of bringing social services to the family, and alerting participating hospitals to the possibility of future injuries.[31]

Although some of the VCC's interventions were on a secondary rather than a primary level—that is, some children have already been injured by the time they are identified—the VCC and the index represented a program that used a coordinated system designed to head off child abuse. For example:

> A 2-month-old boy was brought to a hospital by parents who said the child had fallen out of the crib. A check with the index showed a sibling had been seen a month prior with a slight concussion. In view of this, X-rays were taken of the infant. They revealed five prior fractures of both legs. In the absence of the index, the case might have been dismissed as an isolated and unimportant accident.[32]

Even though the index was useful in alerting hospitals and agencies to potential abuse, it is no longer in use in Brockton or any of the Boston area hospitals. Out of concern that the index might be in violation of laws protecting privacy, administrations ordered the social work staffs to stop keeping the index.[33] This decision reflects the growing concern in the last few years about confidentiality and institutional efforts to protect those rights. It also illustrates how children's rights to safety may be sacrificed to those of their parents to privacy.

Another method of flagging high-risk cases and promoting secondary intervention is to color-code the charts of children who are suspected of being subject to abuse. Since the early 1970s, the South End Community Health Center in Boston has used charts with red covers to identify children who might be at high risk.[34] This permits easy retrieval and periodic review of the chart without using identifying names or diagnostic terms.

Gerald Haas, the medical director of the center, states that the value of the system is in the physician's being alerted to possible danger signs by a red cover on the chart of a child being treated. The nurse, who may know more about the family, can then be consulted and give information about what may be going on in the child's life. If the home situation improves and the child is considered to be no longer at risk, the red cover can be removed.

In the past, some hospitals and clinics put a star on the chart and stamped it with "TRAUMA X," meaning suspected child abuse. The problem with that system was that the patients as well as the staff could figure out that the code meant child abuse. The same does not appear to be true of the visual color coding system. So while most hospitals have abandoned the "TRAUMA X" label on the chart, the red cover system is still working well after nearly 20 years.[35]

SELF-HELP GROUPS

The growth of self-help groups in child abuse was stimulated by several factors: (1) the lack of professional help in many communities, (2) the inadequacy of services in general for abusive parents, and (3) the recognition that many abusive parents have a basic distrust of authority figures (including professionals) and are likely to feel more comfortable around people who have the same problem. As Helfer points out, the self-help group is "a good way to short-circuit abusive habits."[36] Parents change their behavior by modeling themselves after others in the group who have proved that it is possible to stop inflicting violence on children. There may be no major changes in the parents' feelings toward their children or in their understanding of why they abuse them, but their behavior changes. For example, one mother in a self-help group admitted, "I don't beat him any more, but I cannot really say I have any feeling or love for him."[37] Another commented, "Since I joined P.A. (Parents Anonymous), I don't beat my kid any more, but I don't like the little bastard any better."[38] A founder of one Parents Anonymous chapter reflected that she still gets angry at her daughter and feels like "clobbering her, but would I? No, I don't have to be afraid of the urge. I can handle it. If not, I could always call my husband or another P.A. member, or go back to kicking the chair."[39]

Learning to deal with anger and to redirect it is a major concern of self-help groups for abusive parents. Although these parents do not always direct the anger toward the child (it may be toward another adult), they often become so frightened of their rage, which they have frequently vented on the child, that they are afraid of expressing anger toward anyone. In other words, they are afraid of losing control. "Because he was not allowed to express his anger as a child, he may not know how to express it legitimately as an adult nor even understand that anger is an acceptable, normal emotion."[40] The self-help group offers the parent the opportunity to learn that he can express anger without destroying a relationship with another person or losing control of himself. The following excerpt illustrates this point:

> Mrs. N phoned [her caseworker] to say she had been hurt by Mrs. O's remarks at the previous Parents Anonymous meeting and felt that Mrs. O did not want her in the group. Mrs. N was encouraged to express just how she felt, and it was then suggested that it was important for her to express these same feelings to Mrs. O at the next meeting.
>
> Supported by the caseworker's acceptance of her feelings, Mrs. N was able, with great difficulty, to repeat to the group what she had said. The worker's role in the group meeting was to help each of the women clarify how she was feeling and to express these feelings to the others. Mrs. O told Mrs. N that she could accept the fact that her own problems were different from Mrs. N's but that she did want her in group and she did care for her. As they talked out their misunderstanding, the tension subsided. It was a learning experience for the whole group.[41]

In addition to short-circuiting abusive behavior and redirecting anger, self-help groups are effective for two other reasons. They break up the isolation of abusing parents, and the members bail each other out during a crisis.

Whether self-help groups should admit professionals such as social workers or psychologists to their meetings or ask them for advice is an issue that is addressed differently by different P.A. chapters. Parents Anonymous, Inc., of Los Angeles, which began in 1970 under the name of Mothers Anonymous, does use professionals as chapter sponsors. It also relies on the advice and input of other professionals when necessary.[42] Others, such as the Parents Anonymous chapter in New York, which was founded in 1972, did not originally rely on professionals for consultation or advice.[43]

According to Helfer, one drawback of self-help organizations is that the members "lack a model of healthy parenting—a person who understands child development and can provide examples of healthy ways to handle problems as they arise."[44] Because abusive parents had poor parenting themselves, many believe it is essential for them to be exposed to healthy parenting. Another possible drawback of P.A. groups is that they do not address the problems of symbiosis and role reversal, which entails teaching parents how to meet their own needs rather than depend on their offspring.

Some Parents Anonymous chapters expose their members to professional role models to some degree, while others see it as essential that parents learn from those who have overcome their abusive behavior and thus serve as effective examples for others who are still struggling with the problem. Regardless of which position is more valid, self-help groups are proving the value of the Alcoholics Anonymous model, which has led people with many kinds of addictions to band together—Gamblers Anonymous, Narcotics Anonymous, Overeaters Anonymous, Codependents Anonymous.

The idea of a self-help group for abusing parents was greeted with skepticism and a lack of cooperation from professionals when the late Jolly K, then 29, wanted to use her understanding of the problem and her leadership ability to help parents like herself. Despite the lack of support, Jolly went ahead to found Mothers Anonymous, which later became Parents Anonymous of California. Jolly had been reared in 100 foster homes and 32 institutions, had been raped at age 11, completed only 5 years of school, and had worked as a prostitute. After two disastrous marriages, she tried to destroy both herself and "the little slut" she had brought into the world. "Her 'credentials' and cries for help turned off at least nine established agency professionals who found it difficult to accept this form of 'field work' as a suitable criterion for motherhood, much less leadership."[45] Finally, a social worker challenged her to do something herself about the dearth of services for abusive mothers.

In 1974 the initial Parents Anonymous organization that Jolly K founded received a grant from the Children's Bureau to set up additional chapters. It now has 1200 chapters in 42 states and serves 30,000 families.[46] Its goals include (1) redirecting anger onto objects other than children and other people, (2) learning to reach out to other people for help, and (3) altering destructive ways of viewing oneself and one's children.[47] P.A. meetings often deal with how to handle anger nonabusively. As one P.A. member shared with others in her group: "I did it! Last week ... I got so teed off at my son! But instead of abusing him I squashed the milk carton I was holding until the milk went all over the place.... I released my anger in a more positive way and it worked. Now I know I can do other things besides being abusive when I'm uptight."[48]

Jolly K believed that her organization served the typical abusive parent. "We are seeing the very withdrawn, the very aggressive, the isolationist, the uptight, the psychotic.... In short, we are seeing human beings displaying a lot of different 'typical human traits.'"[49] The size of a P.A. group at any one time averages 6 to 10 parents, most of whom remain active for one or more years. Only 25 to 30% of the members are men. When a group learns that a member has been abusive recently, special attention is devoted to that parent. If supportive efforts appear to be unsuccessful in stopping the abuse, authorities are asked to intervene, whether the parent agrees to this intervention or not.

One need of self-help groups is a system of evaluation and follow-up. Jolly K reported what while there has been no formal follow-up on members, "recidivism has been very, very low."

Many P.A. organizations sponsor a telephone hot line in addition to the support groups. The Parents Anonymous chapter in New York City called theirs the Heart Line, which operated 24 hours a day. Even on slow days, there were at least 10 calls, reported Mrs. Gertrude M. Bacon, a former Family Court judge who founded the organization. In Houston, parents reach the hot line by calling Parents Anonymous directly. Their call is received by an answering service operator, who then transfers the call to a professional staff person or volunteer. Parents are listened to and supported, and urged to attend one of the groups for ongoing help.

A third self-help organization, Families Anonymous, was started in Denver by a public health nurse and her husband, a psychiatric social worker, using an Alcoholics Anonymous model.[50] The parents voluntarily met on a regular basis, and their sessions were supervised by professional leaders, who acted primarily as "advisors, counselors and friends." However, when crises arose, the ultimate decision of what action to take rested in the hands of the professionals.

The emphasis in Families Anonymous was on sharing experiences, both positive and negative.[51] Parents were provided with a safe place to express their feelings. The structure varied with the parents' needs. Sometimes it was highly directive and at other times quite free-flowing. By sharing their feelings and experiences, parents learned they were not unique in their frustration with their children. Information on child management techniques was also an important component of the program.

The therapists or group leaders in Families Anonymous played an active role in teaching, being directive in group, and following up on clients because they found that doing so was vital when working with abusive parents—much more so than with nonabusive clients. For this reason, they felt strongly about including professionals in what was essentially a self-help group. One advantage was that professionals could offer the positive "mothering" model that is likely to be lacking or minimal in other self-help groups.

CASEWORK COUNSELING

If any group can be called the infantry in the war against child abuse, it is the children's protective service agency worker. The responsibilities of these men and women run the gamut from investigation of home situations and removing children when necessary to family counseling. They are expected to be many things to many people, and performing all their duties without getting caught between roles is difficult. Some are successful. Others are not. What steps are necessary for successful casework with abusive families?

One of the first hurdles confronting the caseworker is how to establish a relationship with the abusive parent.[52] Since the parents are in all likelihood initially hostile, cold, and defensive, relating to them is no easy task. If, on the other hand, they are likable, the caseworker may tend to deny the seriousness of the accusation of abuse. If these first barriers can be surmounted, the parents' excessive dependency and the crises they are likely to go through in the course of counseling place a heavy emotional burden on the caseworker. In short, any one abusive family is difficult to work with—a discouraging thought for a caseworker whose caseload is almost always stretched to the limit.

> Often workers can't help but feel accusatory or vengeful for what the parents have done to their child. They also feel uneasy about interfering in the time-honored sanctity of the parent–child relationship. This all adds up to a situation in which workers may find themselves confronted by people who don't like them, who are threatening them, and whom they find it hard to like.[53]

The initial anger and hostility that abusive parents feel when confronted can often be reduced if the caseworker is understanding and empathetic. Beneath the parents' anger is fear of what will happen to them and their family. Asking questions that let the parents know their feelings matter eases the fear somewhat. This can be done by asking questions such as: What did your child do that upset you? Is your youngster hard to handle? Does your baby need too much attention? The parents' fears can also be relieved by making certain that they clearly understand what will happen. As Davoren points out, "Offering practical and specific help in contacting family members, finding child care for other children in the family and obtaining transportation—or simply thinking through with parents how they can do these things—will help them be more open to treatment."[54]

Once the caseworker is successful in establishing a relationship with the parents, the next task is to explore more fully the factors that precipitated the abuse. Once these factors are identified, the caseworker and the parents can work together to change the situation or at least devise ways that will help the parents control the abusive behavior. That control may develop as a result of learning the techniques of effective child management, learning about their own feelings, or both. In the process of educating the parents, the caseworker must continually keep their needs in mind and help them to modify their child's behavior without making them feel inferior or inadequate.

Practical information on childrearing and how to deal with anger is important, but the caseworker must also demonstrate consistently to the parents that he or she believes they are worthwhile and is willing to listen to them.

> In many situations the first thing parents need is someone who is willing and able to go to a lot of effort just to see them. Home visits are not only useful in themselves, but may be the only way workers will get to see the parents at all—at least in the beginning.... Sympathetic, responsive, non-judgemental listening is an extremely valuable service. People who have never been listened to before will find it

hard at first to believe that anyone is interested in what
they have to say.[55]

After the abusive parents have developed trust in the caseworker, the worker can begin encouraging them to break out of
their isolation and expand their lives by engaging in some activities, like a self-help group. However, when it is clear to the
caseworker that a child is not safe at home, the worker must
recommend removal from the home to the courts, place the child
in foster care, or, in some instances, initiate termination of parental rights.

What kind of person functions well while carrying out these
varying and sometimes contradictory tasks? Davoren lists the
following characteristics as useful to a caseworker dealing with
abusive parents:

> A person with few, if any, managerial tendencies.
>
> Someone who is willing to put himself out for patients, but
> who does not go around sacrificing himself much to every-
> one's discomfort.
>
> Someone who has a fair number of satisfactions in his life
> besides his job so that he won't be looking to the patients
> to provide these satisfactions.
>
> Someone with a strong working knowledge of child beha-
> vior that can be shared with abusive parents at appropriate
> times.[56]

In short, successful caseworkers are those who are willing
to give much of themselves to the abusive family but not to the
point where they themselves become abused. They must know
what is reasonable to expect of the abusive parents in terms of
change and what they will need in order to change. The job of
providing nurturing may fall to the caseworkers in a community
that cannot provide parent aides or has minimal support services.

> Even when workers feel strong within themselves, and have
> reasonably fulfilling lives of their own apart from their

work, the nurturing of abusive parents can be exhausting. The parents' needs are extensive—at times like bottomless pits. Workers calling on their own emotional resources are constantly aware of themselves, their own upbringing and the way they are raising their own children, if they have any. The awareness can be wearing. But the most draining part of caring for these parents is knowing that a child may be seriously injured or neglected, or even die, if the worker misjudges the parents' capacity to care for the child.[57]

Beyond the emotional drain abusing parents often put on the caseworker is their constant need for assistance with transportation, money, and child care. "If services are not available elsewhere and workers are able to give some of these services themselves, it can be well worth the time."[58]

Thus, being a friend and helper and generating the kind of conditions necessary for effective counseling is a major part of doing casework with abusing parents. In one 4-year child abuse study treatment project involving 46 parents, "the nature of service was primarily supportive in 28 cases, casework was aimed at the development of insight in 11 cases, and eight were receiving psychiatric services."[59]

Caseworkers do considerable treatment of abusive parents in this country. Some are trained social workers, and some are not. Some have parent aides and homemakers to help them. Many do not. A few have psychotherapy resources to which to refer the parents. Arvanian offers the following approach for social workers who must handle treatment on their own:

> Emphasize caring and acceptance of the isolated, depressed people who feel so worthless. Primarily, our tool is the therapeutic relationship between parent and helping person. The therapist becomes the parents' parent; through identification with the therapist—as a loving, caring parent— parenting of their own children is learned. Listen and try to help them sort out their feelings—at home they're really angry, how to love, and how to set limits for their children....[60]

Alone or assisted, trained or not, caseworkers who work with abusive parents must do so within the context of their agency, where heavy caseloads and frequent turnover of personnel may be a fact of life. Generally speaking, caseworkers never have enough time to do the things necessary for the best results for all the families. Doing what is possible with available resources and with an attitude of compassion is the goal to be strived for.

In the ideal situation, the caseworker would have sufficient psychotherapy available to be able to function as an "alternate therapist" to the psychologist or psychiatrist doing the therapy.[61] As an alternate therapist, the worker would be available to the family when the primary therapist was not and would be willing to listen to criticisms and complaints that the parents might be unwilling to express to the primary therapist. Misunderstandings that arise in therapy can be passed through the alternate therapist, and when the family learns that they can express their thoughts and feelings without reproach, they gradually begin to express them directly to the therapist. Most important, because abusive parents are so needy and distrustful, having more than one person available can be an enormous resource for change.

Over and over in this section, we have emphasized the demands that casework counseling places on even the best worker, and that the caseworker has to strike a balance between meeting the needs of the families and one's own needs. A program in Allentown, Pennsylvania, was designed to benefit abusive parents by helping their caseworkers.[62] A psychiatrist and a psychiatric social worker run groups for protective service caseworkers, using as material the problems these workers encounter in their caseloads. We used a similar model in the context of training CPS workers to conduct group therapy with abusive parents. While the workers were primarily training to learn the skills necessary to lead groups, much of the work focused on understanding their own emotional reactions to clients, how to stay out of psychological games with clients, and how to take care of themselves while taking care of others. The skills they learned carried over into many aspects of their work other than leading groups and helped many of them avoid burnout.

WHEN THE SYSTEM FAILS

One major new demand on Children's Protective Services organizations all over the country is the expectation that they will not fail—that no child should die from abuse as a result of having been allowed to stay in a home or returned home. The Steinberg-Nussbaum case in New York in 1988-1989 illustrated the blame a CPS agency undergoes for failing to remove a child when there were several reports on the family and previous CPS involvement. The same kind of accusations were made in another New York case shortly afterward involving a 5-year-old named Jessica Cortez, whose neck was broken by her mother's boyfriend. Sadly, there are children like Jessica all across our nation, and CPS will never be able to protect all of them.

When such a tragedy happens, CPS is blamed and a major investigation often follows. The Harris County Children's Protective Services in Houston underwent a one-year investigation following such an incident. Among the findings of the investigators were recommendations that CPS needed additional staff and additional training for their staff. The blame may be unjustified. As Carroll notes, "We must not construe the death of a child in a county as evidence that the county represents a poor or closed system. Even in the best of services, children, most tragically, will die. In this field of protective services, we are making human judgements; and being human, mistakes will be made."[63]

"Open" CPS systems are defined as those that are responsive to the needs of referred families, progressive in program planning, and open to the involvement of other agencies in the community. The opposite would be characterized as "closed systems."[64] A closed system would minimize the problems of child abuse and neglect in the community, provide little leadership in delivering services to families, and set up barriers within their system against families and other community agencies.

In their frustration and anger at seeing children not being protected from abuse, the public attacks CPS and the front-line social worker. For example, Justice for Children, a children's advocate group in Houston, charges that CPS does not care about children and is more interested in protecting the abusive parents.[65] This leaves the CPS workers in a Catch-22 situation. If they feel the interests of the children are best served by working with the parents and trying to keep the families intact, they are accused of not protecting the children. When they are so overworked that they can investigate only the most critical cases and monitor those cases infrequently, opponents attack them for failing to prevent the abuse or death.

Social service departments have been given the tremendous obligation of protecting children at risk but are provided with little help. They are trying to protect more and more children with lowered budgets and smaller staffs.[66] Workers are put in the demoralizing position of being seen as uninterested in children when a desire for protecting them is what leads many to go into the field in the first place.[67]

The solution proposed by some challengers of CPS is to put the investigation of all cases in the hands of the police, who would first arrest the parents and then call in a social worker if needed.[68] This solution fails to take into account that the intent of most state laws for the protection of children is to call into play two systems when a child is abused. CPS is charged with assessing the present and future risks and needs of the children. The criminal system comes into play to deal with the past tense—to hold the parents accountable for the harm they inflicted on their children. Both may be necessary for the family to be helped. Another problem with the idea of having police handle all child abuse cases is that most cities are faced with a shortage of police and criminal investigators. In Texas, CPS estimated in 1989 that it has half the number of caseworkers and one-tenth the number of criminal officers that are needed to handle the number of cases they have.[69]

A third shortcoming of the proposal to have the police investigate all cases referred to CPS is that half of the referrals are usually cases of neglect, and in many states, including Texas, there is no criminal statute against neglect. Only recently was there even a criminal statute in Texas against abandonment. The solution, too, discounts the emotional trauma to a child that can come from being subjected to the stresses of the criminal process.[70]

Part of the overall problem of handling child abuse cases is that children's programs are often seen as unimportant when it comes time to allocate funds. For their part, social service departments are sometimes at fault for being reluctant to request funding that is actually essential and instead ask for what they think the legislature will bear.[71]

There is much improvement to be made, and a better job by all communities needs to be sought. But there are signs of change in the direction of prevention. In Houston, for example, CPS is in some cases delivering support services to high-risk families who are not in their highest priority group.[72] The answer lies in an attitude of community responsibility for child abuse and not in attacks on CPS workers or expecting them to solve complex problems in which the whole society plays a part. It is time "to think of a larger protective services system encompassing the legal system, schools, health department, child protection teams, public and private hospitals, law enforcement, lay and community groups, parent-consumer groups, medical private practitioners, county and state social service departments, juvenile courts, public and private mental resources, and private social service agencies."[73]

A COORDINATED TEAM APPROACH

Tying all the elements of secondary prevention together into an effective delivery system requires coordination of the highest order. It demands the teamwork of hospitals, community agencies, the helping professionals, and volunteers. One of the biggest problems in the delivery of services is fragmentation and lack of coordination. A number of community agencies may be concerned with child abuse, and if parents are pulled from one to another, the stress in their lives increases and heightens their potential for abuse.[74]

Based on a system outlined by Helfer, the following is one way that a coordinated team approach could ideally work.[75]

Step 1. The problem is recognized when a teacher, nurse, neighbor, policeman, or relative makes a report to a community protective services agency, which in many cities is legally responsible for investigating child abuse cases.

Step 2. The child is taken to the emergency room of a hospital that has a child abuse consultation team. An examination is performed and acute treatment is provided.

Step 3. The child is admitted to the hospital for further treatment, which allows time for the case to be investigated. The family physician, if any, is brought in.

Step 4. The hospital-community SCAN (Suspected Child Abuse and Neglect) consultation team is notified and checks to ensure that a social worker from the protective services agency will assess the family and the home environment. In addition to the agency social worker, the SCAN team includes a public health nurse, a pediatrician, a family physician, and a psychologist or psychiatrist.

Step 5. A diagnostic and treatment planning conference is held by the consultation team 3 or 4 days after the case is reported and the child has been admitted to the hospital. By this time, all relevant information on the child and the family has been gathered. The team considers the following questions at the conference: Does the family meet the criteria for abuse? Is there any evidence that either parent is psychotic? What are the major problems of the family and child in terms of priority? Who will take action on each problem listed; e.g., who will arrange treatment for the parents, what kind of treatment or placement should the child receive, which treatment programs can be used for parents and child, who will help the parents with employment or housing problems, who will act as overall coordinator? (Helfer suggests there should be a friendly family coordinator for each case of child abuse because it is so easy for these families to slip through a crack when several agencies and referrals are involved.) After answering these questions, the team formulates a treatment plan.

Step 6. If it is advisable to remove the child from the home, the protective service agency petitions the courts for the authority to do so. If the child was not hospitalized after the report came in on his suspected abuse, the agency approaches the court immediately to obtain temporary custody if necessary.

Step 7. The treatment plan is put into action. A parent aide—and a homemaker, if necessary—is assigned to the family. The parents are referred for group therapy or begin receiving casework counseling. They also may be advised to join a Parents Anonymous group and to visit a co-op nursery, where they can observe how to play with and manage children. If the abused child remains in the custody of its parents (or if there are other children in the home), the family becomes acquainted with the local crisis nursery or emergency care shelter and the telephone hot line service. Again, a coordinator must be designated to ensure that all these services are marshaled on the family's behalf.

Step 8. Everyone involved in the treatment program meets regularly to report the family's progress, including medical and psychological follow-ups on the child.

Step 9. When the team agrees that the parents have progressed to the point where the home is safe, the child is returned. The court is petitioned at the appropriate time to return legal custody of the child to the parents. The parents remain in group therapy or continue to receive counseling until the child has been back home at least 1 month and any problems of readjustment have been overcome.

Step 10. Treatment ends, but the parents remain in a Parents Anonymous group and the family coordinator checks periodically to determine whether the family is functioning satisfactorily.

This is an ideal kind of coordinated approach to secondary prevention, and, in reality, such a cooperative concentration of services and professionals is difficult to find. The program at the University of Colorado Medical Center is similar in terms of coordination, and the Sinai Hospital Child Abuse project in Baltimore also has a teamwork program.[76] In fact, many large hospitals now have specialized child abuse assessment and treatment teams, but work with most families does not involve hospitals, removal of the child, or the intensive services Helfer recommends. Other coordinated programs that are not based in hospitals were included in the 11 demonstration programs funded by the federal government in 1974 to "test different strategies for tackling the child abuse problem and to study carefully ... the successes and failures of the projects."[77]

The results of the National Clinical Evaluation Study make it clear that all treatment services come with a high price tag. But the study also pointed the way to some cost-effectiveness in the future. One method recommended for reducing costs and improving outcomes is by targeting services according to the type of abuse (physical, sexual, emotional, or neglect). Another strategy is to offer prevention services linked to existing systems, such as schools, public health centers, or churches. Concludes Daro, "Building upon these strategies in jointly expanding our treatment and prevention efforts is a more cost-effective practice and policy path to pursue than simply dealing with the growing number of victims the current system is certain to produce."[78] Prevention of child abuse is ultimately everyone's responsibility—practitioners in public and private settings, caseworkers, police, the judiciary, legislators and decision-makers who establish policies that affect families, and the families themselves.

> No one group or discipline can carry the load alone; it clearly is too heavy a burden. All of the professionals and agencies involved in a community's efforts to deal with the problem of abuse must be tied together in some type of coordinated consortium. Collectively, there is some hope for success; individually, the struggle goes on.[79]

By working together, supporting each other's efforts, and sharing knowledge, we move forward in our goal to heal the abusing family.

Notes

INTRODUCTION

1. U. S. Department of Health and Human Services (1980). *Promoting health/Preventing disease.* Washington, DC: U.S. Government Printing Office.
2. U. S. Department of Health and Human Services (1986). *The 1990 health objectives for the nation: A midcourse review.* Washington, DC: U.S. Government Printing Office.
3. Simmons, J. T. (1986). *Programs that work: Evidence of primary prevention of child abuse.* Houston: Greater Houston Committee for the Prevention of Child Abuse.
4. Mrazek, P. J., & Mrazek, D. S. (1987). Resilience in child maltreatment victims: A conceptual exploration. *Child Abuse & Neglect, 11,* 357–366.
5. Mrazek & Mrazek (1987).
6. Egeland, B. Jacobvitz, D., & Papatola, K. (1987). Intergenerational continuity of abuse. In R. J. Gelles & J. B. Lancaster (Eds.), *Child abuse and neglect: Biosocial dimensions.* New York: Aldine de Gruyter.
7. Simmons (1986).

8. Helfer, R. E. (1982). A review of the literature on the prevention of child abuse and neglect. *Child Abuse & Neglect, 6*(3), 251–261.

9. Gershenson, C. (1984). The cost saving impact of permanency planning. *Child Welfare Research Notes*, No. 6.

10. U. S. Department of Health and Human Services (1980).

11. Hackett, G. (1988, December 12). A tale of abuse. *Newsweek*, pp. 56–61.

12. Zalba, S. (1971, July-August). Battered children. *Trans-Action, 8,* 58–61.

13. Kempe, C. J., Silverman, F. N., Steele, B. F., Droegemueller, W., & Silver, H. K. (1962). The battered-child syndrome. *Journal of the American Medical Association, 181,* 17–24.

14. Felder S. (1971). A lawyer's view of child abuse. *Public Welfare, 29,* 181–188.

15. Laury, G. V. (1970, September). The battered child syndrome. *Bulletin of the New York Academy of Medicine, 46,* 678–681.

16. *Lift a finger: The teacher's role in combating child abuse* (1975). Houston: Education Professions Development Consortium C.

17. Felder (1971).

18. *Texas Penal Code* (7th ed.) (1984). St. Paul, MN: West Publishing.

19. Gil D. G. (1970). *Violence against children: Physical abuse in the United States.* Cambridge, MA: Harvard University Press.

20. Gil (1970).

21. Daro, D. (1988). *Confronting child abuse: Research for effective program design.* New York: Free Press.

22. Justice, B., & Justice R. (1976). *The abusing family.* New York: Human Sciences Press.

23. Caldwell, R. A., Bogat, G. A. & Davidson, W. S. (1988). The assessment of child abuse potential and the prevention of child abuse and neglect: A policy analysis. *American Journal of Community Psychology, 16*(5), 609–624.

24. U. S. Department of Health and Human Services (1986).

25. Straus, M. A., & Kantor, G. K. (1987). Stress and child abuse. In R. E. Helfer & R. S. Kempe (Eds.), *The battered child.* Chicago: University of Chicago Press.

26. Daro (1988).

27. Justice & Justice (1976).

28. Barber-Madden, R., & Cohn, A. H. (1983, November). *Family violence: The role of public health.* Paper presented at the annual meeting of the American Public Health Association, Dallas.

29. Helfer, R. E. (1987). Back to the future. *Child Abuse & Neglect, 11*(1), 11–14.

30. Daro (1988).

31. *NCPCA Fact Sheet* (1986, March). Chicago: National Committee for Prevention of Child Abuse, p. 1.

32. Simmons (1986).

33. Cohn, A. (1983). *An approach to preventing child abuse.* Chicago: National Committee for Prevention of Child Abuse.

34. Daro (1988).

35. Haynes, C. F., Cutler, C., Gray, J., & Kempe, R. S. (1984). Hospitalized cases of nonorganic failure to thrive: The scope of the problem and short-term lay health visitor intervention. *Child Abuse & Neglect, 8,* 229–242.

36. Green W. H., Campbell, M., & David R. (1984). Psychosocial dwarfism: A critical review of the evidence. *Journal of the American Academy of Child Psychiatry, 23*(1), 39–48.

37. Bovard, E. W. (1985). Brain mechanisms in effects of social support on viability. *Perspectives on Behavioral Medicine, 2,* 103–129.

38. Bovard (1985).

39. Straus & Kantor (1987).

CHAPTER 1

1. Light, R. J. (1973). Abused and neglected children in America: A study of alternative policies. *Harvard Educational Review, 43,* 588.

2. Justice, B., Calvert, A., & Justice, R. (1985). Factors mediating child abuse as a response to stress. *Child Abuse & Neglect, 9,* 359–363.

3. Friedrich, W. N., & Wheller, K. K. (1982). The abusing parent revisited: A decade of psychological research. *Journal of Nervous and Mental Disease, 170,* 577–587.

4. Straus, M. A. (1980). Stress and child abuse. In C. H. Kempe & R. E. Hefler (Eds.), *The battered child* (3rd ed, pp. 86–103). Chicago: University of Chicago Press.

5. Straus (1980), p. 87.

6. For a description of the two groups, see B. Justice & D. F. Duncan (1976, March-April). *Public Health Reports, 91,* 110–115.

7. Holmes, T. H., & Rahe, R. H. (1967). The social readjustment rating scale. *Journal of Psychosomatic Research, 11,* 213–218.

8. Straus (1980).

9. Justice, B., & Duncan, D. F. (1975, April-June). Physical abuse of children as a public health problem. *Public Health Reviews, 4,* 183–200.

10. Toffler, A. (1970). *Future shock.* New York: Random House.

11. Straus, M. A. (1980). Justice, B., & Duncan, D. F. (1976). Life crisis as a precursor to child abuse. *Public Health Reports, 91,* 110–115. Justice, B., & Justice, R. (1982). Etiology of physical abuse of children and dynamic of coercive treatment. In J. C. Hansen & R. Barnhill (Eds.), *Family therapy collections.* Rockville, MD: Aspen; Passman, R. H., & Mulhern, R. K. (1977). Maternal punitiveness as affected by situational stress: An experimental analogue of child abuse. *Journal of Abnormal Psychology, 86,* 565–569; Gaines, R., Sandgund, A., Green, A. H., & Power, E. (1978). Etiological factors in child maltreatment: A multivariate study of abusing, neglecting, and normal

mothers. *Journal of Abnormal Psychology, 87,* 531–540; Newberger, E. H., Reed, R. B., Daniel, J. H., Hyde, J. N., & Kotelchuck, M. (1977). Pediatric social illness: Toward an etiological classification. *Pediatrics, 60,* 178–185; Egeland, B., Breitenbucher, M., & Rosenberg, D. (1980). Prospective study of the significance of life stress in the etiology of child abuse. *Journal of Consulting and Clinical Psychology, 48,* 195–205; Doran, L. D. (1981). Mothers' disciplinary responses under controllable and uncontrollable stress: A child abuse analogue. *Dissertation Abstracts International, 42,* 2534A (University Microfilms No. 81–26, 094); Rosenberg, M. S., & Repucci, N. D. (1983). Abusive mothers: Perceptions of their own and their children's behavior. *Journal of Clinical and Consulting Psychology, 51,* 674– 682; Tyler, A. H. (1983). A comparison of child-abusing and non-abusing fathers on measures of marital adjustment, life stress, and social support. *Dissertation Abstracts International, 44,* 1610B (University Microfilms No. 83-19, 376).

12. Caplan, G. (1964). *Principles of preventive psychiatry* (p. 48). New York: Basic Books.

13. The mean score for the abusing parents was 234; for nonabusing parents it was 124. Any score above 150 has been classified by Holmes and Rahe as representing a life crisis. A score of 234 represents more than a mild life crisis but less than a major one (any score above 299) and is classified as moderate. Some abusing parents scored almost 650. The means for the abusing and control groups are significantly different at the .001 level, as determined by *t* test. (See Table 2 for a distribution of life changes scores for the two groups.)

14. Selye, H. (1956). *The stress of life* (pp. 31–33). New York: McGraw-Hill.

15. The difference between the two groups on this item had a chi-square probability of .0117 at 2 degrees of freedom.

16. The difference on this item had a chi-square probability of .0339 at 2 degrees of freedom.

17. Schiff, A. W., & Schiff, J. (1971, January). Passivity. *Transactional Analysis Journal, 1,* 1.

18. Justice, R., & Justice, B. (1975). TA work with child abuse. *Transactional Analysis Journal, 5,* 38–41.

19. The chi-square probabilities for the differences on these items were .0123, .008, less than .0000, and .0271, respectively, at 1 degree of freedom.

20. Auerbach, S. M. (1986). Assumptions of crisis theory and a temporal model of crisis intervention. In S. M. Auerbach & A. L. Stolberg (Eds.), *Crisis intervention with children and families* (p. 15). Washington, DC: Hemisphere.

21. Hiroto, D. S. & Seligman, M. E. P. (1975). Generality of learned helplessness in man. *Journal of Personality and Social Psychology, 90,* 311–327.

22. Justice, B., Calvert, A., & Justice, R. (1985). *Child Abuse & Neglect, 9.*

CHAPTER 2

1. Daro, D. (1988). *Confronting child abuse: Research for effective program design* (p. 46). New York: Free Press.
2. Kempe, C.H. (1971, February). Paediatric implications of the battered baby syndrome. *Archives of Disease in Childhood, 46*, 28–37.
3. Kempe (1971, February).
4. Morris, M. G., & Gould, R. W. (1963). Role reversal: A concept in dealing with the neglected/battered child syndrome. In *The neglected battered-child syndrome: Role reversal in parents.* New York: Child Welfare League of America.
5. Helfer, R. E. (1980). Developmental deficits which limit interpersonal skills. In C. H. Kempe & R. E. Helfer (Eds.), *The battered child* (3rd ed., p. 40). Chicago: University of Chicago Press.
6. Morris, M. G. (1966, January-February). Psychological miscarriage: An end to mother love. *Trans-Action, 3*, 8–13; Bishop, F. I. (1971, March). Children at risk. *Medical Journal of Australia, 1*, 623–628; Bakan, D. (1971). *Slaughter of the innocents.* San Francisco: Jossey-Bass; Gelles, R. J. (1973, July). Child abuse as psychopathology: A sociological critique and reformulation. *American Journal of Orthopsychiatry, 43*, 611–621.
7. Blumberg, M. L. (1974, January). Psychopathology of the abusing parent. *American Journal of Psychotherapy, 28*, 21–29; Paulson, M. J. 1974, Spring), Parents of the battered child. *Life-Threatening Behavior, 4*, 18–31.
8. Spinetta, J. J., & Rigler, D. (1972, April). The child-abusing parent: A psychological review. *Psychological Bulletin, 77*, 299–304.
9. Melnick, B., & Hurley, J.R. (1969). Distinctive personality attributes of child-abusing mothers. *Journal of Consulting and Clinical Psychology, 33*, 746–749; Sanders, R. W. (1972, December). Resistance to dealing with parents of battered children. *Pediatrics, 50*, 853–857.
10. Merrill, E. J. (1962). Physical abuse of children: An agency study. In V. De-Francis (Ed.), *Protecting the battered child*. Denver: American Humane Association.
11. Kempe (1971, February), p. 29.
12. Violent parents. (1971, November 6). *Lancet*, pp. 1017–1018.
13. Lascari, A. (1972, May). The abused child. *Journal of the Iowa Medical Society, 62*, 229–232; Blumberg (1974, January), 22.
14. Woolley, P. V., & Evans, W. A. (1955, June). Significance of skeletal lesions in infants resembling those of traumatic origin. *Journal of the American Medical Association, 158*, 539–543.
15. Lord, E., & Weisfeld, D. (1974). The abused child. In A. R. Roberts (Ed.), *Childhood deprivation* (pp. 64–83). Springfield, IL: Charles C. Thomas.

16. Zalba, S. (1971, July-August). Battered children. *Trans-Action, 8*, 58–61; Friedman, S. B. (1972). The need for intensive follow-up of abused children. In C. H. Kempe & R. E. Helfer (Eds.), *Helping the battered child* (p. 81). Philadelphia: Lippincott.

17. Galdston, R. (1965, October). Observations of children who have been physically abused and their parents. *American Journal of Psychiatry, 122*, 440–443.

18. Laury, G. V. (1970, September). The battered-child syndrome: Parental motivation, clinical aspects. *Bulletin of the New York Academy of Medicine, 46*, 681.

19. Spinetta & Rigler. (1972, April), pp. 296–304; Daro (1988), p. 46.

20. Helfer, R. E. (1974). *A self-instructional program on child abuse and neglect* (Unit I, p. 2). Chicago: Committee on Infant and Preschool Child of the American Academy of Pediatrics, and Denver: National Center for the Prevention and Treatment of Child Abuse.

21. Tracy, J. J., & Clark, E. H. (1974, May). Treatment for child abusers. *Social Work, 19*, 339; Lystad, M. H. (1975, April). Violence at home: A review of the literature. *American Journal of Orthopsychiatry, 45*, 328–345.

22. Hughes, R. C. (1974). A clinic's parent-performance training program for child abusers. *Hospital and Community Psychiatry, 25*, 779–782; Savino, A. B., & Sanders, R. W. (1973, March). Working with abusive parents: Group therapy and home visits. *American Journal of Nursing, 73*, 482–484.

23. Gil, D. G. (1970). *Violence against children*. Cambridge, MA: Harvard University Press.

24. Gil, D. G. (1981). The United States versus child abuse. In L. Pelton (Ed.), *Social context of child abuse and neglect* (p. 294). New York: Human Services Press.

25. Gil (1981).

26. Pelton, L. (1981). *Social context of child abuse and neglect* (p. 32). New York: Human Services Press.

27. *Time*. (1975, March 17) p. 88.

28. Fontana, V. J. (1964, January). The neglect and abuse of children. *New York State Journal of Medicine, 64*, 215.

29. Bennie, E. H., & Sclare, A. B. (1969, January). The battered child syndrome. *American Journal of Psychiatry, 125*, 975–979.

30. Blumberg, M. L. (1964, Winter). When parents hit out. *Twentieth Century, 173*, 39–44; and Steinmetz, S., & Straus, M. (1971). *Some myths about violence in the family*. Paper presented before the American Sociological Association, Denver.

31. Spinetta & Rigler (1972, April), p. 301.

32. Gil, D. G. (1975, April). Unraveling child abuse. *American Journal of Orthopsychiatry, 45*, 352.

33. Lancaster, J. B., & Gelles, R. J. (1987). *Introduction*. In R. J. Gelles & J. B. Lancaster (Eds.), *Child abuse and neglect: Biosocial dimensions* (p. 5). New York: Aldine de Gruyter.

34. Klaus, M. H., & Kennell, J. H. (1976). *Maternal-infant bonding*. St. Louis, MO: C. V. Mosby.
35. Lancaster & Gelles (1987), p. 7.
36. Korbin, J. E. (1987). Child maltreatment in cross-cultural perspective: Vulnerable children and circumstances. In R. J. Gelles & J. B. Lancaster (Eds.), *Child abuse and neglect: Biosocial dimensions* (pp. 38–43). New York: Aldine de Gruyter.
37. Scrimshaw, S. (1978). Infant mortality and behavior in the regulation of family size. *Population and Development Review, 4*(3), 383–403.
38. Straus, M. A. (1980). Stress and child abuse. In C. H. Kempe & R. E. Helfer (Eds.), *The battered child* (3rd ed., pp. 86–103). Chicago: University of Chicago Press.

CHAPTER 3

1. Helfer, R. E. (1974). *A self-instructional program on child abuse and neglect* (Unit I, p. 2). Chicago: Committee on Infant and Preschool Child, American Academy of Pediatrics, and Denver: National Center for the Prevention and Treatment of Child Abuse and Neglect.
2. Bowen, M. (1971). Family therapy and family group therapy. In H. I. Kaplan & B. J. Sadock (Eds.), *Comprehensive group psychotherapy* (pp. 384–421). Baltimore: Williams & Wilkins.
3. Bishop, F. I. (1971, March). Children at risk. *Medical Journal of Australia, 1*, 623–628.
4. Isaacs, S. (1972, July). Neglect, cruelty and battering. *British Medical Journal, 3*, 224–226.
5. Kempe, C. H. (1971, February). Paediatric implications of the battered baby syndrome. *Archives of Disease in Childhood, 46*, 28–37.
6. Justice, B., & Duncan, D. F. (1975, April–June). Physical abuse of children as a public health problem. *Public Health Reviews, 4*, 183–200.
7. Flynn, W. R. (1970, September). Frontier justice: A contribution to the theory of child battery. *American Journal of Psychiatry, 127*, 375–379.
8. Bishop (1971, March).
9. Justice, B., & Justice, R. (1974, February 15). *A psychosocial model of child abuse: Intervention strategies and group techniques*. Paper presented before the Clinical and Research Training Seminar, Texas Research Institute of Mental Science, Houston; Justice & Duncan (1975, April-June).
10. Jenkins, R. L. (1970, February). Interrupting the family cycle of violence. *Journal of the Iowa Medical Society, 30*, 85–89; Lystad, M. H. (1975, April). Violence at home: A review of the literature. *American Journal of Orthopsychiatry, 45*, 328–345.

11. Bowen, M. (1966, October). The use of family theory in clinical practice. *Comprehensive Psychiatry*, 7, 345–374.

12. Anonymous. (1972). Toward the differentiation of a self in one's own family. In J. L. Framo (Ed.), *Family interaction* (p. 119). New York: Springer.

13. Bowen (1966, October), pp. 360–361.

14. Bowen (1971), p. 398.

15. Whitaker, C. (1975, March 21). Family Therapy Workshop. Presented at the Southeast Institute Second Annual Spring Conference, Raleigh, NC.

16. Bowen (1966, October), p. 360.

17. Bowen (1966, October), pp. 359–360.

18. Bowen (1966, October), pp. 359–360.

19. Gordon, T. (1970). *Parent effectiveness training* (pp. 121–138). New York: Wyden.

20. Martin, H. (1972). The child and his development. In C. H. Kempe & R. E. Helfer (Eds.), *Helping the battered child and his family* (p. 104). Philadelphia: Lippincott; Helfer (1974).

21. Steele, B. F., as quoted in Kempe (1971, February), p. 30.

22. Schiff, A. W., & Schiff, J. L. (1971, January). Passivity. *Transactional Analysis Journal*, 1, p. 1.

23. Schiff & Schiff (1971, January), p. 71.

24. Schiff & Schiff (1971, January), p. 72.

25. Schiff & Schiff (1971, January), pp. 72–73.

26. Berne, E. (1966). *Principles of group treatment* (p. 220). New York: Oxford University Press.

27. Steiner, C. (1971). *Games alcoholics play* (pp. 3–4). New York: Grove Press.

28. Schiff & Schiff (1971, January), p. 72.

29. Perls, F. (1969). *Gestalt therapy verbatim*. Lafayette, CA: Real People Press.

30. Paulsen, M. G. (1968). The law and abused children. In R. E. Helfer & C. H. Kempe (Eds.), *The battered child* (p. 185). Chicago: University of Chicago Press.

31. Berne, E. (1972). *What do you say after you say hello?* (pp. 106–107). New York: Grove Press; Berne (1966), p. 36.

32. Justice, B., & Justice, R. (1973, August). *"Siamese-twinning" in scripts of child batterers*. Paper presented before the International Transactional Analysis Association Summer Conference, San Francisco.

33. Steiner (1971), p. 29.

CHAPTER 4

1. Justice, B., & Duncan, D. F. (1975, April–June). Physical abuse of children as a public health problem. *Public Health Reviews*, 4, 183–200.

2. Radbill, S. X. (1968). A history of child abuse and infanticide. In R. E. Helfer & C. H. Kempe (Eds.), *The battered child* (pp. 3–21). Chicago: University of Chicago Press.

3. Light, R. J. (1973, November). Abused and neglected children in America: A study of alternative policies. *Harvard Educational Review, 43*, p. 559.

4. Light (1973, November), p. 559.

5. Gibbon, E. (1899). *The decline and fall of the Roman Empire* (pp. 352–353). New York: Collier.

6. Light (1973, November), p. 559.

7. Zalba, S. (1971, July-August). Battered children. *Trans-Action, 8*, 58–61.

8. Sage, W. (1975, July). Violence in the children's room. *Human Behavior, 4*, 42.

9. Although the New York Society for the Prevention of Cruelty to Children has been in existence for a century now, the latest reports indicate that the Society for the Prevention of Cruelty to Animals still has more contributors; Light (1973, November), p. 559.

10. Katz, S., Ambrosino, L., McGrath, M., & Sawitsky, K. (1977). Legal research on child abuse and neglect: Past and future. *Family Law Quarterly, 11*(2), 151–184.

11. Radbill, S. X. (1968), pp. 3–21.

12. Nelson, B. (1984). *Making an issue of child abuse*. Chicago: University of Chicago Press.

13. Katz, Ambrosino, McGrath, & Sawitsky (1977).

14. Daro, D. (1988). *Confronting child abuse: Research for effective program design* (pp. 15–16). New York: Free Press.

15. Daro (1988), p. 16.

16. Justice & Duncan (1975, April-June), pp. 184–185.

17. Bishop, F. I. (1971, March). Children at risk. *Medical Journal of Australia, 1*, 623.

18. Daro (1988), p. 12.

19. Gil, D. G. (1971, November). Violence against children. *Journal of Marriage and the Family, 33*, 637–648.

20. Straus, M., Gelles, R., & Steinmetz, S. (1980). *Behind closed doors: Violence in the American family*. Garden City, NY: Anchor Press/Doubleday.

21. Straus, M., & Gelles, R. (1986, August). Societal change and change in family violence from 1975–1985 as revealed by two national surveys. *Journal of Marriage and the Family, 48*, 465–479.

22. Gil, D. G. (1970). *Violence against children*. Cambridge, MA: Harvard University Press; Kempe, C. H. (1971, February). Paediatric implications of the battered baby syndrome. *Archives of Disease in Childhood, 46*, 28–37.

23. Helfer, R. E. (1982) A review of the literature on the prevention of child abuse and neglect. *Child Abuse & Neglect, 6*, 251–261.

24. NCPCA [National Committee for the Prevention of Child Abuse]. (1987, July/August). *Memorandum*. Chicago: Author.

25. Burns, R., as quoted in Fontana, V. J. (1973). *Somewhere a child is crying* (p. 19.). New York: Macmillan.

26. Lynch, A. (1975, March). Child abuse in the school-age population. *Journal of School Health, 35*, 141–148.

27. Kempe (1971, February), pp. 28–37.

28. Westat and Development Associates. (1981, September). *National Study of the incidence and severity of child abuse and neglect.* Prepared for the National Center on Child Abuse and Neglect under Contract no. 105-76-1137.

29. Daro (1988), p. 14.

30. American Association for Protecting Children. (1985). *Highlights of official child neglect and abuse reporting.* Denver: American Humane Society; Daro, D., & Mitchel, L. (1987). *Deaths due to maltreatment soar: The results of the eighth semi-annual fifty state survey.* Chicago: National Committee for the Prevention of Child Abuse.

31. Daro (1988), p. 14.

32. NCPCA [National Committee for the Prevention of Child Abuse] (1987, July/August).

33. Helfer (1982), p. 253.

34. Gil (1970), pp. 58–60.

35. Zalba (1971, July-August), pp. 58–61.

36. Gil (1970), p. 116.

37. Bennie, E. H., & Sclare, A. B. (1969, January). The battered child syndrome. *American Journal of Psychiatry, 125*, 975–979; Steele, B. F., & Pollock, C. (1968). A psychiatric study of parents who abuse infants and small children. In R. E. Helfer & C. H. Kempe (Eds.), *The battered child* (pp. 89–133). Chicago: University of Chicago Press.

38. Gil (1970), p. 109.

39. NCPCA (1987, July/August)

40. Jason, J., Andeereck, N., Marks, J., & Tyler, C. (1982). Child abuse in Georgia: A method to evaluate risk factors and reporting biases. *American Journal of Public Health, 72*, 1353–1358.

41. Lystad, M. H. (1975, April). Violence at home: A review of the literature. *American Journal of Orthopsychiatry, 45*, 334.

42. Newberger, E. (1983, April 11). *The helping hand strikes again.* Testimony given before the Subcommittee on Family and Human Services, Committee on Labor and Human Resources, U. S. Senate.

43. Gil (1970), p. 112.

44. Jason, Andeereck, Marks, & Tyler (1982).

45. Gil (1970), pp. 110–111.

46. Daro (1988), p. 53.

47. Gil (1970), pp. 113–114, 117.

48. Green, A. H. (1976, Summer). A psychodynamic approach to the study and treatment of child abusing parents. *Journal of the American Academy of Child*

Psychology, 15, 414–442; and Kempe, R. S., & Kempe, C. H. (1978). *Child abuse.* Cambridge, MA: Harvard University Press.

49. Schilling, R. F. S., Schinke, P., Blythe, B., & Barth, R. (1982, October). Child maltreatment and mentally retarded parents: Is there a relationship? *Mental Retardation, 20,* 205.

50. Daro (1988), pp. 52–53.

51. Olson, R. (1976, January). Index of suspicion: Screening of child abusers. *American Journal of Nursing, 76,* 108–110.

52. Milner, J., & Wimberly, R. (1979, January). An inventory for identification of child abusers. *Journal of Clinical Psychology, 35,* 95–100.

53. Kempe, C. H., Silverman, F., Steele, B., Droegemueller, W., & Silver, H. (1962, July). The battered child syndrome. *Journal of the American Medical Association, 181,* 17–24; Galdston, R. (1965, October). Observations of children who have been physically abused and their parents. *American Journal of Psychiatry, 122,* 440–443; Resnick, P. (1969, September). Child murder by parents: A psychiatric review of filicide. *American Journal of Psychiatry, 126,* 325–334; and Bennie, E. H. & Sclare, A. B. (1969, January). The battered child syndrome. *American Journal of Psychiatry, 125,* 975–979.

54. Gil (1970), p. 105.

55. NCPCA [National Committee for the Prevention of Child Abuse]. (1987, July/August). *Newsletter.*

56. Daro (1988), p. 36.

57. Lynch (1975, March), p. 141.

58. *Lift a finger: The teacher's role in combating child abuse.* (p. 35) (1975). Houston: Education Professions Development Consortium C.

59. Thompson, E. M., Paget, N. W., Bates, D. W., Mesch, M., & Putnam, T. I. (1971). *Child abuse: A community challenge* (p. 109). East Aurora, NY: Henry Stewart.

60. Gil (1970), p. 104.

61. Bishop (1971, March), p. 623.

62. Daro (1988), p. 67.

63. Zalba (1971, July-August), pp. 58–61.

64. Bennie & Sclare (1969, January), pp. 975–979; Gil (1970), p. 110.

65. Light (1973, November), p. 574.

66. Daro (1988), p. 67-68.

67. Thompson (1971), p. 116.

68. Gil (1970), pp. 118–119.

69. Daro (1988), p. 52.

70. Harrington, J. (1972, January). Violence: A clinical viewpoint. *British Medical Journal, 1,* 228–231.

71. Milowe, I. D., as quoted in Gil (1970), pp. 29–30.

72. Justice & Duncan (1975, April-June), pp. 29–30.

73. Martin, H. (1972). The child and his development. In C. H. Kempe & R. E. Helfer (Eds.), *Helping the battered child and his family* (p. 106). Philadelphia:

Lippincott; Flynn, W. R. (1970, September). Frontier justice: A contribution to the theory of child battery. *American Journal of Psychiatry, 127,* 375–379.

74. Smith, J. M., & Smith, D. E. P. (1966). *Child management: A program for parents* (p. l). Ann Arbor, MI: Ann Arbor Publishers.

75. Gil (1970), p. 118.

76. Smith, C. A. (1973, August). The battered child. *New England Journal of Medicine, 289,* 322–323.

77. Gil (1970), pp. 112–113.

78. Gil (1970), p. 118.

79. Thompson (1971), pp. 123–124.

80. Thompson (1971), pp. 123–124.

81. Gil (1970), pp. 118–121.

82. Daro (1988), p. 66.

83. Daro (1988), pp. 67–68.

84. Daro (1988), p. 66.

CHAPTER 5

1. Fontana V. J. (1964, January). The neglect and abuse of children. *New York State Journal of Medicine, 64,* 218.

2. Kiresuk, T. J., & Sherman, R. E. (1968, December). Goal attainment scaling: A general method for evaluating comprehensive community mental health programs. *Community Mental Health Journal, 4,* 443–453.

3. Isaacs, S. (1972, July). Neglect, cruelty and battering. *British Medical Journal, 3,* 224–226.

4. In the majority of abuse cases in Harris County, the court does not intervene and attempts to alleviate the problem are made by child welfare workers who counsel parents while the child remains in the home. In the most serious cases, however, the child is removed.

5. Helfer, R. E. (1974). *A self-instructional program on child abuse and neglect.* Chicago: Committee on Infant and Preschool Child of the American Academy of Pediatrics, and Denver: National Center for the Prevention and Treatment of Child Abuse and Neglect; Kempe, C. H.(1971, February). Paediatric implications of the battered baby syndrome. *Archives of Disease in Childhood, 46,* 34; Kempe, C. H. (1973, April). A practical approach to the protection of the abused child and rehabilitation of the abusing parent [panel discussion]. *Pediatrics, 51,* 791.

6. Cohn, A. H., & Daro, D. (1987). Is treatment too late?: What ten years of evaluative research tell us. *Child Abuse & Neglect, 11,* 433–442, 487.

7. Bradshaw, J. (1988). *Bradshaw on: The family* (p. 6). Deerfield Beach, FL: Health Communications.

8. Ellis, A. (1973). *Humanistic psychology* (pp. 17–19). New York: Julian Press; Lazarus, A. A. (Ed.). (1972). *Clinical behavior therapy*. New York: Brunner/Mazel; Wolpe, J. (1969). *The practice of behavioral therapy*. New York: Pergamon Press.

9. Kiresuk & Sherman (1968, December).

10. Straus, M. A. (1980). Stress and child abuse. In C. H. Kempe & R. E. Helfer (Eds.), *The battered child* (3rd ed., pp. 86–103). Chicago: University of Chicago Press.

11. Daniel, J. H., Hampton, R. L., & Newberger, E. H. (1983, October). Child abuse and accidents in black families: A controlled comparative study. *American Journal of Orthopsychiatry, 53*, 645–653.

12. Lenoski's study also suggested that abusing parents not only avoid other people but were raised to shun pets. Only 4% of the abusive parents reported early exposure to pets, compared with 86% of the nonabusers. Lenoski, E. F. (1973). *Translating injury data into preventive and health care services—Physical child abuse*. Unpublished paper, Division of Emergency Medicine, University of Southern California Medical Center, Los Angeles.

13. Gabarino, J. (1977). The human ecology of child maltreatment: A conceptual model for research. *Journal of Marriage and the Family, 39*, 721–735.

14. Light, R. J. (1973, November). Abused and neglected children in America: A study of alternative policies. *Harvard Educational Review, 43*, 587–588; Merrill, E. J. (1962). Physical abuse of children: An agency study. In V. DeFrancis (Ed.), *Protecting the battered child*. Denver: American Humane Association.

15. Gelles, R. J. (1980). A profile of violence toward children in the United States. In G. Gerbner, C. J. Ross, & E. Zigler (Eds.), *Child abuse: An agenda for action* (pp. 82–105). New York: Oxford University Press.

16. Oates, K. (1986). *Child abuse and neglect: What eventually happens*. New York: Brunner/Mazel.

17. Straus (1980).

18. Mash, E. J., & Johnson, C. (1983, Spring). Sibling interactions of hyperactive and normal children and their relationship to reports of maternal stress and self-esteem. *Journal of Clinical Child Psychology, 12*(1), 91–99.

19. Helfer, R. E. (1974).

20. Kiresuk & Sherman (1968), p. 595.

21. Daro, D. (1988). *Confronting child abuse: Research for effective program design* (p. 121). New York: Free Press.

22. Cohn, A. H., & Daro, D. (1987).

23. Kempe, R. S., & Kempe, C. H. (1978). The untreatable family. In R. S. Kempe & C. H. Kempe, *Child abuse* (pp. 128–131). Cambridge, MA: Harvard University Press.

24. Helfer, R. E. (1974), pp. 4–10.

25. Kempe, C. H. (1973, April). A practical approach to the protection of the abused child and rehabilitation of the abusing parent. *Pediatrics, 51*, 809.

26. Cohn, A. H., Ridge, S. S., & Collignon, F. C. (1975, May-June). Evaluating innovative treatment programs in child abuse and neglect. *Children Today, 4*, 12.

27. Martin, H. P., & Beezley, P. (1974, Fall-Winter). Prevention and the consequences of child abuse. *Journal of Operational Psychiatry, 6*, 72.

28. Kiresuk & Sherman (1968), p. 449.

29. Kempe & Kempe (1978).

30. Jones, D. P. H. (1987). The untreatable family. *Child Abuse & Neglect, 11*, 409–414.

31. Meadow, R. (1977). Munchausen syndrome by proxy: The hinterland of child abuse. *Lancet, 2*, 343–345.

32. Jones (1987).

33. Cohn & Daro (1987), p. 438.

CHAPTER 6

1. Haimowitz, N. R., & Haimowitz, M L. (1973). Introduction to transactional analysis. In M. L. Haimowitz & N. R. Haimowitz (Eds.), *Human development* (pp. 318–352). New York: Thomas Y. Crowell.

2. Cohn, A. H., & Daro, D. (1987). Is treatment too late: What ten years of evaluative research tell us. *Child Abuse & Neglect, 11*, 437.

3. Hightower, N. (1989, March). Working with angry and violent patients in group psychotherapy. *Journal of the Houston Group Psychotherapy Society, 3*,15-33.

4. Schmitt, B. D. (1987). Social support and child maltreatment: A review of the evidence. *Child Abuse & Neglect, 11*, 431.

5. Schmitt (1987), p. 421.

6. Ellis, A. (1973). Rational-emotive therapy. In R. Corsini (Ed.), *Current psychotherapies* (pp. 167–206). Itasca, IL: Peacock.

7. Kempe, C. H. (1969, October). The battered child and the hospital. *Hospital Practice, 4*, 52; Lascari, A. D. (1972, May). The abused child. *Journal of the Iowa Medical Society, 62*, 231.

8. Ellis, A. (1973). *Humanistic psychology* (pp. 17–19). New York: Julian Press.

9. Davoren, E. (1974). The role of the social worker. In R. E. Helfer & C. H. Kempe (Eds.), *The battered child* (pp. 142–144). Chicago: University of Chicago Press.

10. *American heritage dictionary.* (1982). Boston: Houghton Mifflin.

11. Savino, A. B., & Sanders, R. W. (1973, March). Working with abusive parents: Group therapy and home visits. *American Journal of Nursing, 73*, 483.

12. Helfer, R. E. (1974). *A self-instructional program on child abuse and neglect* (Unit 3, p. 14). Chicago: Committee on Infant and Preschool Child of the American Academy of Pediatrics; and Denver: National Center for the Prevention and Treatment of Child Abuse and Neglect.
13. Sanders, R. W. (1972, December), Resistance to dealing with parents of battered children. *Pediatrics, 50,* 855.
14. Pollock, C., as quoted in C. A. David. (1974, October). The use of the confrontation technique in the battered child syndrome. *American Journal of Psychotherapy, 28,* 547.
15. Sanders (1972, December), p. 855.
16. Berne, E. (1964). Games people play. New York: Grove Press.
17. Holmes, S. A., Barnhart, C., Cantoni, L., & Reymer, E. (1975, January). Working with the parent in child abuse cases. *Social Casework, 56,* 5.
18. Davoren (1974), pp. 142–144.
19. Lyon, L. (1987, April). Therapeutic dilemmas in child abuse reporting. *AHP Perspective,* p. 6 Association for Humanistic Psychology.
20. Boyd, M. J. (1988, January). Letter to the *APA Monitor, 19*(2), 2.

CHAPTER 7

1. Bradshaw, J. (1988). *Bradshaw on: The family* (p. 134). Deerfield Beach, FL: Health Communications.
2. Reidy, T. J. (1977). The aggressive characteristics of abused and neglected children. *Journal of Clinical Psychology, 33,* 1140–1145.
3. George, C., & Main, M. (1979). Social interactions of young, abused children: Approach avoidance and aggression. *Child Development, 50,* 306–318.
4. Jacobson, R. S., & Straker, G. (1982). Peer group interaction of physically abused children. *Child Abuse & Neglect, 6,* 321–327.
5. Aber, J. L., & Cicchetti, D. (1984). The socio-emotional development of maltreated children: An empirical and theoretical analysis. In H. E. Fitzgerald, B. M. Lester, & M. W. Yogman (Eds.), *Theory and research in behavioral pediatrics* (pp. 147–205). New York: Plenum.
6. Cicchetti, D., Carlson, V., Braunwald, K. G., & Aber, J. L. (1987). The sequelae of child maltreatment. In R. J. Gelles & J. B. Lancaster (Eds.), *Child abuse and neglect: Biosocial dimensions* (p. 278). New York: Aldine de Gruyter.
7. Egeland, B., & Sroufe, L. A. (1981). Attachment and early maltreatment. *Child Development, 52,* 44–52.
8. Cicchetti, Carlson, Braunwald, & Aber (1987), p. 281.
9. Cicchetti, Carlson, Braunwald, & Aber (1987), p. 281.
10. Bowlby, J. (1985). *Attachment and loss. Vol. I: Attachment.* New York: Basic Books.

11. Sroufe, L. A., & Waters, E. (1977). Attachment as an organizational construct. *Child Development, 48,* 1184–1199.

12. Spitz, R. A. (1965). *The first year of life* (pp. 122–126). New York: International Universities Press.

13. Koblenzer, C. S. (1988). Stress and the skin. *Advances, 5*(4), 27–32.

14. Matas, L., Arend, R., & Sroufe, L. A. (1978). Continuity of adaptation in the second year: The relationship between quality of attachment and later competence. *Child Development, 49,* 547–556.

15. Egeland, B., Jacobvitz, D., & Papatola, K. (1987). Intergenerational continuity of abuse. In R. J. Gelles & J. B. Lancaster (Eds.), *Child abuse and neglect: Biosocial dimensions* (p. 258). New York: Aldine de Gruyter.

16. Bowlby, J. (1980). *Attachment and loss. Vol. 3: Loss, sadness and depression.* New York: Basic Books.

17. Egeland, Jacobvitz, & Papatola (1987), p. 258.

18. Cicchetti, Carlson, Braunwald, & Aber (1987), p. 289.

19. Cicchetti, Carlson, Braunwald, & Aber (1987), p. 293.

20. Cicchetti, Carlson, Braunwald, & Aber (1987), p. 293.

21. Egeland, Jacobvitz, & Papatola (1987), pp. 259–266.

22. Egeland, Jacobvitz, & Papatola (1987), p. 265.

23. Johnson, J. H. (1986). *Life events as stressors in childhood and adolescence.* Beverly Hills, CA: Sage.

24. Cowen, E. L., & Work, W. C. (1988). Resilient children, psychological wellness, and primary prevention. *American Journal of Community Psychology, 16*(4), 596.

25. Egeland, Jacobvitz, & Papatola (1987), p. 267.

26. Egeland, Jacobvitz, & Papatola (1987), pp. 268–275.

27. Kaufman, J., & Zigler, E. (1987, April). Do abused children become abusive parents? *American Journal of Orthopsychiatry, 57,* 186–192.

28. *Yale University News Release.* (1987, September 22). New Haven, CT.

29. Mrazek, P. J., & Mrazek, D. A. (1987). Resilience in child maltreatment victims: A conceptual exploration. *Child Abuse & Neglect, 11,* 357–366.

30. Mrazek & Mrazek (1987), 358.

31. Recklin, R., & Lavett, D. K. (1987). Those who broke the cycle: Therapy with non-abusive adults who were physically abused as children. *Psychotherapy, 24,* 790–798.

32. Coleman, D. (1987). Thriving despite hardship: Key childhood traits identified. *New York Times,* October 13, pp. 19–22.

33. Werner, E. E., & Smith, R. S. (1977). *Kauai's children come of age.* Honolulu: University of Hawaii Press.

34. Garmezy, N. (1985). Stress resistant children: The search for protective factors. In J. E. Stevenson (Ed.), *Recent research in developmental psychopathology. Journal of Child Psychology and Psychiatry. Book Supplement No. 4* (pp. 213–233). Oxford: Pergamon.

35. Anthony, E. J., & Bertram, J. C. (Eds.) (1987). *The invulnerable child.* New York: Guilford Press.
36. Cowen, E. L. (1980). The wooing of primary prevention. *American Journal of Community Psychology, 8,* 258–284.

CHAPTER 8

1. Parke, R. D., & Collmer, C. W. (1975). Child abuse: An interdisciplinary analysis. In E. M. Hetherington (Ed.), *Review of child development research* (pp. 509–590). Chicago: University of Chicago Press.
2. Solnit, A. J. (1980). Too much reporting, too little service: Root and prevention of child abuse. In G. Gerbner, C. J. Ross, & E. Zigler (Eds.), *Child abuse: An agenda for action* (pp. 135–146). New York: Oxford University Press.
3. Cohn, A. H., & Daro, D. (1987). Is treatment too late: What ten years of evaluative research tell us. *Child Abuse & Neglect, 11,* 439.
4. Cohn & Daro (1987), 439.
5. Malone, C. A. (1979). Child psychiatry and family therapy: An overview. *Journal of the American Academy of Child Psychiatry, 18,* 4–21; Mann, E. & McDermott, J. F. (1983). Play therapy for victims of child abuse and neglect. In C. E. Schaefer, & K. J. O'Connor (Eds.), *Handbook of play therapy* (pp. 283–307). New York: Wiley.
6. *Lift a finger: The teacher's role in combating child abuse* (1975). Houston: Education Professions Development Consortium C, p. 35.
7. *Lift a finger,* p. 35.
8. Identifying the battered or molested child (1972). In *Handbook for School Staff Members.* Palo Alto, CA: Palo Alto School District.
9. Identifying the battered or molested child (1972), p. 226.
10. *Lift a finger,* p. 34.
11. *Lift a finger,* p. 34.
12. *Guidelines for schools teachers, nurses, counselors, and administrators* (1971). Denver: American Humane Association, p. 221.
13. Kempe, C. H. (1969, October). The battered child and the hospital. *Hospital Practice, 4,* 45.
14. Kempe (1969, October), 45.
15. Morris, M. G., et al., as quoted in F. M. Nomura (1960), The battered child syndrome. *Hawaii Medical Journal, 25,* 390.
16. Morris, M. G., et al., in Nomura (1960), 389.
17. Mann & McDermott (1983), p. 285.
18. Stewart, M. S., Farquhar, L. C., Dicharry, D. C., Glick, D. R., & Martin, P. W. (1986, April). Group therapy: A treatment of choice for young victims of child abuse. *International Journal of Group Psychotherapy, 36,* 265.

19. Stewart, Farquhar, Dicharry, Glick, & Martin (1986), 266.
20. Mann & McDermott (1983); Solnit (1980); Stewart, Farquhar, Dicharry, Glick, & Martin (1986).
21. Stewart, Farquhar, Dicharry, Glick & Martin (1986), 262.
22. Stewart, Farquhar, Dicharry, Glick & Martin (1986), 273.
23. Stewart, Farquhar, Dicharry, Glick & Martin (1986), 269.
24. Steele, B. F. (1977). *Psychological dimensions of child abuse*. Paper presented before the American Association for the Advancement of Science, Denver.
25. Stewart, Farquhar, Dicharry, Glick & Martin (1986), 270.
26. Suomi, S. J. (1973). Surrogate rehabilitation of monkeys reared in total social isolation. *Journal of Child Psychology and Psychiatry, 14*, 71–77; Suomi, S. J., & Harlow, H. F. (1975). The role and reason of peer friendship in rhesus monkeys. In M. Lewis & L. A. Rosenblum (Eds.), *Peer relations and friendship: ETS Symposium on the Origins of Behavior*. New York: Wiley.; Suomi, S. J., & Harlow, H. F. (1976). Monkeys without play. In J. Bruner, A. Jolly & K. Sylva (Eds.), *Play: Its role development and evolution*. Harmondsworth, England: Penguin Books.
27. Stewart, Farquhar, Dicharry, Glick & Martin. (1986), 274–275.
28. Kistner, M. C., & Patterson, C. J. (1980). Children's conceptions of causes of illness: Understanding of contagion and use of immanent justice. *Child Development, 51*, 839–846.

CHAPTER 9

1. Blum, H. (1974). *Planning for health: Development and application of social change theory*. New York: Human Sciences Press.
2. Helfer, R. E. (1982). A review of the literature on the prevention of child abuse and neglect. *Child Abuse & Neglect, 6*, 251–261.
3. Daro, D. (1988). *Confronting child abuse: Research for effective program design* (p. 124). New York: Free Press.
4. *Crisis in child mental health: Challenge for the 1970s, report of the Joint Commission on Mental Health of Children*. (1970). (pp. 3–4). New York: Harper & Row.
5. Bakan, D. (1971). *Slaughter of the innocents* (p. 119). San Francisco: Jossey-Bass.
6. Kempe, C. H. (1971, February). Paediatric implications of the battered baby syndrome. *Archives of Disease in Childhood, 46*, 36.
7. Olds, D. (1984). Case studies of factors interfering with nurse home visitors' promotion of positive care-giving methods in high-risk families. *Early Child Development and Care, 16*, 149–166.
8. Olds, D., Chamberlin, R., & Tattlebaum, R. (1986). Preventing child abuse and neglect: A randomized trial of nurse home visitation. *Pediatrics, 78*, 65–78.

9. Dawson, P., Robinson, J., & Johnson, C. (1982). Informal social support as an intervention. *Zero to Three: Bulletin of the National Center for Clinical Infant Programs, 3*(2), 1–5; Affholter, D. Connell, D., & Nauta, M. (1983). Evaluation of the child and family resource program: Early evidence of parent-child interaction effects. *Evaluation Review, 7*(1), 65–79; Gray, E. (1983). *Final report: Collaborative research of community and minority group action to prevent child abuse and neglect, Vol. 1: Perinatal interventions.* Chicago: National Committee for Prevention of Child Abuse.

10. Gray, J., Cutler, C. A., Dean, J. G., & Kempe, C. H. (1979). Prediction and prevention of child abuse and neglect. *Journal of Social Issues, 35*(2), 127–139.

11. Frederickson, C., Boger, R. , Stuzok, B., & Hartman, M. (1982). *Parenting: The tender touch.* East Lansing: Michigan State University.

12. Simmons, J. T. (1986). *Programs that work: Evidence of primary prevention of child abuse* (pp. 22–23). Houston, TX: Greater Houston Committee for the Prevention of Child Abuse.

13. Simmons (1986), pp. 32–33.

14. Simmons (1986), pp. 44–45.

15. Craig, W. S. (1946). *Child and adolescent life in health and disease.* Edinburgh, Scotland: E. & S. Livingstone.

16. Kempe, C. H. (1973, April). A practical approach to the protection of the abused child and rehabilitation of the abusing parent. *Pediatrics, 51,* 805.

17. Justice, B., Justice, R., & Kraft, I. A. (1974, April). Early warning signs of violence: Is a triad enough? *American Journal of Psychiatry, 131,* 457–459.

18. Justice, B. (Ed.). (1973). *Your child's behavior.* Project for the Early Prevention of Violence. Houston: School of Public Health, University of Texas.

19. Milner, J. (1980). *The Child Abuse Potential Inventory Manual.* Webster, NC: Psytec Corporation.

20. Murphy, S., Arkow, B., & Nicola, R. M. (1985). Prenatal prediction of child abuse and neglect: A prospective study. *Child Abuse & Neglect, 9,* 225–235.

21. *Highlights of official child neglect and abuse reporting—1986.* (1988). Denver: American Association for Protecting Children, Division of American Humane Association.

22. Helfer, R. E. (1975, May-June). Why most physicians don't get involved in child abuse cases and what to do about it. *Children Today, 4,* 28–32.

23. Morris, M. G. (1966, January-February). Psychological miscarriage: An end to mother love. *Trans-Action, 3,* 11.

24. Bishop, F. I. (1971, March). Children at risk. *Medical Journal of Australia, 1,* 627.

25. Altemeier, W. A., O'Conner, S., Vietze, P., Sandler, H., & Sherrod, K. (1982, May). Antecedents of child abuse. *Journal of Pediatrics, 100*(5), 823–829.

26. Schmitt, B. D., & Kempe, C. H. (1975, March). The pediatrician's role in child abuse and neglect. *Current Problems in Pediatrics, 5,* 35–45.

27. Schmitt & Kempe (1975, March).

28. Kempe, C. H., & Hopkins, J. (1975, March-April-May). The public health nurse's role in the prevention of child abuse and neglect. *Public Health Currents, 15,* 1.

29. Kempe & Hopkins (1975, March-April-May), p. 2.

30. Kempe & Hopkins (1975, March-April-May), p. 2.

31. Kempe & Hopkins (1975, March-April-May), p. 2.

32. Elmer, E. (1967). *Children in jeopardy* (p. 49). Pittsburgh: University of Pittsburgh Press; Klein, M., & Stern, L. (1971, July). Low birth weight and the battered child syndrome. *American Journal of Diseases of Children, 122,* 15–18; Lenoski, E. F. (1973). *Translating injury data into preventive and health care service—Physical child abuse.* Unpublished paper, Division of Emergency Pediatrics, University of Southern California Medical Center, Los Angeles; Martin, H. P., & Beezley, P. (1974, Fall-Winter). Prevention and the consequences of child abuse. *Journal of Operational Psychiatry, 6,* 73; Mussen, P. H., Conger, J. J., & Kagan, J. (1974). *Child development and personality.* New York: Harper & Row; Elmer, E. (1971). Child abuse: A symptom of family crisis. In E. Pavenstedt & V. W. Bernard (Eds.), *Crisis of family disorganization: Programs to soften their impact on children* (p. 55). New York: Behavioral Publications.

33. Powell, G. F., Brasel, J. A., Raiti, S., & Blizzard, R. M. (1967). Emotional deprivation and growth retardation simulating idiopathic hypopituitarism, II: Endocrinological evaluation of the syndrome. *New England Journal of Medicine, 276,* 1271–1283.

34. Scott, S., & Richards, M. (1979). Nursing low birthweight babies on lambswool. *Lancet, 8124*(1), 1028.

35. Nuckolls, K. B., Cassel, J., & Kaplan, B. H. (1972). Psychosocial assets, life crisis, and the prognosis of pregnancy. *American Journal of Epidemiology, 95,* 431–441.

36. Fanaroff, A. A., Kennell, J., & Klaus, M. (1972, February). Follow-up of low birth weight infants—The predictive value of maternal visiting patterns. *Pediatrics, 49,* 280–290.

37. Siegel, E. (1980, August). Hospital and home support during infancy: Impact on maternal attachment, child abuse and neglect, and health care utilization. *Pediatrics, 66*(2), 183–190.

38. O'Connor, S., Vietze, P. M., Sherrod, K. B. Sandler, H. M., & Altemeier, W. A. (1980, August). Reduced incidence of parenting inadequacy following rooming-in. *Pediatrics, 66*(2), 176–182.

39. Helfer, R. E. (1974). *A self-instructional program on child abuse and neglect,* Unit 3. Chicago: Committee on Infant and Preschool Child of the American Academy of Pediatrics, and Denver: National Center for the Prevention and Treatment of Child Abuse and Neglect.

40. Steele, B. F. (1970). Parental abuse of infants and small children. In J. E. Anthony & T. Benedek (Eds.), *Parenthood: Its psychology and psychopathology*

(pp. 449–477). Boston: Little, Brown; Bishop (1971, March); Schmitt & Kempe (1975, March).

41. Landis, C., & Bolles, J. M. (1947). *Textbook of abnormal psychology*. New York: Macmillan.

42. Kagan, J. (1971). *Change and continuity in infancy* (p. 183). New York: Wiley.

43. Jenkins, R. L., Gants, R., Shoji, T., & Fine, E. (1970, February). Interrupting the family cycle of violence. *Journal of the Iowa Medical Society, 60*, 85.

44. Martin, H. P., & Beezley, P. (1974, Fall-Winter). Prevention and the consequences of child abuse. *Journal of Operational Psychiatry, 6*, 74.

45. Light, R. J. (1973, November). Abused and neglected children in America: A study of alternative policies. *Harvard Educational Review, 43*, 587.

46. Toffler, A. (1970). *Future shock*. New York: Random House.

47. Justice, B. (1969). *Violence in the city* (pp. 88–92). Fort Worth: Texas Christian University Press.

48. Andrews, S., Blumenthal, J., Johnson, D., Kahn, C., Ferguson, C., Laster, T. Malone, P., & Wallace, D. (1982). The skills of mothering: A study of parent child development centers. *Monographs of the Society for Research in Child Development, 47*(6, Serial No. 198).

49. Child Welfare League of America. (1986). *Too young to run: The status of child abuse in America*. New York: Author.

50. Lochman, J. E., & Brown, M. V. (1980). Evaluation of dropout clients and of perceived usefulness of a parent education program. *Journal of Community Psychology, 8*, 132–139; and Johnson, D. L., & Breckenridge, J. N. (1982). The Houston Parent-Child Development Center and the primary prevention of behavior problems in young children. *American Journal of Community Psychology, 10*, 305–316.

51. Daro (1988), p. 135.

52. As quoted in Hawkins, R. P. (1972, November). It's time we taught the young how to be good parents (and don't you wish we'd started a long time ago?). *Psychology Today*, p. 40.

53. Lord, E., & Weisfeld, D. (1974). The abused child. In A. R. Roberts (Ed.), *Childhood deprivation* (p. 80). Springfield, IL: Charles C. Thomas.

54. Toffler (1970), p. 216.

55. Daro (1988), pp. 135–136.

56. Hawkins (1972, November), p. 216.

57. Kempe (1973), p. 805.

58. Lord & Weisfeld (1974), p. 80; Hawkins (1972, November), p. 40.

59. Kempe (1973), p. 808.

60. Hawkins (1972, November), p. 31.

61. Broadhurst, D. D. (1975, June). Project protection. *Children Today, 4*, 25.

62. Hawkins (1972, November), p. 40.

63. Toffler (1970), p. 217.

64. Gil, D. G. (1970). *Violence against children* (p. 146). Cambridge, MA: Harvard University Press; Elmer, E. (1971), pp. 54–55.

65. *Study findings: Study of national incidence and prevalence of child abuse and neglect, 1988*. (1988). (pp. 5–35). U. S. Department of Health and Human Services. Office of Human Development, Administration for Children, Youth and Families, Children's Bureau, National Center on Child Abuse and Neglect.

66. Light (1973, November), p. 595.

67. Sever, J., & Janzen, C. (1982, May). Contradictions to reconstitution of sexually abusive families. *Child Welfare, 61*(5), 279–288.

68. Olson, R. (1976, January). Index of suspicion: Screening of child abusers. *American Journal of Nursing, 76*, 108–110.

69. Maslow, A. (1970). *Motivation and personality* (pp. 35–58). New York: Harper & Row; Berne, E. (1964). *Games people play: The psychology of human relationships* (pp. 13–65). New York: Grove Press; Glasser, W. (1972). *The identity society* (pp. 1–101). New York: Harper & Row; Frankl, V. (1960, Spring). Beyond self-actualization and self-expression. *Journal of Existential Psychiatry, 1*, 5–20; White, R. W. (1959, September). Motivation reconsidered: The concept of competence. *Psychological Review, 66*, 297–333.

70. Gordon, N. P., & McAlister, A. L. (1982). Adolescent drinking: Issues and research. In T. J. Coates, A. C. Petersen, & C. Perry (Eds.), *Promoting adolescent health* (pp. 201, 203, 210). New York: Academic Press; Brook, D. W., & Brook, J. S. (1985). Adolescent alcohol use. *Alcohol and Alcoholism, 20*(3), 259.

71. A study of children's attitudes and perceptions about drugs and alcohol. (1983). *Weekly Reader Publications*. Xerox Education Publications, Table 2.

72. Plaut, T. F. A. (1967). *Alcohol problems: A report to the nation by the Cooperative Commission on the Study of Alcoholism* (p. 122). New York: Oxford University Press. See also Ojemann, R. H. (1957). *Four basic aspects of preventive psychiatry*. Iowa City: State University of Iowa Press.

73. Ravenholt, R. T. (1983, March). Addiction mortality in the U. S. National Institute on Drug Abuse. As cited in *Facts on alcoholism and alcohol-related problems*, brochure of Houston Council on Alcoholism.

74. U. S. Department of Health and Human Services : National Institute of Alcohol Abuse and Alcoholism, Public Service. Questions & answers: *Teenage alcohol use and abuse, Prevention plus: Involving schools and the community in alcohol and drug education* (p. xiii). Publication No. CADM841256. Rockville, MD: Author.

75. Daro (1988), p. 197.

76. Daro (1988), p. 198.

77. Gil, D. G. (1975, April). Unraveling child abuse. *American Journal of Orthopsychiatry, 45*, 354–355.

78. Simmons (1986).

79. Sage, W. (1975, July). Violence in the children's room. *Human Behavior, 4*, 43.

80. Straus, M. A. (1980). Stress and child abuse. In C. H. Kempe & R. E. Helfer (Eds.), *The battered child* (3rd ed., pp. 86–103). Chicago: University of Chicago Press.

81. Hyman, I. A. (1988, June). Should children ever be hit? A contemporary answer to an historical question. *Journal of Interpersonal Violence, 3*(2), 227–230.

82. Kempe (1973), p. 810.

83. Routh, T. (1972). *The volunteer and community agencies* (p. 3). Springfield, IL: Charles C. Thomas.

84. Kempe (1973), p. 810.

85. Pollock, C., & Steele, B. (1972). A therapeutic approach to the parents. In C. H. Kempe & R. E. Helfer (Eds.), *Helping the battered child and his family* (p. 3). Philadelphia: Lippincott.

86. Olds, D. (1984).

87. Personal communication with staff of Best Friends program at Jefferson Davis Hospital, February 10, 1989.

88. Kempe (1973), p. 810.

89. Kempe (1973), p. 810.

90. Personal communication with Walter Black, Recruitment Director of the Volunteer Center of Texas Gulf Coast, Houston, TX, February 27, 1989.

91. Kempe (1973), p. 810.

CHAPTER 10

1. Carkhuff, R. G., & Berenson, B. G. (1967). *Beyond counseling and therapy* (pp. 23–24, 46–48). New York: Holt, Rinehart & Winston.

2. Kempe, C. H. (1973, April). A practical approach to the protection of the abused child and rehabilitation of the abusing parent. *Paediatrics, 51*, 807.

3. Hopkins, J. (1970, December). The nurse and the abused child. *Nursing Clinics of North America, 5*, 596.

4. Kempe, C. H., & Helfer, R. E. (1972). Innovative therapeutic approaches. In C. H. Kempe & R. E. Helfer (Eds.), *Helping the battered child and his family* (p. 44). Philadelphia: Lippincott.

5. Kempe (1973, April), p. 808.

6. Helfer, R. E. (1974). *A self-instructional program on child abuse and neglect* (Unit 4). Chicago: Committee on Infant and Preschool Child of the American Academy of Pediatrics, and Denver: National Center for Prevention and Treatment of Child Abuse and Neglect.

7. Personal communication with Dorothy Tasin, Casework Manager, Family Outreach of the Southwest Center, Houston, TX, February 28, 1989.

8. *Escape.* (1988, June-December). [Newsletter of the Exchange Club Child Abuse Prevention Center of Houston, TX], *3*(2)

9. Barnes, G. B., Chabon, R. S., & Hertzberg, L. J. (1974, December). Team treatment for abusive families. *School Casework, 55,* 607–608.

10. Holter, J., & Friedman, S. (1968, January). Principles of management in child abuse cases. *American Journal of Orthopsychiatry, 38,* 133–134.

11. Kempe & Helfer (1972), p. 47.

12. Paulson, M. J., & Blake, P. R. (1969, February). The physically abused child: A focus on prevention. *Child Welfare, 48,* 95.

13. Paulson & Blake (1969, February), pp. 47–48.

14. Kempe (1973, April), p. 804.

15. Kempe & Helfer (1972), p. 48.

16. Cohn, A. H., Ridge, S. S., & Collignon, F. C. (1975, May-June). Evaluating innovative treatment programs in child abuse and neglect. *Children Today, 4,* 10–12.

17. Davoren, E. (1975, May-June). Working with abusive parents—A social worker's view. *Children Today, 4,* 40.

18. Helfer (1974), Unit 4.

19. Cohn, Ridge, & Collingnon (1975, May-June), p. 11.

20. Kempe (1973, April), p. 808.

21. Helfer (1974), Unit 1, p. 2.

22. Savino, A. B., & Sanders, R. W. (1973, March). Working with abusive parents: Group therapy and home visits. *American Journal of Nursing, 73,* 484.

23. Patterson, G. R., & Gullion, M. E. (1968). *Living with children: New methods for parents and teachers.* Champaign: Research Press.

24. Smith, J. M., & Smith, D. E. P. (1966). *Child management: A program for parents.* Ann Arbor, MI: Ann Arbor Publishers; Gordon, T. (1970). *Parent effectiveness training.* New York: Wyden.

25. Helfer (1974), Unit 3.

26. Cohn, Ridge, & Collignon (1975, May-June), p. 11.

27. *Children in danger.* (1974). Austin, TX: State Department of Public Welfare.

28. Sgroi, S. M. (1975, May-June). Sexual molestation of children. *Children Today, 4,* 19.

29. Ferro, F. (1975, May-June). Combatting child abuse and neglect. *Children Today, 4,* inside front cover.

30. Lovens, H. D., & Rako, J. (1975, February). A community approach to the prevention of child abuse. *Child Welfare, 54,* 85.

31. Lovens & Rako (1975, February), p. 85.

32. Lovens & Rako (1975, February), p. 86.

33. Personal communication with Social Services Staff of Goddard Hospital, Brockton, MA, February 25, 1989.

34. Haas, G. (1975). Child abuse, the community, and the neighborhood health center. In N. B. Ebeling & D. A. Hill (Eds.), *Child abuse: Intervention and treatment* (p. 15). Acton, MA: Publishing Science Group.

35. Personal communication with Gerald Haas, M.D., medical director, South End Community Health Center, Boston, February 24, 1989.

36. Helfer, R. E., as quoted in Davidson, S. (1973, March). At last! Help for the abusive parent. *Woman's Day*, p. 190.

37. Kempe & Helfer (1972), p. 53.

38. Helfer (1974).

39. Davidson, S. (1973, March).

40. Holmes, S. A., Barnhart, C., Cantoni, L., & Reymer, E. (1975, January). Working with the parent in child-abuse cases. *Social Casework, 56*, 3–12.

41. Holmes (1975, January), p. 8.

42. Reed, J. (1975, May-June). Working with abusive parents: A parent's view—An interview with Jolly K. *Children Today, 4*, 9.

43. Bacon, G. M. (1975, June 24). Personal communication. New York: Parents Anonymous.

44. Davidson (1973, March), p. 190.

45. Kempe & Helfer (1972), p. 49.

46. Personal communication with Sharon Carey, executive director of Parents Anonymous of Houston, February 3, 1989.

47. Davidson (1973, March), p. 190.

48. Reed (1975, May-June), p. 8.

49. Reed (1975, May-June), p. 9.

50. Smith, R. (1973, January). Now experts are trying to draw out these battering parents. *Today's Health, 51*, 59–64.

51. *Families anonymous.* (1974). Film produced by the National Center for the Prevention and Treatment of Child Abuse and Neglect, Denver.

52. Holmes, Barnhart, Cantoni, & Reymer (1975, January).

53. Davoren (1975, May-June), p. 39.

54. Davoren (1975, May-June), p. 39.

55. Davoren (1975, May-June), p. 40.

56. Davoren, E. (1974). The role of the social worker. In R. C. Helfer & C. H. Kempe (Eds.), *The battered child* (p. 147). Chicago: University of Chicago Press.

57. Davoren (1975, May-June), p. 39.

58. Davoren (1975, May-June), p. 43.

59. Thomson, E. M., Paget, N. W., Bates, D. W., Mesch, M., & Putnam, T. I. (1971). *Child abuse: A community challenge* (pp. 139–140). East Aurora, NY: Henry Stewart.

60. Arvanian, A. L. (1975). Treatment of abusive parents. In N. B. Ebeling & D. A. Hill (Eds.), *Child abuse: Intervention and treatment* (pp. 93–101). Acton, MA: Publishing Science Group.

61. Kempe & Helfer (1972), pp. 13–14.

62. Helfer (1974).

63. Carroll, C. A. (1980). The function of protective services in child abuse and neglect. In C. H. Kempe & R. E. Helfer (Eds.), *The battered child* (3rd ed., p. 276). Chicago: University of Chicago Press.

64. Carroll (1980), p. 275.

65. Burton, R. (1989, February 9). *Can the abused and the abuser live together? A community response.* Panel presentation sponsored by the League of Women Voters, Houston.

66. Carroll (1980), p. 279.

67. Hay, J. (1989, February 9). *Can the abused and the abuser live together? A community response.* Panel presentation sponsored by the League of Women Voters, Houston.

68. Burton (1989, February 9).

69. Hay (1989, February 9).

70. Hay (1989, February 9).

71. Carroll (1980), p. 279.

72. Personal communication with Judy Hay, Director of Community Relations, Harris County Children's Protective Services, Houston, February 25, 1989.

73. Carroll (1980), p. 287.

74. Child abuse and neglect reach epidemic levels: Maze of programs may be promoting the crisis, not attacking it. *Houston Post*, July 2, 1975, p. 4AA.

75. Helfer (1974), pp. 3-2–3-11.

76. Delnero, H., Hopkins, J., & Drews, K. (1972). The medical center child abusive consultation team. In C. H. Kempe & R. E. Helfer (Eds.), *Helping the battered child and his family* (pp. 161–176). Philadelphia: Lippincott; Barnes, G. B., Chabon, R. S., Hertzberg, L. J. (1974, December). Team treatment for abusive families. *Social Casework, 55,* 604.

77. Cohn (1975, May-June), p. 10.

78. Daro (1988), p. 198.

79. Kempe, C. H., & Helfer, R. E. (Eds.) (1980). *The battered child* (3rd ed., p. 274). Chicago: University of Chicago Press.

Bibliography

Aber, J. L., & Cicchetti, D. (1984). The socio-emotional development of maltreated children: An empirical and theoretical analysis. In H. E. Fitzgerald, B. M. Lester, & M. W. Yogman (Eds.), *Theory and research in behavioral pediatrics* (Vol. 2, pp. 147–205). New York: Plenum.

Affholter, D., Connell, D., & Nauta, M. (1983). Evaluation of the child and family resource program: Early evidence of parent-child interaction effects. *Evaluation Review, 7*(1), 65–79.

Altemeier, W. A., O'Conner, S., Vietze, P., Sandler, H., & Sherrod, K. (1982, May). Antecedents of child abuse. *Journal of Pediatrics, 100*(50), 823–829.

American Association for Protecting Children. (1985). *Highlights of official child neglect and abuse reporting*. Denver: American Humane Society.

American heritage dictionary. (1982). Boston: Houghton Mifflin.

Andrews, S., Blumenthal, J., Johnson, D., Kahn, C., Ferguson, C., Laster, T., Malone, P., & Wallace, D. (1982). The skills of mothering: A study of parent child development centers. *Monographs of the Society for Research in Child Development, 47*(6, Serial No. 198).

Anonymous. (1972). Toward the differentiation of a self in one's own family. In J. L. Framo (Ed.), *Family interaction* (pp. 111–173). New York: Springer.

Anthony, E. J., & Bertram, J. C. (Eds.). (1987). *The invulnerable child*. New York: Guilford Press.

Arvanian, A. L. (1975). Treatment of abusive parents. In N. B. Ebeling & D. A. Hill (Eds.), *Child abuse: Intervention and treatment* (pp. 93–101). Acton, MA: Publishing Science Group.

Auerbach, S. M. (1986). Assumptions of crisis theory and a temporal model of crisis intervention. In S. M. Auerbach & A. L. Stolberg (Eds.), *Crisis intervention with children and families*, (pp. 3–37) Washington, DC: Hemisphere.

Bakan, D. (1971). *Slaughter of the innocents.* San Francisco: Jossey-Bass.

Barber-Madden, R., & Cohn, A. H. (1983, November). *Family violence: The role of public health.* Paper presented at the annual meeting of the American Public Health Association, Dallas.

Barnes, G. B., Chabon, R. S., & Hertzberg, L. J. (1974, December). Team treatment for abusive families. *Social Casework, 55,* 600–611.

Bennie, E. H., & Sclare, A. B. (1969, January). The battered child syndrome. *American Journal of Psychiatry, 125,* 975–979.

Berne, E. (1964). *Games people play.* New York: Grove Press.

Berne, E. (1966). *Principles of group treatment.* New York: Oxford University Press.

Berne, E. (1972). *What do you say after you say hello?* New York: Grove Press.

Bishop, F. I. (1971, March). Children at risk. *Medical Journal of Australia, l,* 623–628.

Blum, H. (1974). *Planning for health: Development and application of social change theory.* New York: Human Sciences Press.

Blumberg, M. L. (1964, Winter). When parents hit out. *Twentieth Century, 173,* 39–44.

Blumberg, M. L. (1974, January). Psychopathology of the abusing parent. *American Journal of Psychotherapy, 28,* 21–29.[

Bovard, E. W. (1985). Brain mechanisms in effects of social support on viability. *Perspectives on Behavioral Medicine, 2,* 103–129.

Bowen, M. (1966, October). The use of family theory in clinical practice. *Comprehensive Psychiatry, 7,* 345–374.

Bowen, M. (1971). Family therapy and family group therapy. In H. I. Kaplan & B. J. Sadock (Eds.), *Comprehensive group psychotherapy* (pp. 384–421). Baltimore: William & Wilkins.

Bowlby, J. (1980). *Attachment and loss. Vol. 3 : Loss, sadness and depression.* New York: Basic Books.

Bowlby, J. (1985). *Attachment and loss. Vol. l: Attachment.* New York: Basic Books.

Boyd, M. J. (1988, January). Letter. *APA Monitor, 19*(2), 2.

Bradshaw, J. (1988). *Bradshaw on: The family.* Deerfield Beach, FL: Health Communications.

Broadhurst, D. D. (1975, June). Project protection. *Children Today, 4,* 25.

Brook, D. W., & Brook, J. S. (1985). Adolescent alcohol use. *Alcohol and Alcoholism, 20*(3), 259.

Burton, R. (1989, February 9). *Can the abused and the abuser live together? A community response.* Panel presentation sponsored by the League of Women Voters, Houston.

Caldwell, R. A., Bogat, G. A., & Davidson, W. S. (1988). The assessment of child abuse potential and the prevention of child abuse and neglect: A policy analysis. *American Journal of Community Psychology, 16*(5), 609–624.

Caplan, G. (1964). *Principles of preventive psychiatry.* New York: Basic Books.

Carkhuff, R. G., & Berenson, B. G. (1967). *Beyond counseling and therapy.* New York: Holt, Rinehart & Winston.

Carroll, C. A. (1980). The function of protective services in child abuse and neglect. In C. H. Kempe & R. E. Helfer (Eds.), *The battered child* (3rd ed., pp. 275–287). Chicago: University of Chicago Press.

Child abuse and neglect reach epidemic levels: Maze of programs may be promoting the crisis, not attacking it. *Houston Post,* July 2, 1975, p. 4AA.

Child Welfare League of America. (1986). *Too young to run: The status of child abuse in America.* New York: Author.

Children in danger. (1974). Austin, TX: State Department of Public Welfare.

Cicchetti, D., Carlson, V., Braunwald, K. G., & Aber, J. L. (1987). The sequelae of child maltreatment. In R. J. Gelles & J. B. Lancaster (Eds.), *Child abuse and neglect: Biosocial dimensions* (pp. 277–298). New York: Aldine de Gruyter.

Cohn, A. (1983). *An approach to preventing child abuse.* Chicago: National Committee for the Prevention of Child Abuse.

Cohn, A. H., & Daro, D. (1987). Is treatment too late? What ten years of evaluative research tell us. *Child Abuse & Neglect, 11,* 433–442.

Cohn, A. H., Ridge, S. S., & Collignon, F. C. (1975, May–June). Evaluating innovative treatment programs in child abuse and neglect. *Children Today, 4*(3), 10–12.

Coleman, D. (1987). Thriving despite hardship: Key childhood traits identified. *New York Times,* October 13, pp. 19–22.

Cowen, E. L. (1980). The wooing of primary prevention. *American Journal of Community Psychology, 8,* 258–284.

Cowen, E. L., & Work, W. C. (1988). Resilient children, psychological wellness, and primary prevention. *American Journal of Community Psychology, 16*(4), 591–607.

Craig, W. S. (1946). *Child and adolescent life in health and disease.* Edinburgh, Scotland: E. & S. Livingstone.

Crisis in child mental health: Challenge for the 1970s, report of the Joint Commission on Mental Health of Children. (1970). New York: Harper & Row.

Daniel, J. H., Hampton, R. L., & Newberger, E. H. (1983, October). Child abuse and accidents in black families: A controlled comparative study. *American Journal of Orthopsychiatry, 53,* 645–653.

Daro, D. (1988). *Confronting child abuse: Research for effective program design.* New York: Free Press.

Daro, D., & Mitchel, L. (1987). *Deaths due to maltreatment soar: The results of the eighth semi-annual fifty state survey.* Chicago: National Committee for the Prevention of Child Abuse.

David, C. A. (1974, October). The use of the confrontation technique in the battered child syndrome. *American Journal of Psychotherapy, 28,* 543–552.

Davidson, S. (1973, March). At last! Help for the abusive parent. *Woman's Day,* p. 190.

Davoren, E. (1974). The role of the social worker. In R. E. Helfer & C. H. Kempe (Eds.), *The battered child* (pp. 142–144). Chicago: University of Chicago Press.

Davoren, E. (1975, May-June). Working with abusive parents—A social worker's view. *Children Today, 4,* 40.

Dawson, P., Robinson, J., & Johnson, C. (1982). Informal social support as an intervention. *Zero to Three: Bulletin of the National Center for Clinical Infant Programs, 3*(2), 1–5.

Delnero, H., Hopkins, J., & Drews, K. (1972). The medical center child abusive consultation team. In C. H. Kempe & R. E. Helfer (Eds.), *Helping the battered child and his family* (pp. 161–176). Philadelphia: Lippincott.

Doran, L. D. (1981). Mothers' disciplinary responses under controllable and uncontrollable stress: A child abuse analogue. *Dissertation Abstracts International, 42,* 2534A (University Microfilms No. 81-26, 094)

Egeland, B., Breitenbucher, M., & Rosenberg, D. (1980). Prospective study of the significance of life stress in the etiology of child abuse. *Journal of Consulting and Clinical Psychology, 48,* 195–205.

Egeland, B., Jacobvitz, D., & Papatola, K. (1987). Intergenerational continuity of abuse. In R. J. Gelles & J. B. Lancaster (Eds.), *Child abuse and neglect: Biosocial dimensions* (pp. 255–276). New York: Aldine de Gruyter.

Egeland, B., & Sroufe, L. A. (1981). Attachment and early maltreatment. *Child Development, 52,* 44–52.

Ellis, A. (1973). *Humanistic psychology.* New York: Julian Press.

Ellis, A. (1973). Rational-emotive therapy. In R. Corsini (Ed.), *Current psychotherapies* (pp. 167–206). Itasca, IL: Peacock.

Elmer, E. (1967). *Children in jeopardy.* Pittsburg: University of Pittsburgh Press.

Elmer, E. (1971). Child abuse: A symptom of family crisis. In E. Pavenstedt & V. W. Bernard (Eds.), *Crisis of family disorganization: Programs to soften their impact on children* (pp. 54–55). New York: Behavioral Publications.

Escape. (1988, June-December). [Newsletter of the Exchange Club Child Abuse Prevention Center of Houston, Tx], 3(2).

Families anonymous. (1974). Film produced by the National Center for the Prevention and Treatment of Child Abuse and Neglect, Denver.

Fanaroff, A. A., Kennell, J., & Klaus, M. (1972, February). Follow-up of low birth weight infants—The predictive value of maternal visiting patterns. *Pediatrics, 49,* 280–290.

Felder, S. (1971). A lawyer's view of child abuse. *Public Welfare, 29,* 181–188.

Ferro, F. (1975, May-June). Combatting child abuse and neglect. *Children Today, 4,* inside front cover.

Flynn, W. R. (1970, September). Frontier justice: A contribution to the theory of child battery. *American Journal of Psychiatry, 127,* 375–379.

Fontana, V. J. (1964, January). The neglect and abuse of children. *New York State Journal of Medicine, 64,* 215–218.

Fontana, V. J. (1973). *Somewhere a child is crying.* New York: Macmillan.

Frankl, V. (1960, Spring). Beyond self-actualization and self-expression. *Journal of Existential Psychiatry, 1,* 5–20.

Frederickson, C., Boger, R., Stuzok, B., & Hartman, M. (1982). *Parenting: The tender touch.* East Lansing: Michigan State University.

Friedman, S. B. (1972). The need for intensive follow-up of abused children. In C. H. Kempe & R. E. Helfer (Eds.), *Helping the battered child* (pp. 79–92). Philadelphia: Lippincott.

Friedrich, W. N., & Wheller, K. K. (1982). The abusing parent revisited: A decade of psychological research. *Journal of Nervous and Mental Disease, 170,* 577–587.

Gabarino, J. (1977). The human ecology of child maltreatment: A conceptual model for research. *Journal of Marriage and the Family, 39,* 721–735.

Gaines, R., Sandgund, A., Green, A. H., & Power, E. (1978). Etiological factors in child maltreatment: A multivariate study of abusing, neglecting, and normal mothers. *Journal of Abnormal Psychology, 87,* 531–540.

Galdston, R. (1965, October). Observations of children who have been physically abused and their parents. *American Journal of Psychiatry, 122,* 440–443.

Garmezy, N. (1985). Stress resistant children: The search for protective factors. In J. E. Stevenson (Ed.), *Recent research in developmental psychopathology. Journal of Child Psychology and Psychiatry. Book Supplement No. 4* (pp. 213–233). Oxford: Pergamon.

Gelles, R. J. (1973, July). Child abuse as psychopathology: A sociological critique and reformulation. *American Journal of Orthopsychiatry, 43,* 611–621.

Gelles, R. J. (1980). A profile of violence toward children in the United States. In G. Gerbner, C. J. Ross, & E. Zigler (Eds.), *Child abuse: An agenda for action* (pp. 82–105). New York: Oxford University Press.

Gelles, R. J., & Lancaster, J. B. (Eds.). (1987). *Child abuse and neglect: Biosocial dimensions.* New York: Aldine de Gruyter.

George, C., & Main, M. (1979). Social interactions of young, abused children: Approach avoidance and aggresssion. *Child Development, 50,* 306–318.

Gershenson, C. (1984). The cost saving impact of permanency planning. *Child Welfare Research Notes,* No. 6

Gibbon, E. (1899). *The decline and fall of the Roman Empire.* New York: Collier.

Gil, D. G. (1970). *Violence against children.* Cambridge, MA: Harvard University Press.

Gil, D. G. (1971, November). Violence against children. *Journal of Marriage and the Family, 33,* 637–648

Gil, D. G. (1975, April). Unraveling child abuse. *American Journal of Orthopsychiatry, 45,* 346–356.

Gil, D. G. (1981). The United States versus child abuse. In L. Pelton (Ed.), *Social context of child abuse and neglect*. New York: Human Services Press.

Glasser, W. (1972). *The identity society*. New York: Harper & Row.

Gordon, N. P., & McAlister, A. L. (1982). Adolescent drinking: Issues and research. In T. J. Coates, A. C. Petersen, & C. Perry (Eds.), *Promoting adolescent health* (pp. 201–223). New York: Academic Press.

Gordon T. (1970). *Parent effectiveness training*. New York: Wyden.

Gray, E. (1983). *Final report: Collaborative research of community and minority group action to prevent child abuse and neglect. Vol. 1: Perinatal interventions*. Chicago: National Committee for Prevention of Child Abuse.

Gray, J., Cutler, C. A., Dean, J. G., & Kempe, C. H. (1979). Prediction and prevention of child abuse and neglect. *Journal of Social Issues, 35*(2), 127–139.

Green, A. H. (1976, Summer). A psychodynamic approach to the study and treatment of child abusing parents. *Journal of the American Academy of Child Psychology, 15,* 414–442.

Green, W. H., Campbell, M., & David, R. (1984). Psychosocial dwarfism: A critical review of the evidence. *Journal of the American Academy of Child Psychiatry, 23*(1), 39–48.

Guidelines for schools, teachers, nurses, counselors, and administrators. (1971). Denver: American Humane Association.

Haas, G. (1975). Child abuse, the community, and the neighborhood health center. In N. B. Ebeling & D. A. Hill (Eds.), *Child abuse: Intervention and treatment* (pp. 13–16). Acton, MA: Publishing Science Group.

Hackett, G. (1988, December 12). A tale of abuse. *Newsweek*, pp. 56–61.

Haimowitz, N. R., & Haimowitz, M. L. (1973). Introduction to transactional analysis. In M. L. Haimowitz & N. R. Haimowitz (Eds.), *Human development* (pp. 318–352). New York: Thomas Y. Crowell.

Harrington, J. (1972, January). Violence: A clinical viewpoint. *British Medical Journal, 1,* 228–231.

Hawkins, R. P. (1972, November). It's time we taught the young how to be good parents (and don't you wish we'd started a long time ago?). *Psychology Today, 6,* 28–30, 36, 38–40.

Hay, J. (1989, February 9). *Can the abused and the abuser live together: A community response*. Panel presentation sponsored by the League of Women Voters, Houston.

Haynes, C. F., Cutler, C., Gray, J., & Kempe, R. S. (1984). Hospitalized cases of nonorganic failure to thrive: The scope of the problem and short-term lay health visitor intervention. *Child Abuse & Neglect, 8,* 229–242.

Helfer, R. E. (1974). *A self-instructional program on child abuse and neglect*. Chicago: Committee on Infant and Preschool Child of the American Academy of Pediatrics, and Denver: National Center for the Prevention and Treatment of Child Abuse and Neglect.

Helfer, R. E. (1975, May–June). Why most physicians don't get involved in child abuse cases and what to do about it. *Children Today, 4*, 28–32.

Helfer, R. E. (1980). Developmental deficits which limit interpersonal skills. In C. H. Kemp & R. E. Helfer (Eds.), *The battered child* (3rd ed., pp. 36–48). Chicago: University of Chicago Press.

Helfer, R. E. (1982). A review of the literature on the prevention of child abuse and neglect. *Child Abuse & Neglect, 6*, 251–261.

Helfer, R. E. (1987). Back to the future. *Child Abuse & Neglect, ll*, ll–14.

Highlights of official child neglect and abuse reporting—1986. (1988). Denver: American Association for Protecting Children, Division of American Humane Association.

Hightower, N. (1989, March). Working with angry and violent patients in group psychotherapy. *Journal of the Houston Group Psychotherapy Society, 3*, 15-33.

Hiroto, D. S., & Seligman, M. E. P. (1975). Generality of learned helplessness in man. *Journal of Personality and Social Psychology, 90*, 311–327.

Holmes, S. A., Barnhart, C., Cantoni, L., & Reymer, E. (1975, January). Working with the parent in child abuse cases. *Social Casework, 56*, 3–2.

Holmes, T. H., & Rahe, R. H. (1967). The social readjustment rating scale. *Journal of Psychosomatic Research, 11*, 213–218.

Holter, J., & Friedman, S. (1968, January). Principles of management in child abuse cases. *American Journal of Orthopsychiatry, 38*, 133–134.

Hopkins, J. (1970, December). The nurse and the abused child. *Nursing Clinics of North America, 5*, 596.

Hughes, R. C. (1974). A clinic's parent-performance training program for child abusers. *Hospital and Community Psychiatry, 25*, 779–782.

Hyman, I. A. (1988, June). Should children ever be hit? A contemporary answer to an historical question. *Journal of Interpersonal Violence, 3*(2), 227–230.

Identifying the battered or molested child (1972). In *Handbook for school staff members.* Palo Alto, CA: Palo Alto School District.

Isaacs, S. (1972, July). Neglect, cruelty and battering. *British Medical Journal, 3*, 224–226.

Jacobson, R. S., & Straker, G. (1982). Peer group interaction of physically abused children. *Child Abuse & Neglect, 6*, 321–327.

Jason, J., Andeereck, N., Marks, J., & Tyler, C. (1982). Child abuse in Georgia: A method to evaluate risk factors and reporting biases. *American Journal of Public Health, 72*, 1353–1358.

Jenkins, R. L. (1970, February). Interrupting the family cycle of violence. *Journal of the Iowa Medical Society, 30*, 85–89.

Jenkins, R. L., Gants, R., Shoji, T., & Fine, E. (1970, February). Interrupting the family cycle of violence. *Journal of the Iowa Medical Society, 60*, 85–89.

Johnson, D. L., & Breckenridge, J. N. (1982). The Houston Parent-Child Development Center and the primary prevention of behavior problems in young children. *American Journal of Community Psychology, 10*, 305–316.

Johnson, J. H. (1986). *Life events as stressors in childhood and adolescence*. Beverly Hills, CA: Sage.

Jones, D. P. H. (1987). The untreatable family. *Child Abuse & Neglect, 11*, 409–420.

Justice, B. (1969). *Violence in the city*. Fort Worth: Texas Christian University Press.

Justice, B. (Ed.). (1973). *Your child's behavior*. Project for the Early Prevention of Violence. Houston: School of Public Health, University of Texas.

Justice, B. (1989, February 9). *Can the abused and the abuser live together: A community response*. Panel presentation sponsored by the League of Women Voters, Houston.

Justice, B., Calvert, A., & Justice, R. (1985). Factors mediating child abuse as a response to stress. *Child Abuse & Neglect, 9*, 359–363.

Justice, B., & Duncan, D. F. (1975, April–June). Physical abuse of children as a public health problem. *Public Health Reviews, 4*, 183–200.

Justice, B., & Duncan, D. F. (1976). Life crisis as a precursor to child abuse. *Public Health Reports, 91*, 110–115.

Justice, B., & Justice, R. (1973, August). *"Siamese-twinning" in scripts of child batterers*. Paper presented before the International Transactional Analysis Association Summer Conference, San Francisco.

Justice, B., & Justice, R. (1974, February 15). *A psychosocial model of child abuse: Intervention strategies and group techniques*. Paper presented before the Clinical and Research Training Seminar, Texas Research Institute of Mental Science, Houston.

Justice, B., & Justice, R. (1976). *The abusing family*. New York: Human Sciences Press.

Justice, B., & Justice, R. (1982). Etiology of physical abuse of children and dynamic of coercive treatment. In J. C. Hansen & R. Barnhill (Eds.), *Family therapy collections*. Rockville, MD: Aspen.

Justice, B., Justice, R., & Kraft, I. A. (1974, April). Early warning signs of violence: Is a triad enough? *American Journal of Psychiatry, 131*, 457–459.

Justice, R., & Justice, B. (1975). TA work with child abuse. *Transactional Analysis Journal, 5*, 38–41.

Kagan, J. (1971). *Change and continuity in infancy*. New York: Wiley.

Katz, S., Ambrosino, L., McGrath, M., & Sawitsky, K. (1977). Legal research on child abuse and neglect: Past and future. *Family Law Quarterly, 11*(2), 151–184.

Kaufman, J., & Zigler, E. (1987, April). Do abused children become abusive parents? *American Journal of Orthopsychiatry, 57*, 186–192.

Kempe, C. H. (1969, October). The battered child and the hospital. *Hospital Practice, 4*, 44–57.

Kempe, C. H. (1971, February). Paediatric implications of the battered baby syndrome. *Archives of Disease in Childhood, 46*, 28–37.

Kempe, C. H. (1973, April). A practical approach to the protection of the abused child and rehabilitation of the abusing parent. *Pediatrics, 51*, 791–809.

Kempe, C. H., & Helfer, R. E. (1972). Innovative therapeutic approaches. In C. H. Kempe & R. E. Helfer (Eds.), *Helping the battered child and his family* (pp. 41–54). Philadelphia: Lippincott.

Kempe, C. H., & Helfer, R. E. (Eds.). (1980). *The battered child* (3rd ed.). Chicago: University of Chicago Press.

Kempe, C. H., & Hopkins, J. (1975, March-April-May). The public health nurse's role in the prevention of child abuse and neglect. *Public Health Currents, 15,* 1–4.

Kempe, C. H., Silverman, F., Steele, B. F., Droegemueller, W., & Silver, H. (1962, July). The battered child syndrome. *Journal of the American Medical Association, 181,* 17–24.

Kempe, R. S., & Kempe, C. H. (1978). *Child abuse.* Cambridge, MA: Harvard University Press.

Kempe, R. S., & Kempe, C. H. (1978). The untreatable family. In R. S. Kempe & C. H. Kempe, *Child abuse* (pp. 128–131). Cambridge, MA: Harvard University Press.

Kiresuk, T. J., & Sherman, R. E. (1968, December). Goal attainment scaling: A general method for evaluating comprehensive community mental health programs. *Community Mental Health Journal, 4,* 443–453.

Kister, M. C., & Patterson, C. J. (1980). Children's conceptions of causes of illness: Understanding of contagion and use of immanent justice. *Child Development, 51,* 839-846.

Klaus, M. H., & Kennell, J. H. (1976). *Maternal-infant bonding.* St. Louis, MO: C. V. Mosby.

Klein, M., & Stern, L. (1971, July). Low birth weight and the battered child syndrome. *American Journal of Diseases of Children, 122,* 15–18.

Koblenzer, C. S. (1988). Stress and the skin. *Advances, 5*(4), 27–32.

Korbin, J. E. (1987). Child maltreatment in cross-cultural perspective: Vulnerable children and circumstances. In R. J. Gelles & J. B. Lancaster (Eds.), *Child abuse and neglect: Biosocial dimensions* (pp. 38–43). New York: Aldine de Gruyter.

Landis, C., & Bolles, J. M. (1947). *Textbook of abnormal psychology.* New York: Macmillan.

Lascari, A. D. (1972, May). The abused child. *Journal of the Iowa Medical Society, 62,* 229–232.

Laury, G. V. (1970, September). The battered-child syndrome: Parental motivation, clinical aspects. *Bulletin of the New York Academy of Medicine, 46,* 678–681.

Lazarus, A. A. (Ed.). (1972). *Clinical behavior therapy.* New York: Brunner/Mazel.

Lenoski, E. F. (1973). *Translating injury data into preventive and health care services—Physical child abuse.* Unpublished paper, Division of Emergency Pediatrics, University of Southern California Medical Center, Los Angeles.

Lift a finger: The teacher's role in combating child abuse. (1975). Houston: Education Professions Development Consortium C.

Light, R. J. (1973, November). Abused and neglected children in America: A study of alternative policies. *Harvard Educational Review, 43*, 556–598.

Lochman, J. E., & Brown, M. V. (1980). Evaluation of dropout clients and of perceived usefulness of a parent education program. *Journal of Community Psychology, 8*, 132–139.

Lord, E., & Weisfeld, D. (1974). The abused child. In A. R. Roberts (Ed.), *Childhood deprivation* (pp. 64–83). Springfield, IL: Charles C. Thomas.

Lovens, H. D., & Rako, J. (1975, February). A community approach to the prevention of child abuse. *Child Welfare, 54*, 85–86.

Lynch, A. (1975, March). Child abuse in the school-age population. *Journal of School Health, 35*, 141–148.

Lyon, L. (1987, April). Therapeutic dilemmas in child abuse reporting. *AHP Perspective*, p. 6. Association for Humanistic Psychology.

Lystad, M. H. (1975, April). Violence at home: A review of the literature. *American Journal of Orthopsychiatry, 45*, 328–345.

Malone, C. A. (1979). Child psychiatry and family therapy: An overview. *Journal of the American Academy of Child Psychiatry, 18*, 4–21.

Mann, E., & McDermott, J. F. (1983). Play therapy for victims of child abuse and neglect. In C. E. Schaefer, & K. J. O'Connor (Eds.), *Handbook of play therapy* (pp. 283-307). New York: Wiley.

Martin, H. (1972). The child and his development. In C. H. Kempe & R. E. Helfer (Eds.), *Helping the battered child and his family* (pp. 93–114). Philadelphia: Lippincott.

Martin, H. P., & Beezley, P. (1974, Fall-Winter). Prevention and the consequences of child abuse. *Journal of Operational Psychiatry, 6*, 68–77.

Mash, E. J., & Johnson, C. (1983, Spring). Sibling interactions of hyperactive and normal children and their relationship to reports of maternal stress and self-esteem. *Journal of Clinical Child Psychology, 12*(1), 91–99.

Maslow, A. (1970). *Motivation and personality.* New York: Harper & Row.

Matas, L., Arend, R., & Sroufe, L. A. (1978). Continuity of adaptation in the second year: The relationship between quality of attachment and later competence. *Child Development, 49*, 547–556.

Meadow, R. (1977). Munchausen syndrome by proxy: The hinterland of child abuse. *Lancet, 2*, 343–345.

Melnick, B., & Hurley, J. R. (1969). Distinctive personality attributes of child-abusing mothers. *Journal of Consulting and Clinical Psychology, 33*, 746–749.

Merrill, E. J. (1962). Physical abuse of children: An agency study. In V. DeFrancis (Ed.), *Protecting the battered child.* Denver: American Humane Association.

Milner, J. (1980). *The Child Abuse Potential Inventory Manual.* Webster, NC: Psytec Corporation.

Milner, J., & Wimberly, R. (1979, January). An inventory for identification of child abusers. *Journal of Clinical Psychology, 35*, 95–100.

Morris, M. G. (1966, January-February). Psychological miscarriage: An end to mother love. *Trans-Action, 3*, 8–13.

Morris, M. G., & Gould, R. W. (1963). Role reversal: A concept in dealing with the neglected/battered child syndrome. In *The neglected battered child syndrome: Role reversal in parents.* New York: Child Welfare League of America.

Mrazek, P. J., & Mrazek, D. A. (1987). Resilience in child maltreatment victims: A conceptual exploration. *Child Abuse & Neglect, 11*, 357–366.

Murphy, S., Arkow, B., & Nicola, R. M. (1985). Prenatal prediction of child abuse and neglect: A prospective study. *Child Abuse & Neglect, 9*, 225–235.

Mussen, P. H., Conger, J. J., & Kagan, J. (1974). *Child development and personality.* New York: Harper & Row.

NCPCA Fact Sheet (1986, March). Chicago: National Committee for the Prevention of Child Abuse, p. 1.

NCPCA [National Committee for the Prevention of Child Abuse]. (1987, July/August). *Memorandum.* Chicago: Author.

Nelson, B. (1984). *Making an issue of child abuse.* Chicago: University of Chicago Press.

Newberger, E. (1983, April 11). *The helping hand strikes again.* Testimony given before the Subcommittee on Family and Human Services, Committee on Labor and Human Resources, U.S. Senate.

Newberger, E. H., Reed, R. B., Daniel, J. H., Hyde, J. N., & Kotelchuck, M. (1977). Pediatric social illness: Toward an etiological classification. *Pediatrics, 60*, 178–185.

Nomurra, F. M.. (1966, May-June). The battered child "syndrome." *Hawaii Medical Journal, 25*, 387–394.

Nuckolls, K. B., Cassel, J., & Kaplan, B. H. (1972). Psychosocial assets, life crisis, and the prognosis of pregnancy. *American Journal of Epidemiology, 95*, 431–441.

Oates, K. (1986). *Child abuse and neglect: What eventually happens.* New York: Brunner/Mazel.

O'Connor, S., Vietze, P. M., Sherrod, K. B., Sandler, H. M., & Altemeier, W. A. (1980, August). Reduced incidence of parenting inadequacy following rooming-in. *Pediatrics, 66*(2), 176–182.

Ojemann, R. H. (1957). *Four basic aspects of preventive psychiatry.* Iowa City: State University of Iowa Press.

Olds, D. (1984). Case studies of factors interfering with nurse home visitors' promotion of positive care-giving methods in high-risk families. *Early Child Development and Care, 16*, 149–166.

Olds, D., Chamberlin, R., & Tattlebaum, R. (1986). Preventing child abuse and neglect: A randomized trial of nurse home visitation. *Pediatrics, 78*, 65–78.

Olson, R. (1976, January). Index of suspicion: Screening of child abusers. *American Journal of Nursing, 76,* 108–110.

Parke, R. D., & Collmer, C. W. (1975). Child abuse: An interdisciplinary analysis. In E. M. Hetherington (Ed.), *Review of child development research* (pp. 509–590). Chicago: University of Chicago Press.

Passman, R. H., & Mulhern, R. K. (1977). Maternal punitiveness as affected by situational stress: An experimental analogue of child abuse. *Journal of Abnormal Psychology, 86,* 565–569.

Patterson, G. R., & Gullion, M. E. (1968). *Living with children: New methods for parents and teachers.* Champaign, IL: Research Press.

Paulsen, M. G. (1968). The law and abused children. In R. E. Helfer & C. H. Kempe (Eds.), *The battered child* (pp. 175–220). Chicago: University of Chicago Press.

Paulson, M. J. (1974, Spring). Parents of the battered child. *Life-Threatening Behavior, 4,* 18–31.

Paulson, M. J., & Blake, P. R. (1969, February). The physically abused child: A focus on prevention. *Child Welfare, 48,* 95.

Pelton, L. (1981). *Social context of child abuse and neglect.* New York: Human Services Press.

Perls, F. (1969). *Gestalt therapy verbatim.* Lafayette, CA: Real People Press.

Plaut, T. F. A. (1967). *Alcohol problems: A report to the nation by the Cooperative Commission on the Study of Alcoholism.* New York: Oxford University Press.

Pollock, C., & Steele, B. (1972). A therapeutic approach to the parents. In C. H. Kempe & R. E. Helfer (Eds.), *Helping the battered child and his family* (pp. 3–21). Philadelphia: Lippincott.

Powell, G. F., Brasel, J. A., Raiti, S., & Blizzard, R. M. (1967). Emotional deprivation and growth retardation simulating idiopathic hypopituitarism, II: Endocrinological evaluation of the syndrome. *New England Journal of Medicine, 276,* 1276–1283.

Radbill, S. X. (1968). A history of child abuse and infanticide. In R. E. Helfer & C. H. Kempe (Eds.), *The battered child* (pp. 3–21). Chicago: University of Chicago Press.

Ravenholt, R. T. (1983, March). Addiction mortality in the U.S. National Institute on Drug Abuse. As cited in *Facts on alcoholism and alcohol-related problems,* brochure of Houston Council on Alcoholism.

Recklin, R., & Lavett, D. K. (1987). Those who broke the cycle: Therapy with non-abusive adults who were physically abused as children. *Psychotherapy, 24,* 790–798.

Reed, J. (1975, May-June). Working with abusive parents: A parent's view—An interview with Jolly K. *Children Today, 4,* 9.

Reidy, T. J. (1977). The agressive characteristics of abused and neglected children. *Journal of Clinical Psychology, 33,* 1140–1145.

Resnick, P. (1969, September). Child murder by parents: A psychiatric review of filicide. *American Journal of Psychiatry, 126*, 325–334.

Rosenberg, M. S., & Repucci, N. D. (1983). Abusive mothers: Perceptions of their own and their children's behavior. *Journal of Clinical and Consulting Psychology, 51*, 674–682.

Routh, T. (1972). *The volunteer and community agencies.* Springfield, IL: Charles C. Thomas.

Sage, W. (1975, July). Violence in the children's room. *Human Behavior, 4*, 42–47.

Sanders, R. W. (1972, December). Resistance to dealing with parents of battered children. *Pediatrics, 50*, 853–857.

Savino, A. B., & Sanders, R. W. (1973, March). Working with abusive parents: Group therapy and home visits. *American Journal of Nursing, 73*, 482–484.

Schiff, A. W., & Schiff, J. (1971, January). Passivity. *Transactional Analysis Journal, 1*, 1.

Schilling, R. F. S., Schinke, P., Blythe, B., & Barth, R. (1982, October). Child maltreatment and mentally retarded parents: Is there a relationship? *Mental Retardation, 20*, 201–209.

Schmitt, B. D. (1987). Social support and child maltreatment: A review of the evidence. *Child Abuse & Neglect, 11*, 421–432.

Schmitt, B. D., & Kempe, C. H. (1975, March). The pediatrician's role in child abuse and neglect. *Current Problems in Pediatrics, 5*, 35–45.

Scott, S., & Richards, M. (1979, November). Nursing low birthweight babies on lambswool. *Lancet, 8124*(1), 1028.

Scrimshaw, S. (1978). Infant mortality and behavior in the regulation of family size. *Population and Development Review, 4*(3), 383–403.

Selye, H. (1956). *The stress of life.* New York: McGraw-Hill.

Sever, J., & Janzen, C. (1982, May). Contradictions to reconstitution of sexually abusive families. *Child Welfare, 66*(5), 279–288.

Sgroi, S. M. (1975, May-June). Sexual molestation of children. *Children Today, 4*, 19.

Siegel, E. (1980, August). Hospital and home support during infancy: Impact on maternal attachment, child abuse and neglect, and health care utilization. *Pediatrics, 66*(2), 183–190.

Simmons, J. T. (1986). *Programs that work: Evidence of primary prevention of child abuse.* Houston: Greater Houston Committee for the Prevention of Child Abuse.

Smith, C. A. (1973, August). The battered child. *New England Journal of Medicine, 289*, 322–323.

Smith, J. M., & Smith, D. E. P. (1966). *Child management: A program for parents.* Ann Arbor, MI: Ann Arbor Publishers.

Smith, R. (1973, January). Now experts are trying to draw out these battering parents. *Today's Health, 51*, 59–64.

Solnit, A. J. (1980). Too much reporting, too little service: Root and prevention of child abuse. In G. Gerbner, C. J. Ross, & E. Zigler (Eds.), *Child abuse: An agenda for action* (pp. 135–146). New York: Oxford University Press.

Spinetta, J. J., & Rigler, D. (1972, April). The child-abusing parent: A psychological review. *Psychological Bulletin, 77*, 299–304.

Spitz, R. A. (1965). *The first year of life.* New York: International Universities Press.

Sroufe, L. A., & Waters, E. (1977). Attachment as an organizational construct. *Child Development, 48*, 1184–1199.

Steele, B. F. (1970). Parental abuse of infants and small children. In J. E. Anthony & T. Benedek (Eds.), *Parenthood: Its psychology and psychopathology* (pp. 449–477). Boston: Little, Brown.

Steele, B. F. (1977). *Psychological dimensions of child abuse.* Paper presented before the American Association for the Advancement of Science, Denver.

Steele, B. F., & Pollock, C. (1968). A psychiatric study of parents who abuse infants and small children. In R. E. Helfer & C. H. Kempe (Eds.), *The battered child* (pp. 89–133). Chicago: University of Chicago Press.

Steiner, C. (1971). *Games alcoholics play.* New York: Grove Press.

Steinmetz, S., & Straus, M. (1971). *Some myths about violence in the family.* Paper presented before the American Sociological Association, Denver.

Stewart, M. S., Farquhar, L. D., Dicharry, D. C., Glick, D. R., & Martin, P. W. (1986, April). Group therapy: A treatment of choice for young victims of child abuse. *International Journal of Group Psychotherapy, 36*, 261–277.

Straus, M., & Gelles, R. (1986, August). Societal change and change in family violence from 1975–1985 as revealed by two national surveys. *Journal of Marriage and the Family, 48*, 465–479.

Straus, M., Gelles, R., & Steinmetz, S. (1980). *Behind closed doors: Violence in the American family.* Garden City, NY: Anchor Press/Doubleday.

Straus, M. A. (1980). Stress and child abuse. In C. H. Kempe & R. E. Helfer (Eds.), *The battered child* (3rd ed., pp. 86–103). Chicago: University of Chicago Press.

Study findings: Study of national incidence and prevalence of child abuse and neglect, 1988. (1988). U. S. Dept. of Health and Human Services. Office of Human Development, Administration for Children, Youth and Families, Children's Bureau, National Center on Child Abuse and Neglect.

A study of children's attitudes and perceptions about drugs and alcohol. (1983). *Weekly Reader Publications.* Xerox Educational Publications.

Suomi, S. J. (1973). Surrogate rehabilitation of monkeys reared in total social isolation. *Journal of Child Psychology and Psychiatry, 14*, 71–77.

Suomi, S. J., & Harlow, H. F. (1975). The role and reason of peer friendship in rhesus monkeys. In M. Lewis & L. A. Rosenblum (Eds.), *Peer relations and friendship: EPS Symposium on the Origins of Behavior.* New York: Wiley.

Suomi, S. J., & Harlow, H. F. (1976). Monkeys without play. In J. Bruner, A. Jolly & K. Sylvia, (Eds.), *Play: Its role development and evolution.* Harmondsworth, England: Penguin Books.

Texas Penal Code (7th ed). (1984). St. Paul, MN: West Publishing.

Thomson, E. M., Paget, N. W., Bates, D. W., Mesch, M., & Putnam, T. I. (1971). *Child abuse: A community challenge.* East Aurora, NY: Henry Stewart.

Time. (1975, March 17).

Toffler, A. (1970). *Future shock.* New York: Random House.

Tracy, J. J., & Clark, E. H. (1974, May). Treatment for child abusers. *Social Work, 19,* 339.

Tyler, A. H. (1983). A comparison of child-abusing and non-abusing fathers on measures of marital adjustment, life stress, and social support. *Dissertation Abstracts International, 44,* 1610B (University Microfilms No. 83-19, 376)

U. S. Department of Health and Human Services. (1980). *Promoting health/Preventing disease.* Washington, D. C.: U.S. Government Printing Office.

U. S. Department of Health and Human Services. (1986). *The 1990 health objectives for the nation: A midcourse review.* Washington, D.C.: U.S. Government Printing Office.

U. S. Department of Health and Human Services. National Institute of Alcohol Abuse and Alcoholism. Public Service. *Questions & answers: Teenage alcohol use and abuse. Prevention plus: Involving schools and the community in alcohol and drug education.* Publication no. CADM841256. Rockville, MD: Author.

Violent parents. (1971, November 6). *Lancet,* pp. 1017–1018.

Werner, E. E., & Smith, R. S. (1977). *Kauai's children come of age.* Honolulu: University of Hawaii Press.

Westat and Development Associates. (1981, September). *National study of the incidence and severity of child abuse and neglect.* Prepared for the National Center on Child Abuse and Neglect under Contract no. 105-76-1137.

Whitaker, C. (1975, March 21). Family Therapy Workshop. Presented at the Southeast Institute Second Annual Spring Conference, Raleigh, NC.

White, R. W. (1959, September). Motivation reconsidered: The concept of competence. *Psychological Review, 66,* 297–333.

Wolpe, J. (1969). *The practice of behavioral therapy.* New York: Pergamon Press.

Woolley, P. V., & Evans, W. A. (1955, June). Significance of skeletal lesions in infants resembling those of traumatic origin. *Journal of the American Medical Association, 158,* 539–543.

Yale University News Release. (1987, September 22). New Haven, CT.

Zalba, S. (1971, July-August). Battered children. *Trans-Action, 8,* 58–61.

Index